An Orchestra at My Fingertips

An Orchestra at My Fingertips

A History of the Canadian Electronic Ensemble

Alexa Woloshyn

McGill-Queen's University Press
Montreal & Kingston • London • Chicago

© McGill-Queen's University Press 2023

ISBN 978-0-2280-1733-2 (cloth)
ISBN 978-0-2280-1734-9 (paper)
ISBN 978-0-2280-1839-1 (ePDF)

Legal deposit third quarter 2023
Bibliothèque nationale du Québec

Printed in Canada on acid-free paper that is 100% ancient forest free (100% post-consumer recycled), processed chlorine free

This book has been published with the help of a grant from the Canadian Federation for the Humanities and Social Sciences, through the Awards to Scholarly Publications Program, using funds provided by the Social Sciences and Humanities Research Council of Canada. Funding has also been received from the AMS 75 PAYS Fund of the American Musicological Society, supported in part by the National Endowment for the Humanities and the Andrew W. Mellon Foundation as well as the Stanley and Marcia Gumberg Dean of the College of Fine Arts and the Cooper-Siegel Professorship in the College of Fine Arts at Carnegie Mellon University.

Funded by the Government of Canada / Financé par le gouvernement du Canada  Canada Council for the Arts / Conseil des arts du Canada

We acknowledge the support of the Canada Council for the Arts.

Nous remercions le Conseil des arts du Canada de son soutien.

Library and Archives Canada Cataloguing in Publication

Title: Orchestra at my fingertips : a history of the Canadian Electronic Ensemble / Alexa Woloshyn

Names: Woloshyn, Alexa, author.

Description: Includes bibliographical references and index.

Identifiers: Canadiana (print) 20230132898 | Canadiana (ebook) 20230132901 | ISBN 9780228017332 (cloth) | ISBN 9780228017349 (paper) | ISBN 9780228018391 (ePDF)

Subjects: LCSH: Canadian Electronic Ensemble – History. | LCSH: Electronic music – Canada – History and criticism.

Classification: LCC ML27.C3 C255 2023 | DDC 786.706/071 – dc23

This book was designed and typeset by Peggy & Co. Design in 11/14 Adobe Minion Pro.

Contents

Figures and Tables   vii

Prologue   xi

Acknowledgments   xxi

1. Electrifying Musical Life in Toronto   3
2. A CEE Origin Story: Don't Mistake Us for a Pop Band   26
3. Sounds like the CEE: A Technological and Aesthetic Community   49
4. The CEE Live: Virtuosity, Perceptibility, and Improvisation   84
5. CEE Listening Spaces: Embodied, Embedded, and Virtual Contexts   122
6. A CEE Musical Network: Supporting Musical Life in Canada and Beyond   152

Epilogue   185

Discography   195

Appendix: Listening Guides   197
   Increscents (1972) – David Grimes   202
   Fancye (1973) – David Jaeger   205
   Consequences for 5 (1977) – Norma Beecroft   209
   I Have Come Through (1979) – James Montgomery   216
   Quivi sospiri (1979) – David Jaeger   219

Psalm (1985) – Larry Lake   225
Attention Elk! (1994) – CEE   228
Caspin's Arrival (1998) – CEE   231
Improvisation #4 (2008) – CEE   233

Notes   235

References   243

Index   255

Figures and Tables

Figures

5.1 Channel placement of voices: Bolton's voice in both L and R (perceived as centre), Chan's voice in L, and Jaeger's voice in R (6:58–7:36). 144

5.2 Spectrogram of synthesizer-only Section E3 showing simultaneous, moving layers across a broad frequency range until fade out (9:30–10:06). 145

6.1 Spectrogram of "All We Like Sheep" (mm. 42–5) showing ornamented passagework and descant in synthesizer accompaniment. 167

6.2 Spectrogram of "All We Like Sheep" (mm. 54–64) with electronic flourishes. 168

A.1 Opening violin solo in *Increscents*. Courtesy of David Grimes. 204

A.2 Score excerpt (p. 5) of synthesizer duo in *Increscents*. Courtesy of David Grimes. 204

A.3 Score excerpt (p. 2) showing recurring gestures in *Fancye*. Courtesy of David Jaeger. 208

A.4 Score excerpt from ending of *Fancye*. Courtesy of David Jaeger. 209

A.5 Score excerpt (p. 2) from Sequence II of *Consequences for 5*. Courtesy of Norma Beecroft. 212

A.6 Patch G instructions for *Consequences for 5*. Courtesy of Norma Beecroft. 213

A.7 Fast, descending passagework in *I Have Come Through* (mm. 15–16). Courtesy of James Montgomery. 217

A.8 Performance indications for techniques 2 and 4 in *I Have Come Through* (mm. 63–72). Courtesy of James Montgomery. 217

A.9 Score excerpt (p. 3) of piano part in *Quivi sospiri*. Courtesy of David Jaeger. 222

A.10 Spectrogram of *Quivi sospiri* (ca 1:40–3:00). 222

A.11 Pulse-oriented piano and synthesizer parts on p. 5 of the score for *Quivi sospiri*. Courtesy of David Jaeger. 223

A.12 Spectrogram of *Quivi sospiri* (ca 4:47–5:31). 223

A.13 Four-voice counterpoint in piano in final measures of *Quivi sospiri*. Courtesy of David Jaeger. 224

A.14 Score excerpt demonstrating recurring intervallic, melodic, harmonic, and rhythmic characteristics of *Psalm* (ca 4:45–5:58). Courtesy of the Larry Lake estate. 226

A.15 Score excerpt of two-voice counterpoint (9:26–10:15). Courtesy of the Larry Lake estate. 226

A.16 Spectrogram of *Attention Elk!* (1:05–1:50) with label above "elk calls." 230

A.17 Spectrogram of *Attention Elk!* (6:36–7:44). 231

A.18 Spectrogram of unit 2 of *Improvisation #4*, with a fast-paced, steady groove in both keyboard and drum kit, represented here by thin vertical lines (ca 2:38–3:36). 234

Tables

P.1 List of CEE membership by name, years of membership, and additional notes about pre-membership involvement with the CEE. xviii

2.1 Most frequently performed compositions written by the CEE, 1972–85. 45

3.1 The most-performed CEE pieces by individual members during the trio era. 60

3.2 The most-performed CEE group compositions during the trio era. 61

5.1 Formal outline and description of *This Is This*. 143

6.1 List of composers and musical works commissioned by the CEE. 170

A.1   Formal outline of *Increscents* with descriptions of violin and synthesizer parts.   203
A.2   List of organ stops used in *Fancye*.   207
A.3   Formal outline of *Consequences for 5* with descriptions and technical details.   210
A.4   Formal outline of *I Have Come Through* with descriptions of piano and synthesizer parts.   218
A.5   Formal outline of *Quivi sospiri* with descriptions. Timings based on the recording from the 1990 album *Catbird Seat*.   221
A.6   Formal outline of *Psalm* with descriptions. Timings based on recording from the 1988 album *Shadow Box*.   227
A.7   Formal outline of *Attention Elk!* with descriptions. Timings based on the recording from the 1996 album *Supertrio*.   229
A.8   Formal outline of *Caspin's Arrival*.   232

Prologue

First Encounters

I first heard about the Canadian Electronic Ensemble (CEE) during the first year of my PhD program at the University of Toronto, when I was roommates with founding member David Jaeger's daughter Anna. Knowing that I was far from my family back in Saskatoon, David and his wife Sally hosted me several times during that first year. Our friendship was established, and I continued to stop by a few times a year during the remainder of my doctoral studies.

David is a generous storyteller, and he regaled me with stories from his many decades as a radio music producer for the Canadian Broadcasting Corporation (CBC): his friendship with the late Glenn Gould, commissioning Hildegard Westerkamp for the radio program *Two New Hours*, and recording projects with pianist Christina Petrowska Quilico, among countless others. I knew David first as a composer and producer, but I soon began to understand another significant musical activity of his: the Canadian Electronic Ensemble, the live electronic group he co-founded in 1972[1] and continues to participate in today.

During my doctoral research on Canadian electronic music, I became interested in the sonic, performative, and perceptual aspects of live electronic music that were distinct from studio-based electronic work. The CEE offered an obvious opportunity to study electronic music making in the context of real-time collective creativity. How does a laptop transform from a quotidian tool to a musical instrument? What does rehearsal achieve for a primarily improvisational group? How important is interpersonal or social connection in fostering a musical connection? What impact do the perception and reaction of the audience have on a performance of live electronic music? What is the secret to surviving decades as a group? These questions and many others emerged through my growing curiosity about the CEE.

Documenting a Musical History

Despite the CEE's long history and substantial discography, the group has received little scholarly attention. Not only has there been no in-depth study of the CEE, but they have also been almost entirely left out of articles, chapters, and books about electronic music history and live electronic ensembles. These sources tend to focus on European and US ensembles, with some mention of groups from Japan, and the same names are touted each time: Stockhausen Ensemble (1964), Gruppo di Improvvisazione Nuova Consonanza (Rome, 1964), Musica Elettronica Viva (1966), AMM (British, 1965), Sonic Arts Union (1966) out of the Cooperative Studio for Electronic Music, and the San Francisco Tape Music Center (1961). Given that the CEE has been creating live electronic music for five decades – with multiple recordings, numerous commissions, and members deeply embedded in the Canadian new music scene – its absence from the scholarly record is problematic.

While the CEE largely remains absent in publications focused on North America or those that attempt a broad, global historiography, it does appear in some Canada-centric studies. George Proctor mentions the CEE in his book *Canadian Music of the Twentieth Century* (1980), and Elaine Keillor's textbook *Music in Canada: Capturing Landscape and Diversity* (2006) includes a single sentence on the group.[2] The group's entry in *The Canadian Encyclopedia* provides an overview of its membership, history, and accomplishments, along with lists of commissions, compositions, and recordings. The CEE was such a remarkable ensemble by the early 1980s that David Keane devoted an entire paragraph to the CEE in his essay "Electroacoustic Music in Canada: 1950–1984" (1984), which otherwise centres on the studios and on Hugh Le Caine's legacy. Keane can likely be credited for the CEE's inclusion in a list of recordings in *On the Wires of Our Nerves: The Art of Electroacoustic Music* (1989).

This book argues for the CEE's critical role in new music – especially in Canada but also worldwide – and preserves the stories of this long-standing group. This book is a collection of stories, a pedagogical aid for teaching the history of electronic composition and performance, and a critical study of collective creativity and agency within a live electronic ensemble. Though the stories are about the CEE, they prompt examination and analysis that can enrich our understanding of all live electronic music making.

Book Summary

This book is the outcome of years of fieldwork on the CEE, including rehearsal and performance observations and interviews. Interviews were conducted primarily in person, with additional conversations over email and the phone. Again, I must thank the members of the CEE – past and present – for their generosity and openness. This book considers both the CEE's extensive past and exciting present, only the latter of which have I been witnessing first-hand. I have relied on the memories of CEE members to construct much of this story. I am particularly indebted to Jim Montgomery, who deserves special credit for acting as the unofficial CEE archivist. Due to his labour in preserving and documenting the CEE's concert history, he has constructed a detailed chronology of the CEE's performance history: dates, locations, performers, and repertoire. From these records, I was able to analyze the data, looking for bigger trends emerging from the public side of the CEE's creative practice within its various eras. These tables are publicly available on the CEE's website, and I hope that other researchers will examine additional questions from this data beyond my considerations here. The CEE's present was most closely studied in late February 2020 when the current CEE sextet gathered for a four-day residency at Carnegie Mellon University (CMU) in Pittsburgh for a series of workshops, a public panel lecture, and a concert in collaboration with CMU's Exploded Ensemble. Statements from in-class visits, the public lecture, and interviews are incorporated throughout this chapter and the remainder of the book.

Chapters 1, 2, and 3 provide the chronological foundation for the book through an emphasis on history and biography. Chapter 1 contextualizes a CEE performance within broader histories of electronic music (both in and out of the studio) and experimental music making in Canada, all of which are linked to issues around collective or distributed creativity, listening, and perception. Chapter 2 outlines the origins of the CEE by first establishing the specific contextual factors that coalesced at the University of Toronto and its Electronic Music Studio (UTEMS) in the late 1960s and early 1970s that brought the four founding members to the institution and fostered the formation of the CEE. This chapter also centres on the CEE founding members' compositional and performance activities from 1971 to 1985. Chapter 3 explores the CEE's aesthetics through personnel changes, discussing the CEE members who joined after the departure of founding member David Grimes. It also explains how the technological, aesthetic, and social aspects of music making inform each other in the CEE's activities. I trace the group's equipment across the analog-digital shift, noting a nostalgic return to analog technologies, particularly in the creative practices of members Stillwell and David Sutherland.

The final three chapters of the book are focused on issues related to electronic music, as illuminated by the CEE's specific practice. Chapter 4 addresses the "live" in live electronic music by analyzing the CEE's performance practice and discusses such issues as audience engagement with non-acoustic gesture–sound relationships, new definitions of virtuosity, locating the "human" in "dehumanized" music, and the centrality of improvisation in live electronic music. Musical examples from their two live albums (*Canadian Electronic Ensemble: Live* and *Live in Cabbagetown*) and first-hand accounts of live performances illustrate how the CEE variously solves, exacerbates, or ignores some of the so-called "barriers" to audience engagement with and appreciation for live electronic music. Chapter 5 discusses the CEE's various listening spaces, positioning the members themselves as the first listeners (a musicking strategy central to their performance practice). Chapter 5 captures the stories of experimental music making in Toronto through its spaces for rehearsal, recording, and performance, from the Music Gallery and The TRANZAC to Paul Stillwell's basement (the most recent CEE rehearsal space). This chapter also discusses listening strategies espoused by R. Murray Schafer, Glenn Gould, Hildegard Westerkamp, and John Cage, which establish listening regimes that can narrow listening experiences with music. I also discuss alternate listening spaces such as radio and recordings (including streaming) as intimate listening ecologies.

Chapter 6 expands the scope of the CEE's activities to examine the impact of the group and its individual members on the broader Canadian new music scene, also highlighting the members' other musical contributions, such as Jaeger's many decades as a producer with CBC Radio-Canada and Jim Montgomery's former position as artistic director of the Music Gallery. This chapter contextualizes the CEE's wider impact through a critique of the Canadian music institutions as gendered, racialized, and classist. Such a critique emphasizes the importance of Rose Bolton's EQ mentorship program for women and non-binary individuals in electronic music.

The epilogue picks up on the notion of "legacy" from the prologue, first by providing an overview of the previous fifty years of the CEE, then by summarizing the members' vision for the future of both the CEE and live electronic music in general. In thinking about the CEE's first fifty years and what the future may hold, the reader is invited to dive more deeply into the CEE's music by exploring a collection of listening guides. Various listening strategies are explored and encouraged, with the hopes that students in particular will find an accessible gateway into the CEE's output.

What's in a Name?

The irony of the name "Canadian Electronic Ensemble" is that the group's four founding members – David Grimes, David Jaeger, Larry Lake, and James Montgomery – were all Americans, not Canadians. The members fully recognize this irony, but when I asked them about the name's origins, their memories are a bit hazy. Grimes joked, "I'm pretty sure 'Four Guys in Search of Jumpsuits' was not seriously considered" (personal communication, 2 November 2019), while Montgomery explained, "We decided on 'Ensemble' so that we would not be mistaken for a pop band. Curiously, that was never a problem. 'Electronic' was pretty easy" (personal communication, 24 September 2019). The four original members of the CEE were graduate students at the University of Toronto when they formed the ensemble, having been in Canada for only about a year. They all stayed after their studies – Grimes was the only one who later moved back to the United States – but claiming the label of "Canadian" so soon after their arrival in the country could have been cause for tension and even criticism at the time, given the heightened discourse around Canadian versus US culture.

The arrival of these four young men in Toronto came at a time when thousands of young American men were coming to Canada, fleeing the United States as draft dodgers during the Vietnam War.[3] They arrived only a few years after the nation's centennial in 1967, a celebration that highlighted internal tensions (such as Quebec separatism) and inspired debates about Canada's relationship to its most influential global partners: Great Britain and the United States.

As the world's longest undefended border, the line between Canada and the United States suggests a peaceful and trusting relationship, but political, economic, and cultural tensions have existed for decades. In the reshaping of global power after the Second World War, some, such as Prime Minister Mackenzie King, advocated for "continental solidarity" with the United States. Such an approach aimed to decrease reliance on Canada's colonizer Great Britain and to fight against the Soviet Union, which threatened to make nuclear war with the United States over Canadian skies. Others feared "Americanization," particularly with the strong US cultural influence in Canada via radio, television, and recordings. The Massey Report of 1951 (for the Royal Commission on National Development in the Arts, Letters, and Sciences) characterized Canada's cultural institutions as relatively weak compared with American mass culture and recommended federal financial support so that "a distinctive Canadian culture [would] survive" (Cormier 2004, 6). These fears concerned more than just the influence of US cultural imports, such as television programs and popular music. One fear was that of American influence through reliance on "foreign" professors at the growing number of Canadian universities (Cormier 2004, 2005). As I discuss in more detail in chapter 2, such "foreign" influences were prominent within the music faculty in Toronto in the 1960s and 1970s, whose members were primarily trained in the United States and Europe.

George Grant (2005), in his 1965 essay *Lament for a Nation*, characterized Canada as a "branch-plant economy" (and thus culture) because of Canada's reliance on the US economy (and formerly on the French and British economies). The alternative was presented as "Canadianization," which included adopting a new flag and national anthem, changes that were seen by many, including Prime Minister Lester B. Pearson, as significant steps away from the influence of Great Britain. Building on existing socio-political crises (including the university crisis mentioned above), momentum for "Canadianization" increased as Centennial celebrations and initiatives emerged across the nation, supported by significant amounts of federal money.[4] These efforts also generated specific strategies for protecting so-called Canadian culture, such as the Broadcasting Act of 1968, which created the Canadian Radio and Television Commission (CRTC) (as it was then called) to enforce "Can Con" rules (Thompson and Randall 1997, 260; Johansen 1973, 183). Canadianization advocates saw cultural institutions as particularly important spheres that must be protected against American influence. Cormier explains: "Canadianization supporters pushed for increased opportunities for Canadians to be employed in Canadian cultural institutions" (2005, 356).

For decades, scholars have identified fears among the public about the state of distinctly Canadian cultural products: for example, Litvak and Maule in the 1970s, Robertson in the 1980s, and Cook in the 1990s. Writing early in the new millennium, Kevin V. Mulcahy declared: "The omnipresence of American entertainment products has prompted a near-crisis mentality among some Canadians about the survivability of a national way of life that is not an American derivative" (2002, 267). The notion of Canada as "hinterland" to the United States (Litvak and Maule 1974, 1) incited Canadian cultural nationalists to adopt protectionist responses against American cultural products (Mulcahy 2002). Mulcahy notes that classical music, being less commercialized than other genres, has a weaker "sphere of influence" among American cultural products (2002, 274) and therefore offers the greatest potential for building up Canadian cultural distinctiveness (276).

Though they came to Canada from the United States, the members of the CEE, both within the group and with their other musical activities, have played a significant role in bolstering Canada's cultural distinctiveness within new classical music. The contributions of the CEE are discussed throughout this book, while chapter 6 examines members' other creative contexts and spheres of influence, namely at CBC Radio, the Music Gallery in Toronto, and EQ, a mentorship program for women and non-binary persons in electronic music.

The CEE Legacy

The CEE's personnel has transformed over its five decades, but the core of its practice and mission has remained (see table P.1). Founding members Jaeger and Montgomery are still part of the group as of this writing, and Lake was a member until his death in 2013. Composers Michael Dobinson and Paul Stillwell were the first new members after Grimes's

Table P.1   List of CEE membership by name, years of membership, and additional notes about pre-membership involvement with the CEE.

Name	Years	Notes
David Jaeger	1972–	Founding member
Larry Lake	1972–2013	Founding member
James Montgomery	1972–	Founding member
David Grimes	1972–1985	Founding member
Michael Dobinson	1996–2005	Performed as guest and "resident artist" in early 1996
Paul Stillwell	1996–	Performed with the CEE in Signals Orchestra in 1995 and as "resident artist" in early 1996
Laura Wilcox	1998	Performed as guest in 1995, "resident artist" in 1996, and guest in 1997
Rose Bolton	1999–	Commissioned as composer in 1997
John Kameel Farah	2009–	Performed as guest in 2007 and 2008
David Sutherland	2017–	Performed as guest in 2016

departure in 1985, followed a couple of years later by violist Laura Wilcox to make a sextet. Wilcox stayed only one year officially in the group. Violinist and composer Rose Bolton joined the CEE shortly before the ensemble entered the new millennium; she is also still a member, though she has taken extended hiatuses for her composition projects. Dobinson left the group in 2005, returning the CEE to a quintet. Pianist and composer John Kameel Farah joined the ensemble a few years later. As of 2017, the CEE's most recent member is David Sutherland, a former member of MetaMusic in Montreal.

The CEE began practising live electronic music making during a time when suitable technologies were expensive, prone to breakdown, or not yet invented. The members of the CEE have demonstrated both dedication and ingenuity in finding studio technologies and creating new instruments capable of real-time sound production and in fostering creative and interpersonal methods that thrive under seemingly limiting and unpredictable circumstances. Across their first five decades of electronic music making, the CEE has commissioned and/or premiered over 100 works, and they have toured across Canada and around the world. The CEE has released six group albums between 1977 and 2014, in addition to other recording projects: a 1996 collaborative album with

Trio Collectif, *The Electronic Messiah* (1982, under the name "Synthescope" Digital Synthesizer Ensemble); MEGAJAM: *18 Musicians in Your Head at Once* (2000) with several Canadian composers; and guest appearances on records including John Campbell's 1978 clarinet album *Transcription*. The group has made an incalculable contribution to the live electronic ensemble as a creative outlet for composers, performers, and improvisers, and this book honours that contribution.

    The story of the CEE is one of an ensemble that has persisted in its love of live electronic music and collective music making over five decades, a story that reveals idiosyncrasies of time and place that have informed and shaped the CEE's specific creative practices and the members' other creative activities. But the story of the CEE also illuminates a broader history of live electronic music, and this book examines issues of technology, aesthetics, performance practice, and audience reception that relate to all live electronic ensembles.

Acknowledgments

The members of the Canadian Electronic Ensemble (CEE) welcomed me as the nerdy musicologist who was curious about their creative practice. I cannot express enough my gratitude to each one for their time and openness. They are tremendous musicians and wonderful human beings, and I have appreciated each interaction and performance. This book celebrates their legacy and ongoing contributions as live electronic musicians. I am especially grateful to all of the current members of the CEE for enthusiastically agreeing to visit Pittsburgh and Carnegie Mellon University (CMU) in February 2020. I certainly kept you busy, and it was such a highlight for the School of Music and the broader campus. I'm so glad we had that time together before the world shut down in the weeks that followed. How fun it was to revisit these musical, social, and intellectual relationships for your fiftieth anniversary in 2022 with another collaboration with CMU's Exploded Ensemble (this time through the magic of telematic performance) and a hybrid symposium.

Thanks also to past CEE member David Grimes for answering my questions; your perspective has been vital. To Paul Stillwell, thanks for giving me permission to include some of your wonderful photographs in this book. Enormous thanks to Jim Montgomery: you are the unofficial (or, at least, unpaid!) CEE archivist. Without your records, much of this book would not exist. You also generously sent me copies of CEE albums and answered many questions about the ensemble's past activities.

Certainly, none of this project would have happened at all without David and Sally Jaeger, who generously hosted me at their home over the years. They knew I was far from family, and I deeply appreciated the meals and afternoon teas. Thank you, David, for sharing your CEE adventures with me, and thank you for introducing me to the group and to your music. I love and appreciate you all.

My friends during my graduate studies, first at Western University and then at the University of Toronto, helped me become the researcher and human I am proud to be today: special thanks to Dr Colleen Renihan, Dr Keith Johnston, and Dr Michelle Boyd. Dr Emily Gale: you introduced me to the Jaegers, so I suppose this book is really thanks to you! My PhD adviser, Prof. Robin Elliott, taught me what it means to be a careful and generous scholar. Prof. Sherry Lee also provided me with essential mentorship during and after my PhD. Thank you to my Toronto/Kitchener roommate Patricia for always believing in me and modelling a strong work ethic. To Amy Haldenby: thank you for going to CEE shows with me and letting me crash at your apartment during my many fieldwork visits to Toronto.

I also thank my many generous Bowling Green and Pittsburgh friends for their encouragement: Kara and Rob, Megan and John, Sidra, and Mary. Dr Alaina Roberts, you've been my cheerleader through the final push of this book; thank you for your unwavering belief in me. Witnessing you as a scholar and teacher compels me to do better and to push for change in our institutions and the world around us. Emily Rybinski receives extra thanks, not only for her friendship during this time but also for her stellar tech skills and help with the book's supporting materials. I literally don't know how you do it.

To my CMU colleagues in the School of Music and beyond: your friendship and support have made my first years at CMU amazing. Thanks to Daniel Nesta Curtis, Dr Jocelyn Dueck, Dr Susan Raponi, Dr Stephen Neely, Dr Chris Lynch, and Lance LaDuke – we share a mutual excitement about each other's research and creative and teaching activities, and this community keeps me motivated. A special shout out to the Electronic Music Division (Jesse Stiles, Dr Annie Hsieh, Dr Rich Randall, and Dr Freida Abtan) for being there through the writing crunch of this book. The CEE's residency at CMU, which is weaved throughout the book, could not have happened without you. Thanks also to Dan Martin (Dean of the College of Fine Arts), Denis Colwell (Head of the School of Music), and the Frank-Ratchye STUDIO for Creative Inquiry (especially Golan, Tom, and Bill) for sponsoring the CEE's visit, and thanks to everyone else on campus who helped make it happen. I am grateful to the Berkman Faculty Development Fund and the Cooper-Siegel Professorship for their financial support for this project. The CMU Libraries were instrumental in providing me with the research resources

I needed to complete this book. Special thanks to Music Librarian Kristin Heath: you managed on more than one occasion to track something down that I thought would be impossible, and beyond this librarian magic, you have also been a dear friend and advocate. My gratitude also goes to Andrew Marshall of Interlibrary Loans, who secured me copies of scores from Canada and other essential sources.

I am grateful for the subvention I received from the AMS 75 PAYS Fund of the American Musicological Society, supported in part by the National Endowment for the Humanities and the Andrew W. Mellon Foundation. Thank you for additional publication support from Mary Ellen Poole, Stanley and Marcia Gumberg Dean, College of Fine Arts at CMU, and the Cooper-Siegel Professorship.

So many people were willing to help me with small and large questions along the way: Pierre Couprie, David Dacks, Wendy Earle, Tyler Greenleaf, Liam Kieser, Jeremy Strachan, and Gayle Young. Thank you to Norma Beecroft for answering questions about *Consequences for 5* and sending me materials. Matthew Fava was quick to help me with a photograph question, and, as then director of the Canadian Music Centre (CMC) Ontario branch, he hosted EQ at the CMC's Chalmers House in Toronto. Thank you to other CMC staff for your help in procuring scores. To the participants in the second iteration of Rose Bolton's EQ project: thank you for letting me interview you and observe your sessions.

Thank you to everyone who has had a direct hand in shaping the contents of this book, including the attendees at the Canadian University Music Society (MusCan) in 2015 and 2018; the participants at the International Conference on Mixed Music Pedagogy in 2018; students in the Music since 1945 and Music History III courses at CMU; and, with deepest gratitude, Dr Erin K. Maher for your helpful feedback on multiple versions of this book; it transformed under your careful eye. To the two anonymous reviewers: your feedback was generous and incisive. This book is much stronger because of you. Giving this labour during these times is especially appreciated.

To my editor, Jonathan Crago, Alyssa Favreau, Kathleen Fraser, James Leahy, Lesley Trites, and everyone at McGill-Queen's University Press: thank you for all of your work and guidance in bringing this book to fruition. You believed in the value of a book on the CEE and in my ability to do it justice.

To anyone who takes the time to read this book, thank you. I appreciate your time, and I hope you find it interesting and inspiring. I certainly hope that more scholars will take up the topic of the CEE; there's so much more to say than what would fit into this one book.

To my family back in Saskatoon: my mom, Jessica and Greg, Leif, Annika, Trygve, and Reid. You've kept me laughing with your musicology and PhD jokes, and you've made me feel loved and supported across the long distance.

I want to express my gratitude to a dear and old friend, Josh Peters, who always supported my dreams. He listened with open and curious ears, and he regularly reminded me why I love music so much.

To my dearest Itay, partner, co-conspirator, and love: I have been unsure even to this moment whether to thank you first or last – you deserve more thanks than I could ever express, and I hope you feel my gratitude until the end of my days. I would be absolutely lost without you. Your belief in me is the only reason this book exists. Your feedback, encouragement, and listening ear have meant everything to me. And of course, you're an amazing father to Aviv and you make sure I have time for my work. To my darling Aviv: I started this book long before you existed, but you have witnessed its completion. I hope I make you proud and show you that big dreams are possible – and that weird music is awesome.

The original CEE quartet poses for official group photos in 1972. Photo: Carol Sutton. Courtesy of Andre Fauteux as trustee of Carol Loraine Sutton.

Jim Montgomery sits in front of electronic music gear ca 1972. Private photo courtesy of David Jaeger.

David Jaeger and Jim Montgomery set up for a performance as Possibilities Portmanteau in Carol Sutton's loft ca 1972. Photo courtesy of Sally Jaeger.

David Jaeger and Jim Montgomery pose with their equipment before a performance in Carol Sutton's loft ca 1972. Photo courtesy of Sally Jaeger.

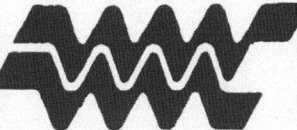

The *Globe and Mail* advertises CEE performances as part of a Multi-Media Concert at the University of Toronto's Edward Johnson Building on 15 December 1972 and for the Toronto Symphony Orchestra's world premiere of Steve Gellman's *Universe Symphony* on 11 January 1986.

ENTERTAINMENT

Under an umbrella: international folk-arts

By MAX WYMAN

CANADIAN ELECTRONIC ENSEMBLE... after the chaos

No short-circuiting of the sins of taste with electronic music

By LLOYD DYKK

Vancouver Sun music critic Lloyd Dykk praises the CEE's "dashing performance" and credits them with "casting a spell of the romance of electronic music" at their Vancouver New Music Society concert on 27 May 1976.

The original CEE quartet rehearses in 1977. Photo: Dick Loek. Courtesy of *Toronto Star* (licensed by Getty Images).

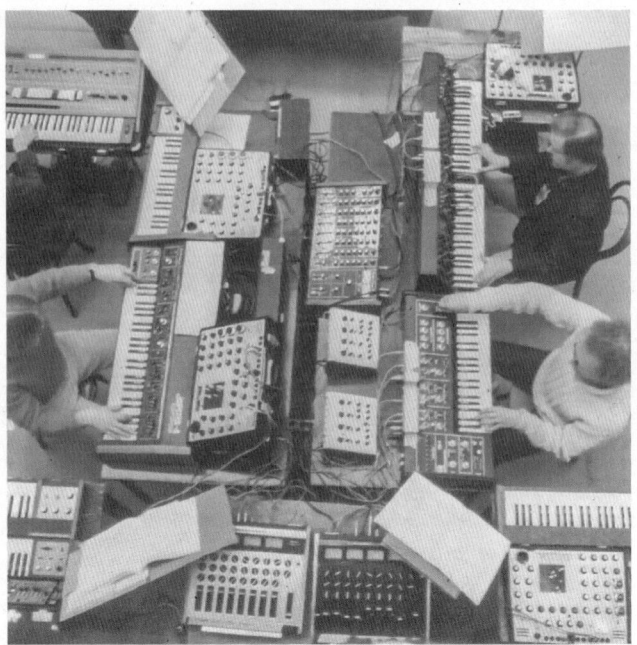

An overhead view of the CEE quartet and their large setup during their 1979 tour in Brussels. Photo: Karen Ann Kieser. Courtesy of The Estate of Karen Ann Kieser.

The Canadian Electronic Ensemble and Trio Collectif combine to form Supertrio during a residency at the Banff Centre in October 1994; image included in the *Supertrio* CD booklet. Photo: Karen Ann Kieser. Box 2. Acc # 2007-04. Item # 7 354 13145 L. Music Programs. Paul D. Fleck Library and Archives, Banff Centre for Arts and Creativity, Banff, Alberta. Courtesy of The Estate of Karen Ann Kieser.

The CEE performs at the Music Gallery ca 2001. Photo courtesy of Paul Stillwell.

Rose Bolton plays the Rosonator at the Music Gallery ca 2001. Photo courtesy of Paul Stillwell.

Jim Montgomery, David Jaeger, Larry Lake, Paul Stillwell, and guest Farhad Nargol-O'Neill perform at the Arts & Letters Club on 29 July 2011. Photo courtesy of Paul Stillwell.

David Jaeger, Jim Montgomery, Paul Stillwell, and Norma Beecroft pose at CMC book launch for *Conversations with Post World War II Pioneers of Electronic Music* on 26 September 2015. Photo courtesy of Matthew Fava.

Jim Montgomery, David Jaeger, and Paul Stillwell pose with Stillwell's Eurorack gear at the Arts & Letters Club on 26 April 2016. Photo: Alexa Woloshyn.

Rose Bolton leads a group session for EQ on 20 April 2017. Photo: Alexa Woloshyn.

David Sutherland performs in his home on 13 October 2017. Photo: Alexa Woloshyn.

John Kameel Farah, David Sutherland, David Jaeger, and Paul Stillwell (not pictured) perform at the CMC on 13 October 2017. Photo: Alexa Woloshyn.

The CEE Sextet poses in front of the College of Fine Arts Lawn at Carnegie Mellon University on 24 February 2020. Photo: Alexa Woloshyn.

The CEE and Exploded Ensemble rehearse in the Media Lab at Carnegie Mellon University on 26 February 2020. Photo courtesy of Paul Stillwell.

Close-up of Paul Stillwell's Eurorack set-up. Photo courtesy of Paul Stillwell.

An Orchestra at My Fingertips

1

Electrifying Musical Life in Toronto

A Canadian Electronic Music Performance in Context

Have you heard the joke about DJs and laptop musicians? The one about checking their email from behind the glowing screen on the stage? Sounds emanate from speakers to the ears of the audience, but the listeners don't know if the DJ is creating the sounds in real time or has simply pressed "play." When the Canadian Electronic Ensemble (CEE) first began performing in the early 1970s, there were no laptops. Their technologies were analog and thus somewhat unpredictable, and creating appealing polyphonic textures required multiple pieces of equipment. But over time, the group members discovered, developed, and incorporated new technologies as they became available. David Jaeger emphasized Larry Lake's leadership in this regard: "Larry was a consummate reader of technical literature" (personal communication, 10 June 2016). Paul Stillwell recalled the changes that the CEE has both witnessed and implemented into the group's collective practice: "so over the time of the CEE, we've gone from having ... synthesizers with fixed signal paths ... fixed control modules to programmable synthesizers, hardware synthesizers. So from analog to digital, programmable, and saveable. We've gone from that into the computer and software synthesizers" (personal communication, 27 January 2016). So, now that laptops are part of the CEE's gear, how do we know if they are *actually* expressing their creative will in real time?

Electronic music making, from analog synthesizers to laptops, presents some challenges in terms of audience engagement and comprehension, especially for those accustomed to the gesture–sound relationships of Euro-American classical acoustic instruments, to which the CEE's gear bears little resemblance. Keyboard interfaces have been ubiquitous in electronic sound technologies (Dalgleish 2016), but even those do not always have the kind of gesture–sound relationship that listeners familiar with the piano would expect. Some key questions therefore arise: From what creative practices do the technologies and performance practice of the CEE emerge? What similarities does the CEE have to Euro-American classical music performed on acoustic instruments? What differences do audiences encounter that shape their engagement with, assessment of, and understanding of the CEE's live electronic music?

The following account of one CEE performance reveals connections to several threads of twentieth-century music history – live electronic music, studio-based electronic/electroacoustic music, experimental and electronic music in Canada, and issues of listening to electronic music – giving us a starting point for contextualizing the CEE's sound, practice, and audiences:

> Author's personal memory. On 26 April 2016, I join a small audience in the Great Hall of the Arts & Letters Club in Toronto. Though there is a stage, the Canadian Electronic Ensemble sets up to perform on the floor, at the same level as the audience. The hall likely seems grand and imposing in the daylight, but with the room lighting dimmed and spotlights only on the performance area, the space feels intimate. On the table at the front of the room is a collection of different live electronic music technologies: Eurorack modular synthesis modules and brightly coloured cables, three laptops, and a midi keyboard controller. The CEE performs as a trio this evening: David Jaeger, Jim Montgomery, and Paul Stillwell. Seemingly without the guidance of a written score, the CEE performs a series of extended pieces (approximately twenty minutes each). After the concert, the consensus of audience members' murmurings is that they enjoyed the sounds created this evening. However, they betray complete confusion about David's contribution behind his two laptops. Audience members are eager to talk with the individual members, especially Paul, who has so many colourful cables. They explain that they saw him turning knobs, plugging and unplugging cables during the performance: he must be the main sound creator in the group.

The various threads of electronic music history underlying this account will be followed in a mostly chronological fashion in this chapter, though they do overlap in time. Because my purpose is to outline the confluence of factors in the late 1960s and early 1970s that influenced the CEE's formation and early practice, each section arrives at this key period for the CEE's genesis. Though electronic technologies for performance and for composition have intersecting histories and mechanics, there are also distinct lineages of electronic tools designed for real-time performance on a concert stage and those for composers in an electronic music studio, both of which are linked to the CEE's practice. I therefore begin by discussing early electronic music instruments and the development of synthesizers, both with and without keyboard interfaces. I then address electronic music composition in the European studios in France and Germany before summarizing both studio-based and live electronic music in Canada from 1959 to the 1970s. Because the CEE's practice relies both on studio-based composition and on live performance, I discuss the temporalities of electronic music composition in electronic music studios in the 1950s and '60s. I situate the CEE's live performance practice within a history of electronic music ensembles, showing traits and approaches both unique to the group and shared with other major ensembles. Finally, I raise the issue of the listener's perspective in electronic music, exploring conceptual issues around agency – namely, intention and effort, which have posed both challenges and opportunities for electronic music performers and composers alike in the past 100 years.

Live on Stage: Performing Electronic Musical Instruments

One might assume that the history of electronic music starts with the twentieth century. However, Collins, Schedel, and Wilson (2013, 26) identify the first electric instrument in the mid-eighteenth century: Václav Prokop Diviš (1698–1765) invented the Denis d'or in 1748, but only one was ever made, and it has not survived. Jean-Baptiste Thillaie Delaborde's Clavecin électrique (1759) is the earliest surviving electric instrument (2013, 26–7). Our fascination with electricity and sound making has a long history, and those details can be found in numerous publications, including *Electronic Music* (Collins, Schedel, and Wilson 2013), *Electric Sound* (Chadabe 1997), and *The Cambridge Companion to Electronic Music* (Collins and d'Escriván 2017).

In the late nineteenth century, the emergence of new communication technologies also resulted in new musical developments, such as AM radio broadcasting, Elisha Gray's Musical Telegraph, and Thaddeus Cahill's Telharmonium. While many of these developments resulted in new listening experiences (over the air waves or through the telephone, for example), these emerging technologies had no capacity for live stage performance. It was in the first decades of the twentieth century that electronic instruments designed for live performance were developed.

The most famous of these new instruments was the theremin. Russian researcher Léon Theremin's invention captured audiences' imaginations through its touchless playing approach, as hands moving gracefully in the air seemed to pluck voice-like melodies from the ether (Leydon 2004). New devices were often tied in some clear way to their musical predecessors, such as the use of the theremin to perform existing vocal repertoire. In his 1937 essay "The Future of Music: Credo," John Cage criticizes inventors for sticking to eighteenth- and nineteenth-century models of design and sound. He praises the innovation of the theremin but decries its performers who "make the instrument sound like some old instrument, giving it a sickeningly sweet vibrato, and performing upon it, with difficulty, masterpieces from the past" (1973, 3–4).

Cage's embrace of found sounds and unusual uses of existing technologies would prove a substantial influence on subsequent electronic music, both live and in the studio. His *Imaginary Landscape* pieces did not use instruments in a conventional sense, either acoustic or electronic. *No. 1* (1939) and *No. 3* (1942) both use variable-speed turntables playing frequency recordings; the former was intended only for radio broadcast or recording, while the latter, which also includes audio frequency oscillators, is a concert piece. *No. 4* (1951) was composed for twenty-four performers at twelve radios whose tunings throughout the work may land on stations playing any variety of music or speech, or even on the white noise in between stations. Today, in the CEE's music, David Jaeger can sample sounds like this (e.g., white noise) easily on his laptop without the need for physical, analog objects.

Another remnant of Euro-American instrument traditions has been the frequent reliance on the keyboard as an interface, such as with the ondes Martenot and Hammond organ. The ondes Martenot, developed by Maurice Martenot in 1928, includes a metal ring that facilitates seamless glissandi and a drawer of switches that enable timbral shifts, functioning similarly to organ stops. The instrument also has a keyboard interface for pitch accuracy in quick passagework. The ondes Martenot remains relatively well known, likely due to a repertoire composed specifically for the instrument, notably including Olivier Messiaen's *Turangalîla-Symphonie* (1946–48). The Hammond organ (1935) was designed for domestic and church use, and it achieved the creators' desired mass production, consumption, and popularity. It was designed to enhance an existing musical instrument and practice rather than to conceive of something entirely unprecedented, but its significance lay in the new timbres it could produce. Collins, Schedel, and Wilson (2013, 41) point to the use of the word "infinite" in advertising claims as evidence of an important shift.

Some inventors in the 1920s rejected the keyboard in order to achieve microtones, designing instruments like Jörg Mager's Elektrophon (1921) and Friederich Trautwein's Trautonium (1928). The goal of the Trautonium, a monophonic instrument, was subtle expressivity in phrasing and articulation (Collins, Schedel, and Wilson 2013, 39). In the 1960s, when Robert Moog and Don Buchla were developing their voltage-controlled synthesizers independently of each other, they still had to decide what place – if any – the legacy of the keyboard interface would have in their new instruments. Moog's original design could be controlled by many different interfaces, but he ended up sticking with the keyboard because that was what consumers wanted (Pinch and Trocco 2002). Buchla, on the other hand, refused to use a keyboard interface, preferring "something more imaginative as a controller ... away from the constraints of the standard keyboard" (Pinch and Trocco 2002, 44). As I discuss further in chapter 3, the Eurorack modular synthesis modules Paul Stilwell uses with the CEE are part of a broader renewed interest in 1960s modular synthesizers.

Each of the inventors above desired to achieve something new, with particular concern for innovations in timbre and pitch. The electronic instruments of the early twentieth century reinforced many aspects of traditional Euro-American classical performance practice and listening contexts, and Nicolas Collins (2017) argues that these instruments did not really change the Euro-American classical music world. Yet "the possibility of musical instruments that can produce 'any' sound raises the question of what exactly makes a sound musical and led many to wonder whether there need be any real limit to this" (Collins, Schedel, and Wilson 2013, 43). Some new sounds were achieved, and sometimes new mechanisms of sound production – though, as outlined above, keyboard interfaces dominated. At the CEE's April 2016 performance, the midi keyboard controller was the ensemble's only keyboard interface (apart from the laptop keyboards); however, other performances across the decades have included numerous keyboard interfaces, pointing to the ongoing prevalence of such interfaces in electronic music.

The new synthesizers created by Hugh Le Caine, Moog, and Buchla made significant strides in the speed and precision of sound synthesis. However, they were still intended for studio composition – for tape pieces – in part because these synthesizers were monophonic. Tape recorders were also conventionally used not as an instrument for live performance but as a way to develop material in the studio (e.g., cut and paste) and then document the final product as a fixed media work. Peter Manning notes that many composers desired to transfer what was happening in the studio to the live concert (2013, 157). This desire reflects a path distinct from electronic (and electric) instruments such as the theremin that largely fit into conventional models of Western classical musical composition and performance. Because the studio offered new notions of music and the musical work, the live electronic music that emerged from studio practice often embraced a diversity of approaches and influences. Mauricio Kagel brought the tape recorder to the live concert stage with *Transición II* (1958–59), as did Karlheinz Stockhausen in *Solo* (1965–66). Alvin Lucier's famous tape piece *I am sitting in a room* (1970) demonstrated the capacities of playback and resonance. Many other composers turned to microphones, amplifiers, and modulators to perform live electronic music.

The CEE experimented first with electronic equipment designed for studio experimentation, unplugging pieces from their stable homes and setting them up on a stage. They used many of the monophonic synthesizers that revolutionized electronic music creation in the 1960s. And soon, the group was adding new, more portable instruments and inventing their own instruments. The CEE's 2016 concert illustrates how their current practice juxtaposes older (i.e., analog) and newer (i.e., digital) tools. A now-ubiquitous digital tool, the laptop is used as both a studio-based composition tool and a live performance instrument. Its capacity for real-time electronic music making, including sampling and live processing, underlines significant developments in live electronic performance technologies in the last century.

Composing Electronic Music: Working and Listening in the Early Studio Era

The Arts & Letters Club in Toronto typically hosts performances of chamber music. Chamber music performances, in both concert and salon contexts, prioritize fixed listening, with the audience in close proximity to the musicians; the account of the April 2016 performance shows the CEE fitting into this practice as a kind of electronic chamber group. However, given their instrumentation, the CEE is also positioned within the performance practice of institutional electronic music, a legacy of the group's origins in the University of Toronto Electronic Music Studio.

In concerts of fixed media electronic/electroacoustic music realized in the studio and then diffused in the concert space, typically with little or no lighting, the "performers" are speakers set up in various configurations within the space. The setup might be very simple, perhaps with just eight speakers encircling the audience, or as complex as the more than 100 channels achieved through the vast collection of loudspeakers in the University of Birmingham's BEAST. The single human "performer" stands behind the mixing board with only a small light, so as not to distract the audience from the immersive sonic space. This is acousmatic music, a listening context in which the sound and source are divorced from each other. The term comes from Pythagoras's concept of akousmatikoi, a part of his pedagogical theory that insisted we concentrate better when we are forced to listen only.

This kind of focused listening was what French composer Pierre Schaeffer desired for his musique concrète, an approach that prioritizes the intrinsic quality of sounds rather than their referential quality. In 1942, the Studio d'Essai (later Club d'Essai) opened in Paris, and under Schaeffer's leadership, it became a musical hub focused on experimental radiophonic approaches. Schaeffer's *Cinq études de bruits*, premiered by broadcast at Radiodiffusion Française (home of d'Essai) on 4 October 1948, marks a deliberate shift in the composer's intentions and their creative results. As Carlos Palombini explains, "Schaeffer started research into noises at the Club d'Essai. Research into noises became publicly known as musique concrète in 1949" (1993, 14). "Noises" (or "bruits") in this context typically denote found sounds, or real-world sounds, though Schaeffer and his associates did not exclude recorded musical or electronic sounds. The formation in 1951 of the Groupe de Recherches de Musique Concrète (GRCM) at Radiodiffusion-Télévision Française reflects both the seriousness of their intent and its respectful reception.[1]

Compared to the limited experimental possibilities of phonograph technology (Manning 2013), tape technology offered Schaeffer, Pierre Henry (who joined him in 1949), and their associates increased ease as well as creative options for manipulating recorded sound. Schaeffer's musique concrète aimed to separate real-world sounds from their purpose (what Griffiths calls their "native associations" [1979, 12]), with the goal "that sounds should be perceived and appreciated for their abstract properties rather than being attached to meanings or narratives associated with their sources and causes" (Emmerson and Smalley 2001). Magnetic tape greatly facilitated this by making it much easier to isolate and combine sounds (a process called "micro-editing" [Teruggi 2007, 217]) and then to process sounds.

The live electronic music of the 1960s and '70s owes much of its technologies to the studio developments of the previous decades, including both Schaeffer's Studio d'Essai and the Nordwestdeutscher Rundfunk (NWDR) in Cologne, West Germany. In the classic studios, much of the equipment was repurposed for musical means. Nowhere was this more apparent than in the experimental studio at the NWDR, which opened in 1952. Here, oscillators and noise generators were the main sound sources, offering synthesized sound for processing and assemblage as opposed to the recorded real-world sounds in the Paris studio. The work of those in the Cologne studio was called elektronische Musik. Though the divide between the Paris and Cologne studios has been rather exaggerated, in the early 1950s, there was indeed a significant distinction in both the basic sound material and the aesthetic goals. Emmerson and Smalley characterize the work in Cologne: "The composers aimed to use electronic resources to construct timbres, thereby extending control to the structure of sound itself, and they envisaged that a musical structure would be planned before realizing it electronically" (2001).

Composers in the Cologne studio worked directly with electronic sound signals, first creating them and then processing them with various filters, gates, and other effects. The early Cologne studio had two single-track tape recorders, a variable-speed tape recorder, and a four-track recording system used for the steps of creating and documenting each sound, then editing, looping, and mixing each in turn. Joel Chadabe characterizes the classic studios as "manual" studios (1967, 107), meaning that each step in working with sound was separate (and time-consuming!).[2] The Cologne composers had the added task of building up timbres from single sound waves until they achieved a complex sound that was appealing.

The overwrought narrative of the "battle" between the French and the Germans for aesthetic and technological domination has formed a well-worn path in electronic music historiography. Such a narrative denies both the aesthetic variety within the two groups and the abundance of activity happening elsewhere in the world at the same time, both within and outside of institutional studios. Indeed, throughout the 1950s, studios were opening in other European centres, such as the Studio di Fonologia Musicale in Milan (1955) and the BBC's Radiophonic Workshop (1958). Composers travelled to the different studios to explore each one's distinctive collection of equipment and approach to technology. In a 1967 article about the analog studios, Chadabe bemoans the lack of standardization across the studios, instead expressing a desire to turn the studio into a "standard instrument" (107) from which innovations and deviations can take place. Nonetheless, it is this lack of standardization that resulted in distinctive works that sonified their place of creation. Furthermore, such idiosyncrasies facilitated a great deal of creative exchange as composers travelled to different studios, including the University of Toronto's Electronic Music Studio, where the members of the CEE first interacted.

The studios of the 1940s and '50s have been criticized for hiding composers away from both performers and audiences. (The advertising of Columbia-Princeton's Mark II, which promised that performing musicians were no longer necessary, might seem to support this claim.) For some composers, though, the motivation was not to isolate oneself from performers and audiences: many musicians used studio technologies to return to the live stage, developing distinct real-time electronic music-making practices. Live electronic music making also occurred outside of the studio context both before and during the classic studio era. However, many of the important live electronic ensembles from the 1960s and '70s, including the CEE, emerged from electronic music studio practice.

Electronic Music in Canada: Studios and Beyond

As Canada's largest city, Toronto is the centre of musical life in Canada, and has been the centre of the CEE's musical life since the group's founding. The city is home to the headquarters of the Canadian Broadcasting Corporation (CBC) (which includes the Glenn Gould Studio, a dual-purpose recording studio and concert hall), the Royal Conservatory of Music, numerous organizations devoted to new music, and the national office of the Canadian Music Centre. These institutions are exclusionary spaces, with networks whose participants and beneficiaries are primarily white, cis male, and class privileged. Certainly large cities like Vancouver, Winnipeg, and Montreal are centres in their own right, especially within their respective regions, but the scope of the cultural infrastructure in Toronto is unrivalled. It is unsurprising that the members of the CEE chose to come to Toronto to study and that this city continues to support their activities both within and outside of the group.

The University of Toronto Electronic Music Studio (UTEMS) was the first electronic music studio in Canada and one of the first in North America. When it opened in 1959, scientist Hugh Le Caine's instruments were a central part of the inventory. Electronic music in Canada owes much to Le Caine and the National Research Council (NRC) in Ottawa, which granted Le Caine space and equipment to pursue his groundbreaking innovations in electronic instruments, all while he continued his primary research in radar and nuclear physics.[3]

UTEMS was a leader in technological, aesthetic, and creative innovation; composers from across the continent visited the studio to work with its unique instruments. Though the names associated with UTEMS – including Le Caine – do not have the same public recognition as names like Robert Moog and Don Buchla, UTEMS and its associated faculty were leaders in the field during these early decades of exploration and innovation. Moog even visited UTEMS in the summer of 1964, and the support of the studio's first director, Myron Schaeffer, was critical in encouraging the young Moog that his basic voltage-controlled synthesizer had potential (Pinch and Truocco 2002).

Beyond the University of Toronto, electronic music in the city also thrived at an electronic studio at the Royal Conservatory of Music Toronto (established in 1966), at which composer Ann Southam frequently worked. Estonian-born Canadian composer Udo Kasemets worked outside of the university institutions, directing important multi- and intermedia arts projects in the 1960s and '70s. Electronic music soon spread out from Toronto across the country. David Keane (1984) credits Hungarian Canadian composer István Anhalt with organizing Canada's first concert of tape music at McGill University in 1959, which included Le Caine's most celebrated composition, *Dripsody*. Anhalt founded McGill's electronic music studio in 1964 – also with the help of Le Caine and his instruments – and Anhalt's own compositions and students helped secure a legacy of Canadian electroacoustic music.

In the subsequent decades, universities across the country opened their own electronic music studios.[4] With the exception of the most eastern provinces and the northern territories, electronic music studios spread to the major urban centres throughout much of Canada, including five in the prairie provinces.[5] Simon Fraser University's studio was founded in 1967 by R. Murray Schafer, and under his leadership, the institution became known for the World Soundscape Project and soundscape composition, with leading composers like Barry Truax (who also directed the studio and made significant strides in digital composition) and Hildegard Westerkamp.

When home studios became viable during the 1970s, many interested composers, such as Norma Beecroft, shifted their working space outside of the academy.[6] However, students have continued to rely on access to institutional electronic music studios to study, experiment, and create. Many individuals in the first generation of Canadian-trained electronic composers opened additional studios, as Kevin Austin[7] did at Concordia University, or took over directorship of existing studios, such as Barry Truax at Simon Fraser and the CEE's James Montgomery at the Ontario College of Education.

Canadian organizations and festivals devoted to new music have typically included programming of electronic and electroacoustic music, including fixed media works for acousmatic concerts or live electronic/ mixed media performances. Winnipeg-based Music Inter Alia (1977–91; renamed GroundSwell in 1991 under new leadership) regularly presented electroacoustic and multi-/intermedia art works, owing to the leadership of co-founders Diana McIntosh and Ann Southam. Other organizations with ongoing series include the Vancouver New Music Society, the Music Gallery in Toronto, and Toronto New Music Concerts.

Among organizations devoted specifically to electronic/electroacoustic music, the Canadian Electroacoustic Community (CEC) was co-founded in 1986 by Jean-François Denis and Kevin Austin. In addition to hosting numerous concerts and festivals and promoting Canada's electroacoustic practitioners on the national and international scenes, the organization publishes an electronic journal *eContact!* (originally a print journal called *Contact!*), which includes articles, interviews, and proceedings from the annual Toronto International Electroacoustic Symposium. The Association pour la création et la recherche électroacoustiques du Québec (ACREQ) was founded in 1978 in Montreal by Yves Daoust, Marcelle Deschênes, and others. ACREQ produces concerts, commissions works, presents workshops in primary and secondary schools, and supports research projects in electroacoustic music.

For the young American musicians who would go on to found the CEE, the Toronto of the early 1970s offered what they were seeking in graduate studies in composition and electronic music. Local organizations like New Music Concerts, the Music Gallery, and Soundstreams have continued to provide creative outlets for members of the CEE over the decades, alongside countless other experimental and electronic composers and performers. In addition, Toronto offers venue spaces including the Canadian Music Centre Chalmers Performance Space, the Arts & Letters Club, and The TRANZAC. I suspect that the CEE has performed in every suitable space across the city.

Electronic Music Creation: Fixed vs Real-Time

In the classic studios, there was a long time period between recording a sound or synthesizing a wave form and completing the final mix of the fixed piece, as this work involved the rather tedious labour of dealing with each parameter – such as timbre or amplitude – separately. Thus, electronic music studios created a different relationship to time and to the notion of the musical work. For example, Barry Schrader's description of how Louis and Bebe Barron created the soundtrack for *Forbidden Planet* (1956) in their home studio clearly illustrates that their collaborative division of labour was time-intensive: "Louis designed and built the electronic circuits for sound generation while Bebe searched the taped material for its musical potential and proposed the application of particular processing and compositional techniques" (2001).

Or consider the timeline of creating a piece using the RCA Mark II synthesizer at the Columbia-Princeton Electronic Music Center (Babbitt 1964). This synthesizer was large, expensive, and cumbersome but also powerful and novel. The Mark II used punch cards that contained the encoded instructions regarding sound synthesis and processing. Rather than process each step separately, as had been required in Cologne, the Mark II could work out several steps simultaneously. But although this synthesizer may have been less time-consuming to use, it still took months to compose a work because of the synthesizer patches required to achieve the desired sound, which often included levels of rhythmic and pitch-based complexity that could not be replicated by a human performer.

The CEE, as a group of individual composer-performer-improvisers, presents a complex system of intentions, choices, coordination, and perception, on multiple time scales. As composers, they write music on a longer time scale than the resulting real-time performance. Sometimes pieces involve experimenting in the studio and creating tracks, resulting in time scales more reminiscent of the Barrons' work and the Mark II's punch cards. The CEE's intended goal, however, has always been real-time collective music making, like what they performed in April 2016.

Live, real-time electronic music making is not the same as its acoustic counterpart. David Tudor, John Cage's frequent collaborator, recognized the importance of embracing the unpredictability and unrepeatability of electronic music, which is reflected in Tudor's indeterminate scores. Cage himself dominates narratives of experimental music in Canada and the United States, with his challenge to conventional notions of a musical sound and the musical work. His aleatory techniques – including graphic notation and chance operations – and his attention to "noise" both positioned music "as a *process* more than a *thing*" (Cecchetto and Strachan 2015, 549).

Invoking Cage's influence in relation to real-time music making necessitates accounting for his dismissive remarks about jazz, which he did not consider "serious" music. George E. Lewis argues that discussions of real-time music making often position "jazz" (in varied and diverging forms) as "Other" in relation to the so-called "Western" composers who are placed in the lineage of "European cultural, social, and intellectual history – the 'Western' tradition" – resulting in "an attempted erasure or denial of the impact of African-American forms on the real-time work of European and Euro-American composers" (2002, 216). Lewis quotes composer Anthony Braxton to underline Cage's deliberate "disavowal of jazz" (2002, 223): "Both aleatory and indeterminism are words which have been coined ... to bypass the word improvisation and as such the influence of non-white sensibility" (2002, 223; original is Braxton 1985, 366).

The concepts of Afrological and Eurological perspectives on real-time music making, as argued by Lewis, allow us to consider each musical belief system and its associated behaviours as "historically emergent rather than ethnically essential" (2002, 217). The Afrological perspective emerges from the practice of "radical young black American improvisers" (2002, 216), but this value system may be practised by any person. Indeed, Lewis identifies several groups and musicians working within the field of "improvised music," such as the Association for the Advancement of Creative Musicians (AACM), European "free" improvisers, and the "downtown (New York) school" (2002, 236). The CEE's relation to Lewis's framework is discussed in chapter 4.

In Euro-American classical music, the composer and the score have maintained hegemony over creativity and agency in music – specifically in how we talk about music, the musical work, and performance (Cook 2018). Nicholas Cook claims that while conservatory students deny they are being creative when they realize musical scores (2018, 199), music as a creative practice is inherently "made out of human actions and interactions" (2018, 1). Whenever music is made in a group, creativity comes from the social, interactive, collaborative, and collective aspects of music making; "intentionality occurs at the level of the group and is dispersed across the players" (2018, 26). Group music making is a complex system, as "at any given moment, there is a multiplicity of choices, each of which branches into a further multiplicity of choices, and so on" (2018, 321), even when a score is part of the performance. Live electronic music further heightens the need to embrace the "given moment." Ronald Kuivila explains that because of the particular "temporal behaviour" of electronic music making, "advanced planning is only partially useful, perfect compliance is impossible, and the concepts of contingency and action are essential" (2009, 111).

Group improvisation highlights the importance of listening: performers create opportunities for one another, or, as Linson and Clarke explain, they "afford one another opportunities for future actions"

(2017, 64). Listening is an essential act of readiness, and this readiness is subjective to the divergent perspectives of each individual. Both listening and responding are outcomes of each performer's particular cognitive, perceptual, and motor skill capabilities and tendencies. Furthermore, the manifestation of their embodied creative practice is deeply tied to their chosen instruments or tools.

Cage encouraged composers and musicians to hear musical potential in seemingly unmusical objects. Doing so requires what Andy Keep describes as "instrumentalizing," which "seeks to discover the performability, intrinsic sonic palette and possibilities for sonic manipulation of objects" (2009, 113). Such a process can apply not only to typically quotidian acoustic sound objects but also to new electronic technologies. In the early decades of electronic music, both in the studio and in live performance, many available technologies did not have set musical purposes. Indeed, those with a particular known technical function (such as an oscillator to produce a pitch with a particular wave form) had musical potential that had to be activated, or "instrumentalized."

The CEE has both instruments and instrumentalized objects at its disposal, and each member brings a unique set of capabilities and tendencies to the ensemble's group music making. Because analog instruments in particular are unpredictable, the electronic tools are even more obvious as co-collaborators rather than merely extensions of the performer, as Euro-American classical instruments are sometimes described. The CEE's network of collaborators sometimes also includes non-CEE composers and performers, further expanding the diversity of perspectives. From this joint effort, questions emerge about how creativity, collaboration, and improvisation manifest within the CEE's musical practice: What makes the CEE successful as a collaboration, or successful as an example of collective creativity? What are the CEE's criteria for success? These questions will be addressed in chapters 3 and 4.

Electronic Music Ensembles: Approaches to Collaboration

During the 1960s and '70s, some musicians believed "live electronic music [appeared] too uncontrolled a medium" (Griffiths 1979, 23). The dream of electronic music had been to achieve limitless sounds – and, for some, limitless control. However, this dream seemed appropriate only in the studio, though even there, "limitless" was not a reality. And in either context – studio or live performance – the electronic musician and composer needed significant technical knowledge to deal with the equipment. While institutional studios had technicians, a composer would struggle without a basic understanding of the science of sound synthesis and how to address frequent issues in the studio, and the live musicians had only themselves. Paul Griffiths explains this performance context and the resulting practice:

> The work of a live electronic ensemble naturally involves a good deal of experiment in building instruments and circuits for special purposes, in finding sounds required and in developing a feeling of ensemble. Moreover, it is difficult to notate sound events which result from devices and performance techniques that have not been standardized. All this has encouraged ensembles very often to concern themselves with more or less free improvisation, and even where this has not been the case, live electronic ensembles have tended to evolve their own styles and their own repertoires … The evolution of live electronic music has been directed principally by composer-performers working with regular ensembles. (1979, 72)

While Griffiths does not mention the CEE specifically, his summary precisely captures the ensemble's approach, one that they have maintained across five decades of live electronic music making.

Most of the early live electronic ensembles in Europe, the United States, and around the world were small ensembles (Griffiths 1979), including the CEE; the group's performance in April 2016 maintained this small ensemble approach with only a trio. Ensemble rather than solo performance was necessitated by the amount of equipment needed to create interesting sounds and textures in the first place. The technology was too complex, and as most synthesizers were monophonic, a solo performance would simply not make for very interesting music during an extended concert performance. In addition, live electronic music breaks down the gesture–sound relationship audiences expect in live performance, particularly in the case of groups like the CEE, as opposed to those who use electronic/electric versions of instruments like electric guitars. With an ensemble, there are more bodies and equipment to look at during a performance, which could make it more appealing for audiences.

The existing histories of electronic music typically mention the following live electronic ensembles: Stockhausen Ensemble (1964), Gruppo di Improvvisazione Nuova Consonanza (Rome, 1964), Musica Elettronica Viva (1966), AMM (British, 1965), Sonic Arts Union (1966) out of the Cooperative Studio for Electronic Music, and the San Francisco Tape Music Center (1961). Manning (2013) expands the typical list to mention Gentle Fire and Naked Software, which both emerged in the 1960s, and Intermodulation, which formed in 1969. In 1958, Takehisa Kosugi formed Group Ongaku, which was devoted to live improvisation. The CEE is never mentioned in these narratives about live electronic ensembles, perhaps because they formed officially in 1972, while these other groundbreaking groups were established in the 1960s. However, the CEE fulfills many of the standard characteristics of live electronic ensembles of this era while also exemplifying the particularities of a group emerging from Toronto, Canada, in the early 1970s.

The CEE is rather unlike Stockhausen's ensemble, for instance. While his studio works such as *Gesang der Jünglinge* receive more attention in the scholarly literature, Stockhausen led a live electronic ensemble that was particularly active in the 1960s and early 1970s. This ensemble's mission was to showcase Stockhausen's works, including *Mikrophonie I* (1964), *Prozession* (1967), and *Kurzwellen* (1968). Peter Manning (2013), Paul Griffiths (1979), and Joel Chadabe (1997) all underscore Stockhausen's emphasis on control and technical precision. Indeed, despite using the phrase "intuitive music," Stockhausen did not embrace "free improvisation" (Griffiths 1979, 80); rather, his group's purpose was to fulfill the composer's intentions, or what Manning refers to as "a coherent realization of his compositional objectives" (2013, 159–60).

Griffiths contrasts "Stockhausen's autocratic rule over his players" with "the perfect democracy sought by such groups as Musica Elettronica Viva" (1979, 80), a group with a much closer resemblance to the CEE. Musica Elettronica Viva (MEV) is one of the best-known experimental ensembles, due in large part to the renown of particular members such as Richard Teitelbaum, Frederic Rzewski, and Alvin Curran. MEV employed intermedia performance strategies of a "highly theatrical nature" (Manning 2013, 162). The CEE and MEV are similar in two main ways: 1) both groups consist of individual composers who have substantial careers outside of the ensemble; 2) the "individual motivations of the players" (Manning 2013, 162) guide the improvisations. However, unlike MEV, the CEE has largely avoided a theatrical performance practice. At one time, they hired someone tasked with keeping the audience engaged during tech set-up between numbers, but this was not a long-term solution. The CEE has also collaborated with artists and dancers, although this is also not a standard part of the group's practice. Another difference is that MEV is not focused on electronic music, but rather uses electronic resources to explore acoustic sound making.

Thus, the CEE also contrasts with Gruppo di Improvvisazione Nuova Consonanza, which focused principally on transforming traditional instruments and voice by expanding the sound resources of acoustic instruments, with the occasional use of oscillators, filters, and ring modulators. The CEE has worked with performers of conventional acoustic instruments throughout its history, and some of its members have also played such instruments alongside the group's synthesizers and other equipment. However, the CEE's creative practice emphasizes dialogue and juxtaposition in its mixed media works more than extending acoustic instruments through electronic processing.

London-based AMM's creative practice was located at the intersection of jazz, avant-garde classical music, and electronic technology, with members Cornelius Cardew, Christopher Hobbs, Lou Gare, Edwin Prévost, and Keith Rowe. Like AMM, the CEE has exhibited an openness to wide-ranging sound sources, though they are not devoted to Cageian instrumentalizations of unmusical physical objects. Rather, they have sought to instrumentalize non-musical electronic technologies and absorb new electronic musical technologies into their aesthetic and creative practice. AMM rejected notation, embraced all sound possibilities, and emphasized "spontaneous interplay between players" (Tilbury 2001). The CEE has not rejected notation entirely, as many works have scores, but much of the group's creative practice is either partially or entirely improvised. Despite the emphasis on improvisation, the CEE also rehearses, with elements of improvisations that emerge during rehearsal resurfacing during live performances.

Manning (2013) notes a creative approach common among European ensembles outside Cologne: "The live electronic ensembles that emerged elsewhere in Europe during the 1960s concentrated for the most part on group improvisation" (161). Improvisation was ubiquitous not only because of the influence of John Cage and other improvisational practices within acoustic ensembles, but also because of the realities of working with analog electronic equipment. A high level of unpredictability meant that ensembles were likely better off embracing the moment and responding to both machine and human input during the performance. The CEE is similar to these European live electronic ensembles: even in composed works with traditional scoring, it has always included group improvisation as a core part of its creative practice. The performances I have attended in recent years have been almost exclusively group improvisations with no notated parts and little direction other than who will start.

Writing in the 1970s, Gordon Mumma placed the innovation of live electronic music not in Europe but in the United States: "Between 1960 and 1965 most live-electronic music activity occurred in the United States. It was nourished not only because of a spirited experimental milieu, but also because the benefits of solid-state electronic technology were more accessible in the United States" (1975, 296). Manning (2013) divides American groups formed in the 1960s into two broad approaches: 1) collectives focused on group projects (such as the San Francisco Tape Music Center); and 2) ensembles with a leader's clear direction (something closer to Stockhausen's approach). The CEE, with its emphasis on group improvisation, aligns mostly with the former. However, as chapter 2 will explain, the group does perform compositions by individual members. Such a practice creates a hierarchy, but the compositions leave deliberate flexibility for each performer, and because each member of the CEE contributes compositions, no one compositional voice dominates.

While the San Francisco Tape Music Center (SFTMC), Once Group, and Sonic Arts Union were all collectives, the CEE distinguishes itself through its true group mentality, with co-composition and improvisation at the core of its creative practice. Contrast the CEE with how Chadabe describes the SFTMC:

> Although group improvisation had been one of its activities at the San Francisco Tape Music Center (SFTMC), it had not been thematic to the center's philosophy. [Morton] Subotnick, [Ramon] Sender, [Pauline] Oliveros, [Tony] Martin, and company in San

Francisco, and for that matter, also the people in the Once Group in Ann Arbor and in the Sonic Arts Union, had come together as groups to pool resources, focus public attention, and cooperate in joint projects. But basically they worked as individuals within the collaborative environments they had formed. (1997, 103)

Each of the individual members of the CEE has a creative life outside of the ensemble, but the purpose of coming together as a group has been to make music together. Even an individually composed work was intended to be realized by the entire ensemble, based on how their individual gear, musical experiences, and aesthetic tendencies would contribute to the collaboration. While they met and first performed through the institutional support of the University of Toronto and its Electronic Music Studio, the Canadian Electronic Ensemble has not aligned itself with any single institution as a means of securing resources or public attention, though its members have had significant institutional associations and opportunities (a topic addressed in chapter 6).

Perceiving Electronic Music: Challenges and Opportunities

Live electronic music is a particular kind of music-making beast. Though it intersects with studies of embodiment, instrumentalizing, collective music making, and audience engagement, live electronic music has some of its own unique qualities. These issues – concerning performance practice, audience perception, notions of virtuosity, and technological interfaces – arise from the breakdown of the gesture–sound relationship in electronic music, and they often overlap. For example, performance practice encompasses not only gesture and technology but also the improvisational practice that the CEE, like most other live electronic ensembles, implements.

Listeners who are familiar with acoustic music making, particularly in the context of Euro-American classical music, understand what a musician is doing with an instrument in order to create sounds, even as they might marvel at the specific talent required to do so. The nineteenth century saw a change in the perceived significance of the musician's body in performance, with the performer regarded as an "artist" whose "job was to interpret the musical work or, better, in a nearly literal sense, to bring it to life through skilled and inspired playing" (Kramer 2012, 231) – that is, the virtuoso. Corporeality is central to virtuosity – the performer pushes the limits of their body and their instrument in the service of expressivity. Lawrence Kramer points specifically to "the demand that the performer's body audibly translate its corporeality into expressivity" (2012, 232–3).

With many (though not all) tools for live electronic music making, corporeality may be reduced to a barely perceivable motion, such as when David Jaeger clicks his laptop's touchpad, a relatively small biomechanical gesture that can have wide-ranging sonic results, depending on what that click initiates in the laptop's software. Audience members often find it difficult to trace human causality in the array of sounds emitted through the loudspeakers, as witnessed at the April 2016 performance, among many others. In the early years of electronic technology, the role of the human in the creative process was still generally one of power, control, and artistic authority. But as computer technology developed, more power was afforded to the machine. A greater interactivity now exists between the human and the machine, which can result in a decrease in perceived human agency. Simon Emmerson argues that the perception of causality is largely up to the listener, though: composers and performers can influence that perception through gestures or other actions that "*imply* a causal link of sound to performer action in the *imagination* of the listener ... What *sounds* causal *is* effectively causal. The distinction of truly real and imaginary lies with the composer and performer, not the listener" (2007, 93). The listener perceives causal relationships that may be "real" – when the performer has causal agency over the sound – or "imaginary," when the performer prepares sound material in such a way that the listener believes there must be a real-time trigger.

Emmerson further explains that "the idea of any 'live' music is increasingly difficult to define, but there stubbornly remains much music which demands human presence and spontaneous creativity (physical and mental) in its production" (2007, 89). The performance practice of the CEE simultaneously challenges and reinforces this "stubborn" idea of "live" music: they incorporate traditional acoustic instruments, use obvious gestures to mark structural points, and perform with keyboard interfaces. But while the presence of keyboard interfaces creates a sense of familiarity for the performer and audience, the resulting expectations might go unfulfilled. A keyboard interface does not necessarily function in the same way as a piano: each depression of the keyboard might produce a single pitch, but it might alternatively be mapped onto sounds and actions completely divergent from acoustic keyboard instruments. Regardless of the specific electronic tool, a single gesture may trigger multiple sounds or, at the very least, complex ones – especially with polyphonic synthesizers and laptops – and the sounds themselves are unfamiliar in their variety and complexity. So, whose intention is sonically manifested in the timbres and textures of live electronic music making? Who has agency: the human or the machine? The relationship is not simple, and yet time and time again I hear audiences at CEE concerts desiring simple answers.

One such recurring desire is for the human presence in electronic music. But what makes technology "humanized"? And, more specifically, what makes the music created with electronic technology "humanized"? When, in 1968, composer John Eaton spoke of the "humanization of electronic music," his solution involved "truly sensitive and immediately responsive" electronic instruments, "capable of being performed 'live'" (101). Real-time capabilities have markedly increased since then. Yet, as Emmerson explains, the default expectation persists of a kind of physical performance that is legible to general audiences.

While the genre of electronic music has earned a niche audience, the breakdown of the traditional gesture–sound relationship familiar from acoustic instruments has alienated listeners because they don't know how to evaluate the music, even as they marvel at the strange electronic sounds. The great performances of the mid-nineteenth century set a new standard, not only in the performance of works deemed to be of the highest quality but also in corporeal virtuosity. The question remains: is there virtuosity in live electronic performance practice? Why might the answer be important to an audience? What might this virtuosity look or sound like? It often does not look like the way a performer impresses us with their corporeal mastery of an acoustic Euro-American classical instrument, as Sergi Jordà describes:

> In traditional instrumental playing, every nuance has to be addressed physically by the performer, although the level of control is almost automatic and unconscious to a trained musician, and acoustics places limits on how separable different aspects of the sound are (for instance, vibrato may enforce a

corresponding tremolo). In digital instruments, all parameters can indeed be varied without restriction, but moreover, the performer no longer needs to control directly all these aspects of production of sound, being able instead to direct and supervise the computer processes that control these details. (2017, 87)

The technological endeavours, performance practices, and legacy of the CEE reveal a group with its own style and repertories whose output highlights the continuing challenges of performing live electronic music. As to the audience, the effort seems minimal compared to the sounds created; and the machine's will seems to trump the humans' own intentions.

From the Global Stage to a Toronto Classroom

The CEE story that opens this chapter is typical in many ways of the CEE's performance practice and reception: small ensemble in a chamber music–like setting; improvised pieces; digital and analog equipment, some with keyboard interfaces; and an interested but perplexed audience. This chapter provided a historical and global foundation for examining the CEE's creative practice and the many additional stories of CEE performances discussed throughout the book. The next chapter shifts scales from the global to the local by outlining the origins of the CEE, starting with their time at the University of Toronto as students in the early 1970s. Institutional history, including curriculum, infrastructure, and personnel, contextualizes the young musicians' arrival at the University of Toronto and their subsequent education.

2

A CEE Origin Story
Don't Mistake Us for a Pop Band

The Centre in a "Country of Margins"

Writer Robert Kroetsch characterized the entire country of Canada as "a country of margins" (1989, 62), and indeed, Canada's history as a European colony and then a quasi-colony of the United States supports this notion of marginality. Yet within the nation-state, a centre clearly exists – one established through a concentration of power and wealth in southern Ontario. Ottawa is the capital of the country, while Toronto has long been the largest city in English-speaking Canada (and, as of the late 1990s, the largest city in the entire country). Thus, Toronto has consolidated considerable cultural and social power for decades (see also chapter 6).

Toronto's leadership role – its position as centre – in Canada's history of music training and electronic music cannot be denied. Curricular initiatives at the Royal Conservatory of Music and the University of Toronto's Faculty of Music served as models for schools across Ontario and then across Canada. This chapter thus begins by outlining how musical training opportunities in Toronto enticed four young American musicians to this Canadian city for training in composition and electronic music. Following some historical background to emphasize the Faculty of Music's significant transformation in the first decades of the twentieth century, I highlight the importance of Arnold Walter, John Weinzweig, and Gustav Ciamaga in establishing the University of Toronto's reputation as a premier place of musical studies in composition and electronic music. The changes in the Faculty of Music starting in the 1950s accelerated in the 1960s as the entire nation of Canada looked towards its centennial in 1967. Significant efforts were made to support and celebrate "home-grown" contributions, including music, in order to fight against the years of brain drain that had seen Canadian talent leave to train in another country – and often remain abroad.

David Grimes, David Jaeger, Larry Lake, and James Montgomery did not know one another before arriving at the University of Toronto, yet, like many graduate cohorts, they bonded quickly. Late-night sessions in the University of Toronto Electronic Music Studio (UTEMS) sealed their lifelong friendship and creative collaboration. The quartet officially became the Canadian Electronic Ensemble (CEE) in 1972, and the next fourteen years were immensely productive, especially considering that each member maintained full-time employment outside of the CEE. This chapter discusses each member's musical background and articulates the balance between individuality and collectivity in the CEE's activities from 1971 to 1985 (when Grimes left the group). The group did not formalize as the "Canadian Electronic Ensemble" until 1972. While the common narrative about the CEE is that they formed in 1971, I position that first year as a transition time: the students who would become the CEE's founding members were composing and performing in ways that anticipate the CEE but remain distinct from the actual ensemble.

Music at the University of Toronto

The music program that drew the young members of the CEE to the University of Toronto had radically transformed over the previous decades; their experience there would not have been possible even ten years earlier. In Toronto, higher education in music was largely the purview of the Toronto Conservatory of Music (TCM; renamed the Royal Conservatory of Music of Toronto in 1947), which offered practical studio-based training. King's College (renamed the University of Toronto in 1850) had started giving BMus and DMus degrees in the 1840s, but no formal syllabi or examinations were attached to these degrees (Green and Vogan 1991). The University of Toronto formed its Faculty of Music in 1918 and took control of the TCM in 1919. Like others in the province of Ontario at the time, the University of Toronto's program was aimed principally at training organists and private teachers. It followed the British tradition (i.e., Anglican), which faculty members such as Healey Willan and Sir Ernest MacMillan exemplified in both their compositional and teaching lives.[1] Canadian universities overall were devoted "chiefly to the transmission of a European cultural heritage" (Clokie 1942, 470), and the specifically British orientation of the University of Toronto's music program was due in large part to the fact that most Canadian musicians were trained abroad, even into the 1920s and '30s; many of them went to Great Britain, though others went to continental Europe.

Finally, in the 1930s, the University of Toronto's Faculty of Music offered its first formal courses to music students, and in 1936, it created its first intramural honours BA degree in music. Toronto was fast becoming a centre for countering the brain drain that had led Canadian musicians to leave the country for training and work. Instead, as J. Paul Green and Nancy F. Vogan note in their book *Music Education in Canada*, "University Avenue and College Street, the site of the Toronto Conservatory and the Faculty of Music, became the cultural crossroads for the English-speaking community" (1991, 402).

The 1950s saw the most significant changes toward creating the kind of Faculty of Music that would attract the future members of the CEE. First, Arnold Walter assumed the role of director of the Faculty of Music (1952–68), and his changes ensured that the Faculty "attained international stature" (McMillan et al. 2008). He expanded program specializations to include musicology and composition, prioritized the creation of a comprehensive music library,[2] secured a new building (Edward Johnson Building, 1962), and directed Canada's first electronic music studio (1959).

Second, John Weinzweig joined the Faculty of Music in 1952 to teach undergraduate composition after having taught at the TCM since 1939. He taught for the newly formed MusM in composition starting in 1954, including a Contemporary Techniques course by the early 1960s. When the future CEE members arrived as young students a decade later, he was also teaching Advanced Composition. Weinzweig's stature as a *Canadian* composer (i.e., not simply a respected composer from abroad) made his presence particularly influential in the 1960s and '70s. According to former student John Rea, "Weinzweig's presence there [at the University of Toronto and specifically at the Edward Johnson Building] attracted many new students to the university both at the graduate and undergraduate levels" (2011, 88). Weinzweig taught for four decades, and his impact on generations of composers in Canada – including all four founding members of the CEE – cannot be overstated. Weinzweig has been called the "dean of Canadian composers" not only for his multi-generational teaching but also for his leadership in the Canadian League of Composers and the Canadian Music Centre.

Weinzweig is also recognized as Canada's first serialist composer, having studied serialist works independently while a student at Eastman School of Music in Rochester, New York (1937–38). While serialism was not formally taught at Eastman at this time, the school did teach twentieth-century music, exposing Weinzweig to music that he had not studied at the University of Toronto (1934–37). Weinzweig had little positive to say about his undergraduate training, which Rea characterizes as a "miseducation" that Weinzweig tried to avoid in his own teaching as he "endeavoured to heal the injury of his poor training" (2011, 80). Weinzweig criticized the program for teaching him rules and requiring him to imitate models of old music rather than inspiring and guiding his creativity. Rea does not mince words about Weinzweig's student experiences: "Because from Weinzweig's long-range perspective, the predilection for English pastoral music together with any inordinate fondness for high classical music not merely disciplined 'living' genius by hindering its flight, clipping its wings; it effectively *killed* it: Weinzweig was a survivor" (2011, 84).

Weinzweig's role as a teacher has been written about since the 1960s by journalists, students, musicologists, and even the composer himself. Rea frames his 2011 essay on Weinzweig, "The Teacher," with a quotation from Blaik Kirby's *Toronto Daily Star* article published on 17 September 1960: "If you don't like 'modern' Canadian music, blame him – he teaches most of the other composers." This growing list of composers taught by Weinzweig would soon come to include David Jaeger, Larry Lake, Jim Montgomery, and David Grimes.

As a pedagogue, Weinzweig aimed to inspire creativity rather than to enforce discipline. Reflecting on his earlier days teaching at the TCM, he declared: "I tried to instill in my pupils a creative approach to all assignments and a psychological awareness of the relationship between composer and listener. The classics were for study, but not models ... I never imposed my own music on my pupils" (quoted in Rea 2011, 81). Many (though not all) of Weinzweig's former students praised his pedagogical approach as encouraging rather than dictatorial. For example, Montgomery explained to me: "[John] was a very good teacher. He didn't impose anything on you. He felt his role was mostly to make sure that your craft was up to snuff ... He very rarely would say 'No, this idea: it's not going anywhere, and you should throw that out and do this instead.' He didn't do that kind of thing" (personal communication, 26 February 2016).

UTEMS

Weinzweig's presence at the University of Toronto was not the only draw for the four young musicians: there was also the Electronic Music Studio. The University of Toronto Electronic Music Studio (UTEMS) was founded in May 1959 under director Arnold Walter. The technical adviser was Hugh Le Caine, whose remarkable instruments would become part of UTEMS's inventory, as they would in the electronic music studios at McGill University (1964), Brandeis University (1961), and the Hebrew University in Jerusalem. UTEMS was originally staffed by Walter, Myron Schaeffer, and Harvey Olnick. It was groundbreaking at the time, as it was not just the first electronic music studio in Canada but also only the third institutional studio in North America (after the Columbia-Princeton Electronic Music Centre and the University of Illinois's Experimental Music Studio, both established in 1958).[3] The University of Toronto was building a strong reputation for innovation in music composition and electronic music; as David Keane later declared, "UTEMS ... quickly became one of the world's ten or so most important studios" (1984, 66).

UTEMS was filled with much of the equipment common to electronic music studios at the time, such as oscillators for various wave types, mixers, filters, a splicing block, a patch bay, and tape recorders (Schaeffer 1963). However, it also included some unique pieces, most notably Le Caine's Multi-Track Tape Recorder (or Special Purpose Tape Recorder), which could "play six tapes simultaneously, changing the playback speed of each tape independently and recombining the resulting sound into a single recording" (Young 1999),[4] and Schaeffer's Hamograph, which was capable of nuanced and complex control (Schaeffer 1963). UTEMS was also highlighted in a 1962 episode of *The Lively Arts* on CBC Television, hosted by Henry Comor, in which Helmut Blume discusses electronic music with Walter and Schaeffer. Schaeffer also demonstrates how he might compose a piece in UTEMS, using the Hamograph and the Multi-Track Tape Recorder.

In 1963, composer Gustav Ciamaga joined the Faculty of Music, becoming the director of the Electronic Music Studio in 1965. He came to Toronto from Brandeis, where he had organized a new electronic music studio (with some coordination with Le Caine). When Jaeger, Lake, and Montgomery arrived at the University of Toronto in 1970 (followed by Grimes in 1971), Ciamaga was still the main teacher of electronic music. Most of his compositions are for tape, and he also developed some exciting new technologies, such as the Serial Sound Structure Generator (developed with Le Caine) and a groundbreaking computer-analog synthesizer hybrid, PIPER (developed with James Gabura), which allowed real-time editing. Montgomery recalls Ciamaga as a key figure for all University of Toronto composition students at the time. He explains that in class, Ciamaga would bring in pieces by François Bayle and Paris musique concrète composers for listening and discussion. Montgomery recognizes the importance of this class: "I think that course completely changed the direction of what I was doing in terms of music" (personal communication, 26 February 2016). Montgomery explained to me that prior to his arrival at the University of Toronto, he composed music that sounded like Shostakovich. He thought Roger Sessions was "contemporary music."[5]

Ciamaga published an essay in *Anuario* in 1967 about his approach to teaching electronic music, giving us a fairly vivid idea of what these four young musicians experienced under his tutelage. He explained that graduate students met for two-hour weekly seminars in addition to at least six hours of private studio instruction each week. The historical and theoretical elements of electronic music instruction focused on the following: 1) terminology of electronics, audio engineering, and audio-acoustics; 2) fundamentals of mathematics related to the acquired terminology; 3) a survey of experimental music techniques, both acoustic and electronic; 4) what he called the "new" music theory. Students would listen to an abundance of electronic music and study their scores, as available. Alongside this reading, listening, and discussion, students practised making electronic music in incremental stages: first, they learned about tape recording, starting with what Ciamaga termed "standard musical repertoire" (71), then moving onto recording real-world sounds, and finally recording purely synthesized sound. Ciamaga's essay advocates for students to learn how to cut and splice tape even if the student will ultimately focus more on "real-time" equipment. Students then learned various methods of sound modification, such as filtering and reverberation, based on the equipment in the studio. Ciamaga found that his students were eager to work independently without a technician and could usually handle the technological demands within a month of study. The final aspect of his electronic music pedagogy was providing a public platform for students to share their works, not principally for the purpose of peer feedback but rather as an opportunity to think about concert venues as spaces for listening and audience engagement.

Founding Members of the CEE

The University of Toronto Faculty of Music had utterly transformed following the Second World War – from a conservative, English-oriented music curriculum focused on harmony and counterpoint to a modern music school embracing academic rigor in musicology, creativity in composition, and cutting-edge technologies in electronic music. Most critically, by the early 1970s, John Weinzweig and Gustav Ciamaga created the kind of composition program that attracted four young men from the United States to head to Canada – and stay.

Such composers as Pauline Oliveros, John Cage, and Tzvi Avni visited UTEMS in its first decade to take advantage of its unique and groundbreaking technology. It should come as no surprise, therefore, that in the early 1970s, aspiring musicians – even those from the United States – were enticed by the possibilities. Montgomery intended first to go to McGill because a friend had praised the lower price of living and tuition; his GI Bill benefits of $212 a month would not have covered tuition at a US university. As luck would have it, McGill was closed when he arrived in Montreal so he drove to Toronto instead and stopped by the university, where he met some graduate students who encouraged him to consider enrolling. Montgomery explained to me that although he didn't have a background or particular interest in electronic music heading into the program, it hooked him:

> The attraction was just physical. We wound up – Jaeger and I wound up, and Larry [Lake] … we just wound up in the studio all the time. We'd be there until four or five o'clock in the morning [laughs], just doing stuff, 'cause it was just magical, I mean it was just … It had a … It's difficult to describe, actually, what that attraction is and why … Most people are completely immune to it [laughs]. (Personal communication, 26 February 2016)

Jaeger's path to Toronto was less serendipitous: after he had won the Woodrow Wilson Fellowship, several graduate schools competed for him. He explains: "The Chair of Graduate Studies at the U of T Faculty of Music, Harvey Olnick, made an intense pitch for me to come to U of T. He was very persuasive, and after I had checked out the campus and the studio, I quickly decided on U of T" (personal communication, 1 August 2019).

The paths that led each of the four founding members of the CEE to the University of Toronto are divergent, and it seems like more than luck that they found themselves there together. While the CEE's lineup has changed over the subsequent decades, the core of the CEE's creative practice was forged during this first period as an amalgam of the four founding members' musical experiences, talents, and curiosities.

DAVID JAEGER

David Jaeger (b. 1947) has earned a reputation as one of Canada's most important classical music producers and new-music advocates. For his contributions, Jaeger was appointed a member of the Order of Canada in 2018. Born in Green Bay, Wisconsin, he studied piano privately beginning at the age of seven, adding pipe organ lessons with his family's church organist while he was in high school. In junior high, he also played cornet in the school band, becoming accomplished enough to win some school music competitions. Jaeger received his Bachelor of Music from the University of Wisconsin–Madison (1970) where he majored in music history and theory (the School of Music did not allow undergraduate students to study composition) and continued his organ studies. After completing his Master of Music at the University of Toronto in 1972, Jaeger remained in Canada, joining the CBC in 1973 as a radio music producer. He has lived with his family for decades in their home in the Riverdale neighbourhood, and he officially retired from the CBC on 1 January 2013. From his time at the CBC, Jaeger is well known for *Two New Hours*, a CBC Radio 2 program he created with Larry Lake in 1978. The program was devoted to contemporary art music, and it commissioned numerous works, including Hildegard Westerkamp's *Beneath the Forest Floor* (1992), which itself has earned a central place in the soundscape composition canon.

Jaeger's output as a composer is dominated by works that include an electronic component, often with mixed media in which an acoustic instrument is combined with either live processing (e.g., *Favour* for viola and signal processing, 1980) or a fixed track (e.g., *Quanza Dueto* for two guitars and tape, 1976). Other works are purely fixed media (e.g., *Crunch*, 1970; *The Studio*, 1991), and he has also composed works for acoustic instruments only, such as *Aria* for cello and piano. Many of his most recent works are unaccompanied solo pieces (e.g., *The Echo Cycle* for solo soprano, 2017; *For Chelsea* for solo baritone saxophone, 2014), and solo pieces with fixed electronic tracks (e.g., *Constable and the Spirit of the Clouds* for viola and tracks, 2021). The CEE became a main compositional outlet for Jaeger, with works like *Quivi sospiri* (1979).

LARRY LAKE

As Jaeger highlighted in his October 2013 memorial for Larry Lake published in *Wholenote*, Lake (1943–2013) arrived at the University of Toronto with three degrees already in hand. Born in Greenville, Pennsylvania, and raised in Florida and Georgia, Lake received a Bachelor of Music (1964), Master of Education (1968), and Master of Music in musicology (1970), all from the University of Miami. Yet he was still required to complete the University of Toronto entrance exam alongside Jaeger and Montgomery. Jaeger exclaimed: "Why the U of T Faculty of Music felt he needed to be examined for graduate study is still, to me, a bit of a mystery" (Jaeger 2013).

While Lake's entry in *The Canadian Encyclopedia* states that he came to the University of Toronto to study electronic music, Jaeger explains that Lake was actually a PhD candidate in musicology. The Faculty of Music's first courses in musicology date back to 1954 with the arrival of Harvey Olnick, and due to Arnold Walter's emphasis on the music library, musicology was a viable specialized study by the time of Lake's arrival in 1970. However, as Jaeger tells it, "Larry seemed more interested in electronic music than in the degree program he was enrolled in, which was as a PhD candidate in musicology. And he was far more intrigued by the challenges of contemporary composition than those of settings of Medieval Latin" (Jaeger 2013). Before entering the program, Lake had some exposure to electronic music during brief studies with Robert

Moog and Lejaren Hiller at Southern Illinois University. He was then strongly influenced by Ciamaga in Toronto, where he studied from 1970 to 1972 but ultimately did not complete a degree. Instead, he joined CBC Radio as a producer and later as a consultant. He co-founded *Two New Hours*, serving as a writer and as host (1996–2007).

Evan Ware and David Olds (2009) explain that prior to 1975, Lake's compositions were entirely electronic (e.g., *Eight Studies for Electronic Tape*, 1971). Like many of his colleagues, though, he shifted to acoustic-electronic combinations and the possibilities of live performance. For example, *No More Blues* (1976) is composed for trombone, two synthesizers, and tape. He composed for a variety of acoustic instruments in combination with tape and/or synthesizer: viola (*Slowly I Turn*, 1982), accordion (*Sticherarion*, 1984), oboe (*Psalm*, 1985), flute (*Israfel*, 1987), bassoon (*Helices*, 1988), and clarinet (*Partita*, 1989). He composed for the Evergreen Club Gamelan Ensemble *(Three Bagatelles*, 1986) and for Gayle Young's uniquely designed percussion instrument, the columbine (*The Columbine*, 1980). This heterogeneous list of compositions emphasizes Lake's interest in diverse timbres.

On 17 August 1979, Lake married British-born pianist Karen Kieser (1948–2002), who was a frequent collaborator with the Canadian Electronic Ensemble. Her three degrees from the University of Toronto are a testament to her exceptional talent as a pianist and scholar. Kieser hosted *Music Alive* and *Themes and Variaions* (1973–77) on CBC Radio, and she became an advocate for new music and emerging musicians. In 1986, she became the youngest person and first women to serve as Head of Music for CBC Radio Music, a position she held until 1992, making her its longest-serving director. When Kieser died in 2002, Lake – with the support of friends and colleagues – established an annual award for a graduate student in composition at the University of Toronto. The Karen Kieser Prize commenced in 2002 and includes a cash prize, a concert performance of the winning work, and a broadcast of the performance on *Two New Hours* (while it was on the air). Kieser's death after five years with ovarian cancer created a significant hole in the Canadian music community. Lake's illness and subsequent death in 2013 represented a similar loss for the new music community and particularly for the Canadian Electronic Ensemble.

JAMES MONTGOMERY

James Montgomery typically goes by Jim – or "Mudfish" to his close friends. He was born in 1943 near Akron, Ohio, in the small city of Ravenna. He studied horn at the Baldwin Wallace Conservatory of Music, originally intending to be a professional horn player. However, a sixteenth-century counterpoint class in his third year of undergraduate studies changed his musical path. He told me the story of his "eureka" moment:

> When I was a kid, in high school and even earlier, I had played around, because both of my parents were musicians, so I had played around with writing little ditties and little songs and stuff. The notion that you could actually write stuff and be a composer had never occurred to me, until that sixteenth-century counterpoint course, and I started writing stuff. The prof was a really interesting guy named Delbert Beswick. The classroom had blackboards all the way around it with staves on them. He's talking, and he starts writing this motet, this three-part motet, and he just goes across. It was a real revelation. (Personal communication, 26 February 2016)

Montgomery extended his musical studies by a year to include a double major in performance and composition. He then started graduate studies at Northwestern University while also playing in the Chicago Civic Orchestra, but he did not complete these studies because he was drafted to fight in the Vietnam War. Because of his horn proficiency, he was able to play in an army band, which he said "made it significantly less horrendous than it would have been otherwise." His experience in Vietnam "was a revelation," and he gladly took the opportunity to study in Canada (personal communication, 26 February 2016). He completed his Master of Music from the University of Toronto in 1972.

Montgomery has thrived primarily in three different roles: performer (including in the CEE), composer, and administrator. He served as the managing director of the CEE from 1976 to 1983; after that, he was the administrative director of New Music Concerts from 1984 to 1987, and then the artistic director of the Music Gallery from 1987 to 2005. The significance of his work with the Music Gallery is discussed in chapter 6. Montgomery has composed for diverse forces, including chamber groups (e.g., *White Fire* for amplified brass quintet, 1974), large ensemble (e.g., *Reconnaissance* for string orchestra, 1982), and theatre (e.g., *Nightbloom*, 1984). Many of his pieces include some kind of electronic element, though the specifics of the electronics reflect technological developments over time. Acclaimed experimental composer Udo Kasemets described Montgomery's music as follows: "The instrumental language itself covers a full gamut from dodecaphonic counterpoint to special sonic effects drawn from the physical and acoustical makeup of the instrument. His explorations in the realm of music created by 20th-century technological means have evolved over the years, moving from traditional studio techniques through various synthesizing processes to computer programming" (Kasemets 2006).

For the past twenty-five years, Montgomery has also been practising martial arts, and he credits the mindfulness aspect of this discipline with helping him as an improviser. Montgomery embraces the unknown in his music, including indeterminacy. In a conversation with Norma Beecroft, he elaborates on what he considers to be a great partnership – electronic sounds and randomness:

> One of the things that make electronic timbres more interesting, at least to my ear, is the introduction of some sort of indeterminacy in the patch, in the manner in which the sound is created, and one of the easiest ways to do this is to introduce feedback at some point in the signal path, because what it does is add the kind of random harmonics to the sound that you get when you expose the sound acoustically, and you create that same effect electronically by using electronic feedback. (Beecroft 2015, 434)

DAVID GRIMES

David Grimes arrived in Toronto a year later than the other three men, but he quickly joined them in the studio and, soon enough, in live performance. Jaeger and Montgomery had performed together at concerts featuring the tape music of Jaeger, Montgomery, and Lake in mid-1971 and early 1972. The first concert under the title "Canadian Electronic Ensemble" added Grimes to the lineup.

Grimes was born in in 1948 in Salem, Massachusetts, and he has since returned to his home state. In middle school, he was a drummer, but he switched to trombone based on his love for big band music. He earned a Bachelor of Music in Composition and Arranging from the Berklee School of Music in 1971 (now called the Berklee College of Music), where he also studied trombone with Phil Wilson. At Berklee during the 1969 Vietnam War draft lottery, he and his roommate both had high numbers (317 and 365, respectively), so they knew they would not be drafted. However, the war influenced his decision to leave the United States as protest and to continue his studies at the University of Toronto, where he was eager to study electronic music.

Grimes earned his Master of Music in 1972 following studies in electronic music with Gustav Ciamaga, whom he fondly remembers, and composition with John Weinzweig. Grimes recounts a story in which he presented a piece for clarinet and viola to Weinzweig, who remarked: "We don't write music like that anymore."

Grimes made a name for himself as a composer early in his career, placing third in the CBC National Radio Competition for Young Composers in 1976 for his composition *Increscents* (1972). Alongside his work with the CEE, he was also the first host of *Two New Hours*. He left the CEE in 1985 and returned to the United States the following year; he taught as an adjunct professor at Northeastern University from 2005 to 2010. Through his own company, David Grimes Music, he continues to license his music for film, video games, and other media. Like his CEE colleagues, Grimes often combines acoustic and electronic sound sources. He still plays the trombone, an interest that surfaces in some of his works.

The First Decade of the CEE

FIRST PERFORMANCES

The earliest concerts of music by Lake, Jaeger, and Montgomery were filled with the sonic outcomes of their feverish work in UTEMS, specifically tape pieces. In her book on alcides lanza, Pamela Jones describes a visit the composer took to UTEMS: "When lanza visited the University of Toronto studio in 1971 he was surprised by its pristine appearance, and asked how they managed to keep it so clean; the director replied that students were rarely allowed to touch the equipment" (2007, 129). When I asked Jaeger about how his experience compared with lanza's remarks, he declared: "We didn't pay attention to any restrictions, if we heard them. We proceeded to touch what ever we wished. I can't actually recall hearing any such restrictions, anyway" (personal communication, 1 August 2019). Montgomery's memory of this time is similar; Grimes credits Dave MacKenzie with the meticulous maintenance of the studio, though he also recalls being encouraged to experiment with all of the available equipment.

Since the earliest studio days in Europe, electronic music has involved humans experimenting – often through time-consuming and tedious trial and error – to achieve something musically satisfying. Much of the available technology consisted of equipment that was not designed for musical purposes, and certainly not for real-time live music making; wielding the electronic equipment in the studio was difficult enough for fixed media works. Great strides had been made by Hugh Le Caine and Myron Schaeffer to offer real-time responsivity in UTEMS, but the equipment was still cumbersome and capricious. Building a satisfying musical work of textures, timbres, rhythms, and structure – this was generally the realm of the studio, as Montgomery explained in an interview with Norma Beecroft: "You could get a very wide variety of sounds, but you had to set one up, record it, and set the next one up, and record it, so that the time that it took to get you from one texture or timbre or event to the other was much longer than, well, it was so long that it made live performance impractical with that equipment" (2015, 432). The resulting fixed media works would then be projected through loudspeakers in live concert.

The idea of gathering an audience to listen to music in a concert hall without live performers on stage was relatively new and, for some, alienating. While these young composers did not dislike hearing music from loudspeakers, they were ultimately musicians: they wanted to perform music. For electronic music, this required an entirely new array of equipment.

In order to translate studio work to live performance, Jaeger, Montgomery, and Lake (and soon Grimes as well) built much of their own equipment or repurposed pre-existing equipment. Montgomery explained to Norma Beecroft: "We devised our own instruments at first using some of the equipment which was found in the normal synthesizers, some of which wasn't" (2015, 432). The dream of live electronic music performance was achieved in large part thanks to the EMS Synthi A, a compact synthesizer that was released in 1971. In this portable object there were three oscillators, a noise generator, filters, a trapezoid envelope generator, a ring modulator, and reverberation. Montgomery explains the significance of the Synthi A:

> It occurred to us that here was what we had been doing in the studio in a small package and we could actually take it out of the studio and take it onto the stage ... with a certain amount of expertise, it gave you the ability to get you from one of those sounds to another one very quickly, which you couldn't do in a tape studio. (Beecroft 2015, 432)

The three concerts Lake, Jaeger, and Montgomery produced before the formalizing of the CEE were dominated by tape works. The first one on 13 August 1971, in the Edward Johnston Building included live improvisation before the concert. Lake and Montgomery each had two tape pieces on the concert, and Jaeger had one. For their second concert on 6 January 1972, Jaeger, Lake, and Montgomery each performed a tape piece from the first concert, and the program also included works by fellow graduate students John Fodi and Clifford Ford. These first two concerts both featured a guest dancer (Dennis Simpson, then Richard Pochenko) performing to Jaeger's tape piece *Space to Move Around In*. One important development in these early concerts is a live performance of "Putney Duo N" by Jaeger and Montgomery under the performance name Possibilities Portmanteaux. Both this duo name and the title for their improvised performance are references to the EMS Synthi A: EMS was located in the London suburb of Putney, and the instrument fit into a suitcase. Later that month on 29 January, "Putney Duo N" opened another concert of mostly tape music, which featured works by John Fodi and Howard Knopf; one new piece each by Jaeger, Lake, and Montgomery; and Clifford Ford's film *Opus II*.

That 29 January performance was the last concert before Grimes joined and the group officially took on its name. Grimes may have joined in the electronic music merriment later than Jaeger, Lake, and Montgomery, but soon enough, they were a quartet. Grimes recalls his transition into the group as being easy: "We all shared the same sense of humor and musical outlook" (personal communication, 2 November 2019). The Canadian Electronic Ensemble held its debut concert on 15 May 1972 at Windfields Junior High School in Toronto.

THE CEE TOURS AND LPS

During the fourteen years that the original quartet was together, the CEE performed over one hundred concerts – in Toronto, across Canada, on a large European tour, and during a residency at the 1985 Holland Festival. The CEE composed prolifically (both as individuals and as a group); commissioned new works; collaborated with numerous non-electronic musicians; and established the aesthetic, performance practice, and close friendship that has allowed the CEE to thrive. Alongside all of this activity, each CEE member was working full-time elsewhere, which impacted the frequency with which the group could perform and tour. Nonetheless, when perusing the large quantity of concerts and repertoire during the CEE's first decade and a half, it is clear that the ensemble was a vital creative outlet for its members. As Jaeger explained, the members realized the CEE was an addition to their other musical activities, but nonetheless, "something that we were not only willing to but quite eager to add to our mix of activities" (personal communication, 10 June 2016).

As a Toronto-based group, the CEE performed frequently across the city often at the Winchester Street Theatre, Comus Theatre, and Toronto Free Theatre with its main Theatre Downstairs and smaller Theatre Upstairs. Above all, the Music Gallery proved essential for the CEE; in addition to the space itself, the organization and its audience were a match for the kind of aesthetic experience the CEE aimed to create. The CEE's performance spaces are discussed in more detail in chapter 5.

Already in January 1973, the CEE journeyed outside the boundaries of Toronto to give a concert at the University of Guelph. The group first left the province of Ontario to perform at Concordia University in Montreal on 19 May 1975 for the Week of New Music. The following spring found the CEE in British Columbia with concerts in Vernon (22 May) and Vancouver (29 May). Their Canadian travels increased the following year to Halifax, St John's (Newfoundland), and Montreal (2–6 October 1977), and in March 1979, they returned to British Columbia with performances in Nanaimo, Vancouver, and Burnaby's Simon Fraser University (16–19 March). In all, over the course of these fourteen years, the CEE performed in eighteen Canadian cities across seven provinces. The performances of early 1979 in particular, though, were building up to a much bigger achievement: a European tour.

From 15 April to 15 May 1979, the CEE toured in seven European cities: Stockholm, Copenhagen, Ghent, Paris, Brussels, Treviso, and Belgrade. Across the eight concerts, the CEE was joined by guests Karen Kieser (piano) and Billie Bridgman (soprano). When asked to identify the highlight of the trip, Jaeger recalls the concert in Treviso on 8 May 1979:

> It took place in a ruin that was once a church, but was then a community events venue with stage and sound system. It was completely filled with an excited, enthusiastic audience. The performance was broadcast live in the local (AM I believe) radio station. I think I have never experienced such high energy excitement at any other CEE event. We even received fan mail – a young woman who had come backstage for an autograph had taken down the postal address written on our road cases and sent an adoring letter a few months later. It was a sweet surprise – completely unexpected. (personal communication, 11 August 2019)

Montgomery's remarks on the tour reflect his sense of humour and suggest that this tour was definitely a good time for all involved: "To paraphrase Robin Williams: if you remember it, you weren't there" (personal communication, 24 September 2019).

Live electronic music in the 1970s was tricky at best: technical glitches were to be expected. Touring was even trickier as gear was constantly being set up and torn down, then packed up and moved to the next city and venue. Grimes exclaimed: "Roadies would have been welcome for sure" (personal communication, 2 November 2019). Jaeger shared one particularly memorable story from the tour when they were performing at the Carlsberg Glyptotek in Copenhagen on 24 April 1979:

> The concert was sponsored by the Danish Society for Electronic Music, who had established a concert series in this grand old botanical garden in central Copenhagen, the Carlsberg Glyptotek. We arrived, having driven from Stockholm, and unloaded our gear. We set-up and conducted a sound check, and then we took a dinner break. Upon our return David Grimes discovered, to his horror, that the condensation from the glass roof of the Glyptotek had dripped into his Roland SH-5 synthesizer. It was saturated with water – David tipped the synth and water streamed out of

it! He was obviously reluctant to switch on the power, and had to play the concert without the use of the instrument. (personal communication, 10 August 2019)

This tour also underlines the stressful realities of international travel against the backdrop of Cold War geopolitics. Jaeger recalls a dramatic experience at the Italy-Yugoslavia border when he attempted to walk across to request an entry visa:

> I had not obtained one [an entry visa] in advance, because my passport had been at the Hungarian embassy for another visa application. This was a mistake. The Yougoslav [sic] border officers took me to be a vagrant, and refused to issue me a visa and turned me back. When I re-appeared as a passenger in one of the CEE vehicles, they became angry, dragged me out of the car, hit me with their gun-stocks and escorted me back across the frontier. It took intervention from the Canadian Embassy in Rome to get things sorted out. When I departed Belgrade on May 13th, I couldn't have been more relieved. (personal communication, 10 August 2019)

While the international tours were certainly exciting and prestigious, the work and stress they entailed also made staying in Canada a lot more appealing. The CEE performed domestically for the remainder of Grimes's time in the group, with the exception of a concert in Holland on 11 December 1981 and five concerts at the Holland Festival in 1985. The CEE released two self-titled LPs during this time (in 1977 and 1981), in addition to a collaboration with James Campbell and John York entitled *Transcription*, a recording of *Consequences for 5* on Norma Beecroft's *Anthology of Canadian Music* volume, and an album with the Elmer Iseler Singers, *The Electronic Messiah*, which is a recording of Handel's famous oratorio arranged for choir and synthesizers (the last two of which are discussed in chapter 6).

The four members of the CEE were united in the goal of not only composing electronic music but also performing it live, as both predetermined (or "composed") and improvised works. Beyond the consideration of performance, the CEE has always been an outlet for both individual and collective compositional creativity. During the first fourteen years of the CEE, each of its four members contributed several compositions to its live performances, and collaborations between two or more members were also common. Clearly, the CEE was an ensemble in which the individual and the group could thrive creatively.

In its original quartet configuration, the CEE performed close to seventy different compositions composed by one, two, or three of its members, along with a dozen compositions credited to the entire ensemble.[6] Table 2.1 lists the most frequently performed pieces composed by members of the CEE, demonstrating that no single creative voice dominated the group's aesthetic and performance practice.[7] Montgomery explained one of the practical reasons for this balance: "We were all composers in [an] era when royalties for 'classical' works were still relevant to one's income, so we were pretty rigorous about equal representation" (personal communication, 24 September 2019).

The CEE released its first self-titled LP in 1977. The electronic gear included EMS Synthi As, ARP Odyssey analog synthesizers, the Roland Sh-5, and the Dyno-Soar. The album featured many acoustic instruments as well, including trumpet (Lake), trombone (Grimes), French horn (Montgomery), and piano (Kieser and Montgomery); Montgomery also used ping-pong balls. This first LP includes the frequently performed pieces *Arnold* (for four microphones, brass, and synthesizers) and Piano Quintet (featuring ring modulation of various piano effects), both recorded live at the University of Saskatchewan on 23 September 1977. Between these two group compositions is the CEE's first tape composition, *Whale Oil* (1973), which was presented at the 4th International Festival of Experimental Music in Bourges, France, on 28 May 1974.

Arnold is a mammoth work, running almost twenty-seven minutes. These four musicians are able to achieve wide-ranging textures and timbres and sustain interest across the work's distinct sound worlds. That this is a live recording – and not the result of studio composition, which can create material at its own pace – is a testament to the CEE's technical capabilities and musicianship. Unlike Piano Quintet, which features the acoustic instrument as soloist throughout the piece, the brass instruments in *Arnold* join the texture only in the final third of the work, adding a striking contrast of sustained pitches over the electronic beat pulsing beneath. *Whale Oil* mostly avoids dense textures and slowly transitions sounds in and out of the mix. By contrast, Piano Quintet is a highly dramatic work. The middle section in particular exploits the piano's capacity for cacophony, an effect that is exaggerated

Table 2.1 Most frequently performed compositions written by the CEE, 1972–85, in descending order of frequency.

Title	Composer	Performances	Notes
Chaconne à son goût	CEE	23	
F.A.C.E.	Lake	16	
Bord du Son	Jaeger and Montgomery. Also credited to the CEE.	14	Also spelled "Le board du son"
Arnold	CEE	13	
Walter	Grimes and Montgomery	12	
Piano Quintet No. 5	CEE	11	With Karen Kieser; referred to as "Piano Quintet" on the 1977 LP
All Wounds	Grimes	10	With Kieser and Billie Bridgman
Quivi sospiri	Jaeger	10	Features piano
I Have Come Through	Montgomery	10	
Sotto voce	Grimes	6	
Cavatina	Jaeger and Lake	5	
Increscents	Grimes	5	Third place in CBC National Radio Competition for Young Composers
The Devil in the Desert	Lake	5	
Body Peek	Montgomery	5	
Ritual IV: The Uses of Power	Montgomery	5	
Novellette	Lake	5	
A Wave and a Bird	Jaeger	5	

by the live piano processing and synthesizer accompaniment. This first album establishes some CEE features that persist across the decades: collaboration with acoustic soloists, the virtuosity of the CEE members on both electronic and acoustic instruments, and a repertoire comprising both purely electronic and mixed media.

In 1981, the CEE released a second self-titled LP, featuring Billie Bridgman (soprano) and Karen Kieser (piano), in addition to the four members of the CEE quartet. The album includes the group's most frequently performed piece, *Chaconne à son goût* (1978; revised several times in subsequent years), composed by the CEE, as well as *All Wounds* (ca 1979), composed by Grimes for the 1979 European tour, and involving both Bridgman and Kieser accompanied by the CEE. This album, like its predecessor, shows CEE's wide range. Both tracks are noteworthy for their tonal references (in comparison to the CEE's broader output), such as a beautiful passage for piano with synthesizer accompaniment and the closing untexted vocal material in *All Wounds*.

The title *Chaconne à son goût* is a play on the original French phrase "chacun à son gout," replacing the word "chacun" (meaning "each") with the Baroque variation genre "chaconne." Lake explains in his liner notes, though, that the title also refers to the meaning of the original French phrase, as each member of the CEE performs within the group "to his own taste." While they are a collective, their individuality remains.

The work opens with an assertive C minor chord (resembling the *forte* synthesizer chords of the *Phantom of the Opera* theme, a connection reviewer Gaynor Jones also noted in his *Toronto Star* concert review published on 8 December 1985), and this tonality resurfaces at other points in the piece. The pitch material does not remain within any particular key, however, and many solo passages are focused on timbre and texture rather than pitch. In the liner notes, Lake explains the overall formal design of the piece:

> Formally, *Chaconne à son goût* is actually more of a toccato and chaconne. It begins with a series of episodes in which tutti chords alternate with solo and duet passages of increasing complexity, climaxing in a solo by David Jaeger which leads directly to the chaconne. The chaconne theme is presented, and variations are introduced. Each variation leads farther from the tonal centre of the theme, until it is finally obliterated. Suddenly, the C minor chord from the beginning reappears, is established, and the piece is over.

The CEE's next project was *The Electronic Messiah* (1982), which is discussed in detail in chapter 6. Walter Pitman explains that when the Elmer Iseler Singers premiered this electronic re-visioning live at Expo '86, the results were mixed: "*Electronic Messiah* ... horrified some conservative choral enthusiasts but delighted many who saw this as an example of Elmer's courage" (Pitman 2008, 166). Though the album credits "A CBC Synthescope Production," the electronic arrangements were indeed made by the CEE quartet. Given the prominence of the Elmer Iseler Singers, this album was a significant step both for electronic music and for the CEE.

With a second European tour, this time to the acclaimed Holland Festival for a week in June 1985, the CEE proved that there was still an international audience for their brand of electronic avant-garde music. During its five concerts as featured performers, the CEE performed many of its "classics" including *Chaccone à son goût*, *Davies*, *Quivi sospiri*, and *I Have Come Through;* the two piano pieces were performed with Monica Gaylord. Lake's newly composed *Psalm* was performed by Thomas Indermühle. The remainder of 1985 was quiet for the group, with the exception of two concerts in December 1985.

The possibilities within electronic music sparked curiosity and excitement, seeming to represent an important new stage in the progression of music. In 1979, American composer and violinist Yehudi Menuhin (1916–1999) hosted eight hour-long episodes in a CBC series entitled *The Music of Man*, in which he traces the development of music within diverse musical traditions around the world. One episode, "Sound or Unsound," features the CEE as an example of electronic music, one of the paths of postwar music discussed in the series. The swirling sounds of the CEE fade in (starting at 4:16) over the nonsensical recitation of a sound artist. At 4:23, we see the ensemble, first with Jaeger in the centre and Montgomery behind him. The documentary shows the CEE in its earliest configuration: four men around a table, each with his own station of monophonic synthesizers, including many keyboard interfaces, and mixers. Menuhin narrates their performance:

> Will our own music on earth by then have totally abandoned the organic? The prime need of our animal nature for sensual satisfaction? Or for our spirit for the metaphysical? The electronic music so often heard today seems to me a way station on the road to an unknown destination. [performance with no narration] Somehow with its synthetic means and abstract method, this at least does seem to me a music appropriate to an age of travel to the moon and Mars.

Menuhin reluctantly accepts electronic music's position within broader technological developments and dreams. The members of the CEE, in contrast, needed no convincing that electronic music, with or without acoustic instruments, was a viable and rewarding path for a performer-composer.

The Original CEE Quartet: An Ending and a Beginning

When David Keane wrote his summary of electroacoustic music in Canada from 1950 to 1984, he was sure to emphasize the importance of the CEE, devoting an entire paragraph to their achievements and leadership in electronic music since the early 1970s:

> Significant among these younger composers are David Grimes, David Jaeger, Larry Lake, and James Montgomery who met at UTEMS just at the beginning of the 1970s and in 1971 formed the Canadian Electronic Ensemble (CEE) ... The Ensemble has performed several hundred works including over 30 works by one or more of the member composer-performers ... Among the many new works commissioned by the CEE for their rather singular instrumentation have been compositions by Robert Bauer, Norma Beecroft, Derek Healey, Udo Kasemets, David Keane, Norman Symonds, John Thrower, Steve Tittle, Barry Truax, and Gayle Young. (1984, 67)

To some ears, the sonic worlds of the CEE's works during this period betray their origins in the 1970s, and thus perhaps suggest aesthetic irrelevance or obsolescence. Such an attitude not only does a disservice to the CEE's richly textured output but also misses the opportunity to appreciate how innovative the CEE was at a time when live electronic music performance was still a daunting task. The CEE's performance schedule is a testament not only to their dedication to live electronic music but also to their technological, aesthetic, and collaborative achievements.

Following Grimes's departure from the group in 1985, the CEE remained a trio until Michael Dobinson and Paul Stillwell joined in 1996. Since that time, four additional musicians have joined the CEE, some of whom have since departed. The next chapter discusses all of these personnel changes while demonstrating how the CEE's aesthetics (the CEE "sound") persist across technological shifts in their creative practice over the decades.

3

Sounds Like the CEE

A Technological and Aesthetic Community

In Christopher Small's groundbreaking book *Musicking*, he reminds us of something we live out each day but often forget in our musical discourse: "Music is not a thing but an activity, something that people do" (1998, 2). The history and creative practice of the Canadian Electronic Ensemble resists narrow discussions of its live electronic music that would restrict it to formal performances, specific composed works, or even a self-contained improvisation. The CEE is constantly rejecting "thingness." To music, or to live electronic music, for the CEE is to converse about musical and non-musical topics at rehearsal, to drink whisky during a recording session, to record, edit, mix, and master, to rehearse, to perform, to listen, to produce and present, and to experiment. The CEE is a community mediated by electronic technology that achieves a particular aesthetic result. In the end, what matters most to the CEE? The gear? The sound? The people? This is an impossible question, because the CEE cannot be reduced in such a manner.

This chapter explains how the technological, aesthetic, and social aspects of music making inform each other in the CEE's activities. The CEE has had ten different members over its five decades, ranging in size from a trio to a sextet (refer back to table P.1). To explore the CEE's aesthetics across and despite these personnel changes, I first review the group's original configuration as a quartet, then the trio era (1986–96) that followed the departure of founding member David Grimes. I then discuss the CEE members who joined in the 1990s (Paul Stillwell, Michael Dobinson, Laura Wilcox, and Rose Bolton) and 2000s (John Kameel Farah). I trace the group's equipment across the analog–digital shift, noting a nostalgic return to analog technologies, particularly in the creative practices of members Stillwell and the CEE's most recent addition, David Sutherland.

The CEE Community

The CEE is more than a performing ensemble. The members view themselves as a community, a family even. Stillwell explains: "The CEE is like family for me. It isn't all roses all the time and that is ok, we are still there for each other" (personal communication, 20 May 2020). This attitude manifests not only in social aspects, like hanging out together and attending important personal events; it is at the core of their creative practice. Stillwell explains: "The CEE has always embraced both the ensemble and the individual musicians who make up the ensemble. There are voices that all of us have that seem to be reserved for playing with the CEE. We are more like a band or a family than a musical ensemble" (personal communication, 20 May 2020). Potential new members need to be sonically compatible with the group. To ensure this, each new member went through a trial period in which they performed as guests before being invited to join officially. When I inquired about specific criteria for membership, the CEE members struggled to articulate specifics. For them, it's more of a vibe factor, something that resists tangible description.

While sonic compatibility is key to the group's cohesion, the social aspect remains important. The founding members were and are particularly close – for example, David Jaeger was Larry Lake's best man at his wedding. Farah discussed with me how much he values the CEE as a community in contrast to his solo practice (personal communication, 21 May 2020); he also expressed his love of Stillwell's mother's oatmeal cookies and hanging out in Stillwell's basement (i.e., the CEE's current rehearsal space). Bolton describes the CEE as a community of great friends, a community that extends beyond the musicians themselves to their families. Lake, who passed away in 2013, was core to the CEE family, and not only because he brought in Dobinson and Stillwell as members. The CEE members recall with affectionate laughter Lake's proclivity for choosing nicknames for individual members, some of which are not permitted to be shared beyond the CEE itself. Farah laughs when he remembers that Lake called him "dude," which he sees as a sign that Lake thought of him as a cool, younger guy. The CEE members agree that nicknames were a sign of Lake's affection, even if they were not generous on the surface. Jaeger declared: "Larry's special talent was to get your goat" (personal communication, 25 February 2020).

The CEE likes to create a casual atmosphere for themselves when they rehearse or perform. While they have certainly performed in tuxes and other formal concert attire, these days most of them prefer the comfort of a t-shirt or a collared shirt with the top buttons loose. They talk freely with friends, family, and other audience members before and after performance. Any witness to a CEE rehearsal or performance, live or in photo documentation, will notice the centrality of alcohol to the ensemble's creative practice, the presence of which also creates a sense of informality and social connection. When I asked Stillwell about this, he responded: "I knew that Whisky would make an appearance in these questions somewhere! There is usually a nice bottle of some kind of whisky on hand as most of us are fans" (personal communication, 20 May 2020). Stillwell describes feeling euphoric and energized after rehearsals: "it's time for another round of scotch! …If you look at the photos of our recording sessions, you'll notice that the scotch bottles feature prominently" (personal communication, 27 January 2016). Farah also appreciates this aspect of rehearsals, as it helps to establish the CEE's relaxed approach. Even Bolton, who told me she doesn't like drinking too much, enjoys "a taste of the fine scotch that Paul or Jim might offer" (personal communication, 23 June 2020).

Sutherland perceives rehearsals a bit differently from the other members: "You know, there's very little conversation. It's remarkably wonderful … But I swear, playing with Paul and David and Jim: it's just like, 'Any beer? Okay.' And then somebody goes first" (personal communication, 13 October 2017). By contrast, Stillwell explained to me that "conversation is hugely important … It happens while we are rehearsing and playing as well as when we aren't" (personal communication, 20 May 2020). This difference in perspective is likely due to the length of time each member has spent with the CEE: while Sutherland joined in 2017, Stillwell has been part of the group for twenty-five years. Regardless of each individual's perception of the CEE and its social activities, all members value the group as a creative space. Sutherland explained: "This music isn't about earning a living. This music is, in some strange way, sort of a community spiritual activity" (personal communication, 13 October 2017).

The CEE Sound

The potential aesthetics produced in any given electronic music are as varied as the tools used to create them. David Keane blames the practical considerations of electronic music studios for the dominance of certain aesthetic features, such as rapid glissandi and loudness: "The number of knobs in the electronic music studio are perhaps an even greater obstacle to the composer than the numbers of sonic possibilities. Electronic compositions very frequently evolve using a logic of knobs and switches – proceeding in directions that are suggested by the physical ease of the control of sound manipulation, rather than in directions suggested by the sound itself" (1979, 196). The CEE's aesthetic must similarly be shaped by its tools. Yet the tools are only one component; the resulting sounds are also guided by each individual's decisions.

During the CEE's early quartet years, the group established the principle of highlighting each member's distinct compositional and performance aesthetic, as examined in chapter 2. In addition to this diversity within the ensemble, the CEE frequently collaborated with acoustic performers, resulting in numerous distinctive works that feature the capabilities of the specific guest performers. So, given this intentionally cultivated variety, is there a CEE sound?

Taking the group's output as a whole, some common tendencies become apparent. The CEE's sound focuses more on texture and timbre than on melody and harmony. The sound worlds are a collection of sonic gestures that punctuate the relatively slowly emerging time and space of any given piece. For example, the tracks on the two CEE albums of the quartet era are relatively long, such as *Arnold* (26:30) and *Chaconne à son goût* (17:22). The CEE's music is generally through-composed. My descriptions of specific works in the previous chapter (as well as in subsequent discussions) indicate that I hear sectional divides and, in some cases, conventional classical form (such as the ABA' structure of *I Have Come Through*). Such structural descriptions, however, likely reflect more strongly the emphasis on structural listening in Euro-American classical music analysis. I discuss the limitations of teleological listening in the listening guides. The CEE employs general concepts of repetition and variation. Nonetheless, in the absence of repeated close listening, the CEE's sound is likely to be perceived as continuous rather than circular or recapitulatory, with individual punctuations of the texture – some more dramatic than others.

The CEE's sound does not adhere to conventional Western pitch-based structures, such as common practice functional tonality or dodecaphony. Some pieces have clear tonal centres: some frame the beginning and ending, while others change throughout the course of a piece. Pitch material, particularly through drones, establishes stability and familiarity within the CEE's broader electronic sound world. Oftentimes, pitch material is included likely not so that listeners will be drawn to specific pitch-based harmonic and vertical relationships but rather so that pitches might be incorporated for the purposes of shifting densities or creating a sense of cacophony; in the latter case, individual pitches and their intervallic relationships become too difficult to trace aurally. Pitch material is often used to create a collection of short motives that are implemented throughout a piece.

Owing to their original quartet set-up with a collection of monophonic synthesizers, it's unsurprising that the CEE's sound is often polyphonic. While individual members may take on the role of "soloist" at various times, the CEE sound is produced from equitable collaboration. In the composed pieces, such polyphonic textures are deliberately specified; in improvisational contexts, achieving an electronic polyphony relies both on the ears of each performer and on the co-operation of the gear at that moment. In pieces composed for a solo performer, by contrast, the CEE's contribution often shifts into more of an accompaniment role. The CEE's version of polyphony, though, is not about a simultaneity of melodic lines. As I have already explained, the CEE's sound is not driven by melody but rather by motives. Furthermore, the independent lines here are an amalgam of timbral, textural, rhythmic, and pitch-based elements (including aperiodic sound waves, a type of noise). This description bears some resemblance to Edgard Varèse's concept of a sound mass in which a grouping of sounds is characterized not so much by melody but by specific timbres, textures, rhythms, and registral placements that are relatively stable or transform over time. In many ways, this concept captures what any given member of the CEE quartet had to offer to a group piece, whether composed or improvised, because the components of sound are compartmentalized into discrete knobs and patches, each of which could be changed slowly or suddenly.

While electronic music is ubiquitous, the application of electronic tools in musical practices is varied. For example, the CEE's music does not fall into the category of EDM (or Electronic Dance Music), an umbrella term for a diverse set of dance-oriented electronic music genres. This is not a value statement; rather it underlines an important element of the CEE's sound, along with much of the electronic music whose lineage is experimental Euro-American music and the classic electronic studios: the CEE does not create primarily pulse-based music. Ben Neill declares: "[The] aesthetic approaches [of high art and popular electronic music] are most clearly defined in terms of the presence or absence of repetitive beats" (2002, 3), with so-called "high art" electronic music predominantly lacking repetitive beats.

When I asked Jaeger about this topic, he responded: "I don't think we felt any particular reluctance to create regular-pulsed music. But I think it was always understood that a balance should be maintained. So it does happen from time to time" (personal communication, 10 June 2016). While the CEE's attitude may be open to regular pulses, their overall practice engages little with it. Thus, the concept of metre has little relevance to their music. In the instances in which steady pulses are present, they are typically used in sections designed to contrast with the rest of the piece and are relatively slow (as opposed to a fast pulse that might establish a dance-like groove). For example, in the listening guides, I discuss four works with steady pulses: material in both *I Have Come Through* and *Psalm* has clear pulses and rhythmic subdivisions of those pulses; *Quivi sospiri* uses the Roland DC-10 Analog Echo, which creates a pulsed echo of the piano part; *Improvisation #4* has a relatively long unit with a steady drum beat presented through the timbres of a drum kit. The CEE's 2012 performance of John S. Gray's *No Dim Pearls* also includes a synthesized drum kit pattern.

One word that frequently comes up when the CEE discusses their sound is "weird." "Weird" is not a constant CEE aesthetic, but rather one they value for occasional expressive power. That is, the CEE aims to have "weird moments." Bolton describes the CEE's practice of weirdness as follows: "We have perhaps never (to my knowledge) attempted to have a piece that settles into some kind of constant ... If it starts to, someone will create a sound that will shake us out of it ... Often what happens is that if there is a point that some semblance of a tonal structure, or a rhythm or some kind of pattern seems to be taking hold, someone will burst in with a sound that completely throws havoc into that" (personal communication, 8 January 2021). Bolton here emphasizes the importance of the unexpected – of the CEE's members being surprised by moments in their performances. Her use of the word "havoc" reflects how the group embraces what they consider risk and the unknown within their creative practice. I see the notion of "weird" manifesting in the CEE's practice in terms of both aesthetic context and genre, or on micro and macro levels. At the level of an individual performance by the ensemble, "weird" can be understood as the unexpected, based on whatever sound world exists at any given moment: something stands out and demands a response. In a broader sense, the CEE also mobilizes the notion of weirdness to situate themselves outside of the norms of acoustic contemporary classical music and improvisation as well as beat-oriented electronic music. Compared with acoustic contemporary classical music and improvisation, the CEE's mostly electronic timbres are "weird," a concept connected not only to timbral quality but also to perceptual mysteries ("What is that sound? Who is making that sound?"). Compared to beat-oriented electronic music, the CEE generally avoids regular pulses, and any instances of pulsing generally avoid metrical implications. The CEE's desire for weirdness has guided both technological and personnel choices for the ensemble, as I will outline below.

Shifting Technologies: Analog to Digital

There's something wonderfully intuitive about analog instruments: the continuous rather than discrete electronic signal means that every physical gesture with a knob, slider, or switch will result in a corresponding change to the sound. But it also increases instability and unpredictability. For instance, intonation was a challenge in early analog instruments, as Chadabe explains: "Tuning, in general, was a significant problem with analog technology. Analog synthesizers were neither precise nor impervious to temperature change" (1997, 157).

When the CEE began performing in the early 1970s, monophonic analog synthesizers were the only option for live performance. This initial performance practice is documented on the CEE's 1977 album. They used EMS Synthi As (which can be seen on the back cover), ARP Odyssey analog synthesizers, a Roland SH-5, and the Dyno-Soar (an instrument made by Jaeger and Montgomery that can create continuous feedback loops). EMS (Electronic Music Studio) was a leading company in voltage-controlled synthesizers in the 1960s and 1970s; the Synthi A, small enough to fit in a suitcase, was designed to be portable. Montgomery still owns and performs on a Synthi A; Sutherland sometimes plays the Synthi A's sibling, the Synthi AKS, which comes with a built-in sequencer.

These EMS devices use resistance pins in a grid of pinholes rather than patch cords. Chadabe explains, though, that "the pins often broke or got lost on a tabletop, and in any case, it took time to decide where in the grid to insert them. These were not optimal performance-oriented systems" (1997, 153). The CEE persevered with them as performance-oriented systems nonetheless, though Montgomery has bemoaned his lost pins and the near impossibility of replacing them. The ARP Odyssey analog synthesizers were designed to be compact, user-friendly, and relatively inexpensive, all with a good sound. Unlike the Synthi A's three oscillators and rotary knobs, the ARP Odyssey has two oscillators and sliders. The Roland SH-5 combines rotary knobs and sliders with a keyboard interface. This monophonic synthesizer is capable of portamento and pitch bending, and it has a mixer section and stereo panning in the VCA section, among many other features. Jaeger described the Dyno-Soar to me as follows:

> A Dynaco preamp was wired such that the output fed back into the input, via a level controller (aka a pot) in the circuit path. The feedback loop was kept in an unstable state, via the pot, and the resulting oscillations became the output of the device. It was, generally speaking, a source of raucous signals, which would often run out of control at any moment, given the instability of the circuit. (personal communication, 10 August 2019)

Though all of the synthesizers described above could certainly create "weird" sounds, the instability of the Dyno-Soar lent itself particularly well to the CEE's desire for occasional weirdness due to its instability: the instrument surprised the musicians, forcing them to react and adjust in real time.

As early as the 1960s, attempts were made to apply digital control through computers to analog synthesizers. The goal was to maintain the beloved sounds of the analog synthesizers but to achieve greater stability and control through digital processing. The University of Toronto's Gustav Ciamaga and James Gabura created the first hybrid synthesizer (*Piper*) in 1965–66, but hybrid synthesizers weren't widely available until the 1970s.

Another main goal of synthesizer developers during the 1970s was expanding from monophonic to polyphonic capabilities. The Synthi

As and ARP Odyssey synthesizers discussed above were monophonic. Chadabe explains: "Although [synthesizers like the Minimoog and portable ARPs] were successful, they were also limited, and there was an increasingly urgent need felt during the early 1970s for the development of a polyphonic synthesizer that could generate several different sounds simultaneously" (1997, 155).

Comparing the CEE's gear list from its 1977 album to a photo from a 1979 performance in Brussels (published in the *Music of Man* booklet) illustrates these rapid changes in live electronic music performance practice. In the photo, each member is positioned at an individual work station, with at least two synthesizers at his disposal and the keyboard as a common interface. Synthi As and a Roland SH-5 are still visible, but they have added a polyphonic, eight-voice Yamaha CS-60 analog synthesizer, which has a ribbon controller for pitch bends; a polyphonic Korg vocoder to filter vocal or non-vocal sounds; and Oberheim Synthesizer Expander Modules (SEM), a keyboard-less module that can be played by a digital sequencer at the same time that it is patched to a keyboard being played.

Regardless of these developments in polyphonic synthesizers, hybrid tools, and soon enough, fully digital devices, a live electronic performance ensemble of the 1970s and '80s was going to have a lot of gear. Montgomery joked about the realities of live performance: "The performances were an afterthought, and what we were really doing was setting up and tearing down!" (personal communication, 26 February 2016).

Nonetheless, the desire to explore new technologies has been central to the CEE's practice throughout its five decades. Jaeger explains: "Whenever a new piece of hardware came in to the CEE – it could have been a new synth or it could have been a new piece of processing equipment like a delay or even a bigger, more complete mixer. Whenever there was a new piece of hardware, it would inevitably spawn new pieces" (personal communication, 10 June 2016). Yet, as members of the group have remarked, keeping up with new technologies requires both space and money, something that the CEE has always had to reckon with. In conversation with students at Carnegie Mellon University (CMU) in February 2020, Montgomery and Jaeger recall securing gently used equipment from celebrated Canadian pianist Oscar Peterson, who was always buying the latest electronic gear. They confess that they would not have been able to afford such pieces otherwise. As for space, in further conversations at CMU, the CEE explained their rule: Something new in? Something's gotta go.

There's a danger, though, in always bringing in new gear. When musicians understand how their electronic gear works, then they can develop a control intimacy. According to Andy Keep, "this in turn can lead to practiced operational skills, more decisive excitation and more subtle sound-shaping of timbral nuances" (2009, 125). Stillwell expresses deep affection for certain modules that he uses; he has developed such familiarity with them that he considers them extensions of himself: "[With certain modules,] I love them, I use them a lot, and they become a part of me" (personal communication, 8 May 2020).

Throughout the 1980s, the CEE's equipment list became more digitized though analog tools were still present, such as the beloved Roland DC-10 Analog Echo and its "bucket brigade" technology. One result of the constant development of new technologies and tools is that, over time, the previous ones often become obsolete – not in aesthetic terms but in technical terms. Take the Synthi A I mention above: its pins have become nearly impossible to replace. For a predominantly improvised practice, to which the CEE would devote itself more and more over the coming decades, such technological obsolescence does not stymie the creative practice, as they use whatever tools are in front of them at any given moment. However, for the CEE's composed repertoire, with specific parts assigned to specific tools, it can be difficult to keep performing certain works. In some cases, the original piece of music may have been captured in tape form in the first place for playback, which allows that era of performance practice to be sustained in later performances (though the playback medium needs to be updated). Some pieces, like Jaeger's *Quivi sospiri*, require reworking from the composer, in the manner of an arrangement. Jaeger's *Quivi sospiri* (see listening guides) was composed during the CEE's monophonic analog synthesizer era and subsequently updated for its 1990 recording. Christina Petrowska-Quilico recorded this work again for her 2017 album *Worlds Apart*; she also included on the piece on her 2021 album *Vintage Americana,* which CBC Music included in its list of Canada's top 21 classical albums of 2021. As electronic technology is often victim to the passing of time, Jaeger reworked the synthesizers' parts into a digital version to accompany the piano part. Joseph Auner identifies a "tendency for electronic sounds and techniques to become stuck in time" (2013, 216). What will happen when Jaeger is unable to provide updates for future performers? Furthermore, as Auner states in reference to a different electroacoustic piece, "it is likely that a significant dimension of the original impact of the work has been lost as the stage has been cleared of equipment [and] cables" (2013, 227).

In the 1990s, laptops with synthesizer software ("soft synths") became accessible and offered satisfying sounds to the group. After two and a half decades of hauling around cumbersome equipment, the utility of the laptop was welcome. But even as the CEE became a laptop-oriented group, additional keyboard interfaces and other hardware didn't completely disappear; I will discuss the reintroduction of analog technologies to the CEE later in the chapter. Jaeger is now the only CEE member to use a laptop exclusively. Several members, including Montgomery, use a laptop in combination with other tools; for Bolton, a violin, effects, and other synthesizers, and for Farah a piano, synthesizers, and sound processing. Of those who use primarily analog equipment, Stillwell has a relatively enormous Eurorack set-up, while Sutherland performs with a Buchla Music Easel and occasionally a Synthi AKS.

Throughout all these stages of personnel and tools, the CEE's activities and aesthetics have remained rather consistent. In the remainder of this chapter, I summarize the CEE's concerts, repertoire, discography, and collaborations in its three most recent eras: trio (1986–96); quintet/sextet/quintet (1996–2008); sextet (2009–present).

The Trio Era: *Catbird Seat* and *Supertrio*

The Canadian Electronic Ensemble was officially a trio from 1986 until late in 1996. Over this decade, the concertizing activities of the CEE as a trio decreased slightly in comparison to the early quartet days, with sixty or so concert performances in Toronto, Ottawa, Vancouver, Quebec, Kingston, Montreal, and Guelph. The trio era was still an exciting and productive time, however, with a CEE album (*Catbird Seat*, 1990), a collaborative album (*Supertrio*, 1996), two European tours, and a Banff residency.

Many of *Catbird Seat*'s tracks are the CEE's most frequently performed works of this trio era, including *Hut, Israfel, Quivi sospiri*, and the title track *Catbird Seat*. *Hut* and *Catbird Seat*, in addition to Lake's *Psalm* and Montgomery's *Affinity Groups*, were featured works during the CEE's 1989 European tour.

Table 3.1 The most-performed CEE pieces by individual members during the trio era, in descending order of frequency.

Name	Composer	Performances	Notes
Psalm (1985)	Lake	6	For oboe and tape
Hut (1987)	Montgomery	6	On *Catbird Seat*
Affinity Groups (1988)	Montgomery	6	
Israfel (1987)	Lake	5	On *Catbird Seat*
Quivi sospiri (1979)	Jaeger	3	On *Catbird Seat*
Favour (1980)	Jaeger	3	
Shadow Box (1986)	Jaeger	3	For accordion and electronic delay
Talisman (1988)	Montgomery	3	

During this era, the CEE performed and presented two dozen unique pieces by its individual members and another two dozen by the whole trio. Table 3.1, listing the pieces by individual CEE members that were performed most frequently at CEE concerts during the trio era, illustrates that the ensemble still emphasized sharing its platform and not allowing any one voice to dominate the group's activities.

The Canadian Electronic Ensemble is a group that knows how to mobilize like-minded musicians. During the 1970s and '80s, this was achieved primarily through collaborations with solo artists. On 24 May 1992, the CEE presented MEGAJAM, a concert of live improvisation featuring eighteen electronic musicians for a concert of live improvisation, which was later released as an album in 2000. Many of the musicians for MEGAJAM previously had and continue to have long-standing relationships with the CEE, including Tim Brady, William Buxton, John Celona, Gustav Ciamaga, John Gzowski, Wes Wraggett,[1] and Gayle Young. In addition to the MEGAJAM collaboration, the CEE also produced six Guitar Boogie concerts, initiated in 1987 by the CEE's then-manager Jon Siddall.

The trio era also featured collaborations with ensembles and performances of works by non-CEE members. On 3 October 1992, the CEE performed with Upstream from Halifax.[2] Upstream (1992–), or the Upstream Music Association, is a multi-genre performance organization that performed its inaugural concert on 27 September 1992 – only days before their collaboration with the CEE. Standing Wave – who, as

Table 3.2 The most-performed CEE group compositions during the trio era, in descending order of frequency.

Title	Performances	Notes
Catbird Seat	9	Title track of 1990 album
Le chat serré	4	As Supertrio; first performance in 1992 is credited as CEE and Trio Collectif
Café Liberté	4	As Supertrio
Chaconne à son goût	3	Last performed in 1988
Mont Cascade	3	As Supertrio
Rock Music	3	As Supertrio
Beef Flat	3	As Supertrio
Attention Elk!	2	From Supertrio album

Jaeger explains, were "fellow community members, and seen as natural collaborators" (personal communication, 18 July 2020) – took part in a performance with the CEE on 31 March 1995.[3] Several months later, on 17 June, the CEE produced a concert entitled "Signals" that included one piece for the Signals Orchestra, which included the CEE trio and future members Laura Wilcox and Paul Stillwell, as well as Sergio Barroso and John Celona, who had both composed for the CEE (including a CEE commission from each for this concert).

The most frequently performed CEE group compositions in the trio era were *Catbird Seat* (the title track from the 1990 album) and the repertoire developed by Supertrio for their performances (table 3.2). In the early years of the CEE trio, *Chaconne à son goût* was repeatedly performed, a holdover from its popularity during the early quartet days.

The most frequently performed piece composed by a non-CEE member was *Universe Symphony* by Steve Gellman (five productions). The CEE developed relationships with a number of composers, including Paul Inston and Richard Sacks, and performed their works during this period. The CEE continued to commission several different composers and premiere their works: some examples include Michael Bussière's *Hypothesis of Memory* (1987) and Bruno Degazio's *On Growth and Form* (1988). Chapter 6 discusses the CEE's commissions in more detail.

The CEE also presented – but did not perform – the music of several different composers during their concerts. Jon Siddall was frequently featured on CEE-produced concerts in the 1980s; as the group's manager, he wanted to participate artistically in the group's activities. The CEE also presented multiple pieces by Tim Brady, John Celona, David Mott, Ann Southam, and Steve Tittle. Southam's piece *Re-tuning* for solo viola was performed at a number of concerts during the trio era because violist Rivka Golani frequently performed as a guest musician on CEE concerts.

Catbird Seat (1990) is the CEE's first CD release, issued on the Canadian Music Centre's label Centrediscs. This six-track album features the CEE trio and a collection of guest musicians: Armin Strings on *Wildfire*,[4] Robert Cram (flute) on *Israfel*, Christina Petrowska Quilico (piano) on *Quivi sospiri*, Lawrence Cherney (oboe) on *Hut*, and Joseph Petric (accordion) on *Davies*. The title track is the only one performed by the CEE trio alone. This album demonstrates the CEE's long history of performing with soloists and composing new music to feature an acoustic-electronic collaboration.

The most important aspect of the CEE's trio era was the multi-year relationship with improvisational group Trio Collectif (Pete Enrnrooth, Bernard Donzel-Gargand, and Philippe Moënne-Loccoz), which hosted them in Annecy, France, during the CEE's European tour in 1989. That first concert was then followed up by performances together in Toronto and Kingston in 1992, tours in Quebec and Europe (1994 and 1996, respectively), a three-week residency at the Banff Centre for the Arts under the name "Supertrio" (October 1994), three workshops for Inner City Angels in Toronto, and an album (*Supertrio*, 1996). According to Montgomery, who recalls knowing of Trio Collectif before their collaboration, the two groups were well suited to collaboration: "They were (are) excellent musicians and our connection was the same one that has informed almost all of our musical relationships; an immediate and unarticulated understanding of how we wanted to make music and what music we wanted to make" (personal communication, 19 May 2020).

Jaeger fondly recalls their time at Banff:

> The mystique of the Banff Centre for the Arts has a wide reach, and I believe [Trio Collectif] had already heard about it. If that wasn't the case, we must have mentioned it, and the mere thought of hanging out there in such a cool place, doing stuff together, was pretty unstoppable. So, the idea was instantly conceived as a sequence of events – we would get ourselves invited to Banff, where we would make a master for a CD, and then we'd tour the

work in both Canada and in France/Switzerland, with the new CD in hand. That was the idea, and it was also exactly what we did. We had a great time doing it, too! (personal communication, 20 May 2020)

Montgomery credits Lake's wife, Karen Kieser, with making the Supertrio collaboration a success. Kieser was in many ways a full CEE member, albeit unofficially, and she performed frequently with the group, including on tour. Montgomery reflects: "In subtle ways, she enabled the transformation (which took less than a week) from two groups jockeying for position to six guys in search of excellence. Boys, after all, will be boys, and we could have spent the entire period pissing on each other's shoes, but under her gentle guidance, from insisting on the communal table in the Dining Hall to ensuring that evenings were rehearsals instead of drinkathons, focus was maintained" (personal communication, 2 June 2020). This story suggests that Kieser sometimes took on a kind of den mother role for the CEE, which, as a result, reinforced a gendered role of invisible labour (Daniels 1987; Erickson 2005). Chapter 6 examines gender inequality in the major music institutions in Toronto, including the CBC, Kieser's employer. Kieser was not only background support of the CEE, however; she was a featured soloist and had a prominent career.

Immediately following this residency, Supertrio conducted three workshops for Inner City Angels in Toronto and performed in Quebec City and Montreal. They returned for one last concert in Toronto and a celebratory dinner. Montgomery recalls: "Everybody had a good time. Nobody died" (personal communication, 1 June 2020). The CEE trio headed over to western Europe, where the members of Trio Collectif resided, for a three-concert tour in Annecy, Geneva, and La Chaux-de-Fonds.

This multi-year collaboration (and alcohol-fuelled bond) is preserved on the album *Supertrio*. The album contains seven tracks, five of which are performed by Supertrio: *Roc Peace, Instrumental One, Clusters, Instrumental deux,* and *Wapiti Sextet*. One track, *La rivière de l'arc,* is for Trio Collectif only, clearly reflecting that ensemble's particular sound, while *Attention Elk!* is a CEE-only track. Two tracks reference an animal – the elk, or wapiti – that populates the Rocky Mountain range. Jaeger describes this source of inspiration: "The presence of the elk on the Banff campus was striking, especially to the Europeans. Somehow, it seemed simply unthinkable that these grand creatures would run free among the otherwise civilized campus. I think the focus on the natural effects of the environment was just a natural reaction to us urbanites being there in the rocky mountain paradise" (personal communication, 20 May 2020).

The CEE in Flux: New People, New Sounds

Though the CEE was officially a trio for a decade, the group was consistent in its commitment to collaborating with other performers and composers. Jaeger explains: "I think we were cautious about finding replacements, since the toolkit for potential new CEE members was highly specialized" (personal communication, 20 May 2020). When the CEE did begin to expand, the ensemble would bring in musicians to jam, or sometimes to guest perform or write a piece for the CEE; then, when the musical and social connection felt right to the existing members, that individual was asked to join the group officially. Stillwell, who became an official member in 1996 after going through his own "audition" process, explains: "There have been a lot of musicians we've either performed with spontaneously at a concert or we have performed with in our studio at a rehearsal or in a rehearsal space like my basement. Things just didn't click. And we never did that again, because we knew they didn't get it. They didn't get what we did, how we did it. It's always worth trying if somebody gets it. But if they don't get it, and you don't think they're gonna get it, then you don't need to pursue" (personal communication, 27 January 2016).

The period of the CEE from late 1996 until the end of 2008 marks the least stable lineup for the ensemble, with four additions to the group and two exits. Performances also became less frequent, with less than half the number of concerts compared with the previous decade, which had already shown a decline from the early quartet era. However, this era is significant for three main reasons. First, the CEE released a live album with its first sextet lineup (*Canadian Electronic Ensemble: Live*, 1998); the ensemble also recorded *Live at Cabbagetown* in 2008, though it was not released until 2013. Second, the CEE held two residencies, one with dancer Lina Cruz (2000) and the other at the XII Sound Symposium in St John's, Newfoundland (July 2004); current members of the CEE still speak with great passion about these two experiences. Finally, in what I think is the most important shift from the first twenty-five years of the CEE, the group increasingly emphasized group improvisations and CEE member-composed works over pieces by non-CEE composers.

During this era, the CEE's repertoire consisted primarily of pieces composed by individual CEE members, most of which were performed only once. *Stonehenge* by Montgomery and Stillwell and *Last Man Standing* by Montgomery, which both appear on *Canadian Electronic Ensemble: Live*, and Montgomery and Stillwell's *Dojo* were all performed more than once. In the same span of time, the CEE performed only two works by non-CEE composers, one of which was by Rose Bolton before she was an official member: *The Chalet in Ke-Wald-Dun-Dot Valley*, performed on 15 March 1997. The other piece was *Three Old Friends* by John S. Gray, composed for the CEE and premiered by the group on 24 October 2004.

Improvisation had been a central part of the CEE's performance practice since its inception. In earlier periods, though, the CEE's concert programs were predominantly filled with compositions that were created and performed with specific frameworks for performance (e.g., *Chaconne à son goût*), and some had conventionally notated elements (e.g., *Quivi sospiri*). During the CEE's quintet/sextet era, almost a quarter of the CEE's repertoire was free improvisations. In the group's current era (2009 to present), this emphasis on free improvisation dominates even more. With the addition of four new CEE members during the 1990s, the CEE's practice needed to be fluid to welcome each member's particular interests in and comfort with collective electronic music making. This next section of the chapter explores the CEE's practice since the 1990s through the lens of each new addition to the group.

MICHAEL DOBINSON

Michael Dobinson (b. 1968) first performed with the CEE on 24 February 1996 as a "resident artist," a designation that indicates the CEE's interest in a potential member. He was made an official member with a concert on 2 November 1996. A composer and performer from Scarborough, Ontario, Dobinson completed a bachelor of fine arts (honours music) from York University in Toronto, then a master of music in composition from Western University in London, Ontario (then called the University of Western Ontario). In his official artist biography, Dobinson notes diverse influences in his musical style, including

John Cage, Iannis Xenakis, Balinese gamelan, and Indian music; York University's strong programs in ethnomusicology and Euro-American classical music can be credited for these formative musical experiences.

Dobinson composed and co-composed works for the CEE and performed with the ensemble until 2005. The current CEE members credit Dobinson with contributing some of the ensemble's weirdest sounds. Jaeger explains: "He was a reliable source of, if you will allow me, 'weirdness' in what he brought to the table. But as such, it was pretty much a welcome voice, given the overall aesthetic of the group" (personal communication, 20 May 2020). Bolton perceived that Dobinson's sound was very unique: "The textures that he added were a relief, a nice contrast" (personal communication, 25 February 2020). Stillwell describes Dobinson's creative voice as follows:

> Mike has his style which he reserved mostly for his own compositions which can be brilliant! He would weave these incredibly complex tapestries with sounds and phrases that are performed live being stored and pulled from the depths of whatever processing to re-emerge minutes later in a different context. This was realized through very complex Reaktor ensembles and in the context of improvising with 5 other people those things don't necessarily work that well" (personal communication, 8 May 2020).

Since 2008, Dobinson has worked with the Canadian Conservatory of Music's (CNCM) Summer Sizzle Keyboard Amp & Pedagogy Symposium hosted annually across Canada. CNCM has developed its own curriculum in coaching, composition, piano, theory, and history, and Dobinson has composed numerous pieces for the piano repertoire across its various levels. The M level of CNCM's "Music for Everyone" program is called the "Michael Level," named in honour of Michael Dobinson.

Dobinson is also a founding member of *mmmm* (2009–), an organization dedicated to the compositions and performances of its four Ms: organist and pianist Michel Allard, electronic and film composer Michelle Wells, composer and organist Marco Burak, and Dobinson. Their programs also include special guest composers and performers. *mmmm* typically produces a spring and fall concert each year in Stratford, Ontario, initially at St Paul's Anglican Church and moving to Zion Lutheran Church in 2011.

LAURA WILCOX

Laura Wilcox is a violinist/violist and artistic/executive director (2014–) of Miami Youth for Chamber Music (MYCM). She began her studies on violin at the age of five, going on to study at McGill University and SUNY-Purchase. She has held a number of administrative, instructional, and performance positions, including teaching at the Conservatory of Music at Lynn University, working as music director of the ArtSouth Ensemble, and performing with the Florida Grand Opera and the Miami City Ballet orchestras.

Wilcox first performed with the CEE as part of the Signals Orchestra on 17 June 1995. She was designated a "resident artist" for the 24 February 1996 concert, alongside Michael Dobinson and Paul Stillwell. Wilcox remained a guest performer in 1997 and became an official member with the CEE's concert on 8 February 1998. She had a short stint with the group, though, with Rose Bolton replacing Wilcox in 1999 as the CEE's string musician.

Wilcox is not an electronic musician. The CEE has worked with many acoustic musicians as guest soloists, but a consistently acoustic timbre within the ensemble is rare. As Stillwell described it to me, his work with her in the studio involved "developing effects patches on an Ensoniq DP-4. These patches included distortion, delay, reverb, chorus, phasing, etc. and allowed her to adapt her voice to fit within the context of the CEE" (personal communication, 8 May 2020).

Wilcox currently plays viola in the Deering Estate Chamber Ensemble (2006–), which she co-founded with her husband, pianist Jose R. Lopez, Ross Harbaugh (cello), and Scott Flavi (violin). She also teaches at the Coral Reef Montessori Academy in Miami, Florida, through MYCM.

PAUL STILLWELL

CompuServe, a pre–World Wide Web platform, became a popular medium for online moderated forums in the early 1990s. Through this platform, Paul Stillwell (b. 1965) met Larry Lake, and he was invited to compose a piece for the CEE. The CEE performed *Helipad* on 17 June 1995, with Stillwell performing in the same concert as part of the Signals Orchestra. He gained the status of "resident artist" at a concert on 24 February 1996, and first performed as an official member of the CEE on 2 November 1996.

Along with being a composer and musician in diverse genres of electronic music, Stillwell is an IT engineer working in the area of network security. Stillwell grew up in Kitchener-Waterloo, Ontario, where his first instrument was the piano accordion, which he played from the age of eight until his early twenties. He joined the local drum and bugle corps at age twelve, eventually joining the Northstar Drum and Bugle Corps. In these ensembles, Stillwell played the two-valve soprano bugle. In high school band, Stillwell played trumpet (or, as he says, he "took on the 3rd valve"; personal communication, 8 May 2020). Stillwell attended Humber College as a jazz student but did not complete the program.

Stillwell first met Larry Lake because he had been sharing some of his compositions on CompuServe, and Lake invited Stillwell to compose a piece for the CEE. It went well, and Stillwell has remained with the group ever since (1996–). Stillwell often performs solo under the name "Intrepita." He is the co-organizer for the annual Toronto Sound Festival (2016–) and curates for the monthly workshop series Frequency Freaks (2016–). He also performs with David Sutherland, the most recent addition to the CEE's lineup.

Stillwell prefers to call himself a "musician" because it encompasses the many hats he wears, including composer, performer, improviser, and recording engineer. For example, on the CEE's 2014 album *Bluffer's Lookout*, he contributed as composer and performer, as well as in recording, mixing, editing, and mastering.

Stillwell's preferred tools of electronic music have shifted over the years. In the 1990s, he used digital tools, like the Korg Wavestation, as well as tools that he used to create sounds in his home rather than live at rehearsal, such as a Roland Sound Canvas for his PC. When laptops became accessible and practical for live electronic music, Stillwell switched to software synthesizers and other non-realtime tools like Cecilia for granular synthesis. But then Stillwell experienced what he calls "Patch Paralysis." He explains: "So many synthesizers providing thousands of presets when creating music I would think to myself that someone else must have already made a sound that will fit here with what I am looking for … Then I would spend a couple of hours trying things and completely lose the creative flow due to the technology getting in the way" (personal communication, 8 May 2020). This is when he acquired the Chapman Stick: it permitted guitar-based gestures and sounds but, as Stillwell says, "made sense to a keyboard player" (personal communication, 8 May 2020). The Chapman Stick is a polyphonic electric stringed-instrument (typically ten or twelve strings) that resembles a wide and long electric guitar fretboard. The strings are struck at their desired locations rather than plucked, which is what allows the instrument to be polyphonic. He enjoyed it for a couple of years, but was soon more interested in modular synthesizers. In his own practice, he uses 5U/MU, Eurorack, Serge, and Ciat-Lonbarde modular and semi-modular devices; hardware synthesizers (ARP Odyssey, Korg MS-20, Yamaha CS-40); and newer devices like the SOMA Lyra-8 and Elektron's Analog Keys and Octatrak, the latter of which creates weird sounds due to the ease with which the audio can be manipulated in unexpected and extreme ways.

ROSE BOLTON

Rose Bolton (b. 1971) first interacted with the CEE as a composer: on 15 March 1997, the CEE quintet performed her *The Chalet in Ke-Wald-Dun-Dot Valley* with special guest Laura Wilcox. On 29 March 1999, Bolton first performed as a full member of the CEE, having replaced Wilcox.

Bolton is a Juno-nominated composer, electronic musician, and violist. She prefers the term "sonic landscapist" because it "makes a suggestion to the listener about what the experience of my music might be" (personal communication, 23 June 2020). She studied composition as an undergraduate at the University of Western Ontario (now Western University) in London, Ontario, and she received her bachelor of music (honours) in 1995. She received her MA in composition from McGill University in 1999.

Since 2008, Bolton has composed the scores for several documentaries directed by her partner, Marc de Guerre. Bolton has also participated in a number of large-scale live installation-performances, including works at the 2013 X Avant festival at the Music Gallery, a multimedia installation at the Gladstone Hotel's Grow Op event, and Toronto's 2011 Nuit Blanche. In 2016, Bolton, de Guerre, and poet Don McKay premiered *Song of Extinction* (produced by Music in the Barns) at Toronto's Luminato Festival. Alongside Norah Lorway, Bolton also co-composed the score for the award-winning documentary ANTHROPOCENE: *The Human Epoch*, which premiered at the Toronto International Film Festival in 2018. Bolton's 2018 work *The Coming of Sobs*, performed and produced by Music in the Barns, was nominated for Classical Composition of the Year at the 2020 Juno Awards.

In the spring of 2016, Bolton, with the support and coordination of the Canadian Music Centre–Ontario branch and its then director Matthew Fava, implemented the project EQ: Women in Electronic Music to build community and skills for women in electronic music making. It had three iterations, with a total of nineteen participants and guest facilitators. I will speak in more detail about Bolton's EQ project in chapter 6 to interrogate electronic music as a gendered space.

When Bolton first began performing with the CEE, she used a Fishman pickup on her acoustic violin processed through an Ensoniq DP-4 effects unit. In the 2010s, she switched to processing her violin through a Boss ME-70. Since 2018, Bolton has performed with an electric violin (which is more portable), and she obtained a MacBook Pro to use Ableton Live and Reason; she also performs with a Roland SE-02 analog synthesizer. Bolton emphasizes that "budget was the main factor influencing what was available to me. I would use whatever I could get my hands on" (personal communication, 23 June 2020). Bolton enjoys "the richness of all of the timbres" the CEE creates, a richness that she sees influencing her other compositions (personal communication, 23 June 2020).

Due to Bolton's demanding schedule of composition commissions, she has been mostly on hiatus from the CEE since 2005. She did perform with the CEE on 20 December 2007, which was Farah's first guest performance. She also participated in Lake's last CEE performance (4 May 2012), the recording of *Bluffer's Lookout* and subsequent CD launch in 2014, and the CEE's residency at CMU in February 2020.

QUINTET/SEXTET/QUINTET OVERVIEW

As stated above, the quintet/sextet/quintet era of the CEE was relatively unstable in comparison with the previous two and half decades. The 2000s in particular were a time of transition and preoccupation with non-CEE activities for many of the members. Stillwell recalls asking the other CEE members to permit him a break to concentrate on his young family and career. Lake and Jaeger were often busy travelling for their show *Two New Hours*, leaving a quartet version of the CEE behind to perform (for example, at the memorable 2000 concert with dancer Lina Cruz), when there were concerts at all. Karen Kieser died in 2002 after being sick with ovarian cancer, and Lake would spend much of the end of the decade sick himself. In 2005, due to arts funding cutbacks, the

CEE lost the funding that had been supporting the rental of a studio space. During 2006, the CEE did not perform at all; this proved a natural pause for the group, and Dobinson left at that time. In the late 2000s and early 2010s, Bolton became increasingly busy with her compositional activities, so she performed less frequently with the ensemble.

In 2000, the CEE produced the *MEGAJAM* album from the 1992 performance, and the Cabbagetown Arts Festival concert from September 2008 was released as a live album in 2013. Otherwise, the CEE did not release any albums during the 2000s. This is likely due not only to the overall decrease in activity and shifts in space and personnel, but also to funding loss. With an ensemble as long-standing as the CEE, it seems reasonable that such periods of flux and lulls in activity would occur; otherwise, the entire group would burn out and abandon the endeavour altogether. The CEE has never been a full-time job for its performers, so other demands have always competed for its members' time and focus. Thus, performances during the 2000s could feature any combination of the CEE membership.

Approaching Fifty Years

Since John Kameel Farah's official addition to the CEE in 2009, the ensemble's activity has continued the slowdown that occurred across the first decade of the new millennium. Its members have all been busy with other musical activities, such as Stillwell's leadership in the Toronto modular synthesis community. The public activities of the CEE have been reserved for more special occasions, such as the release of their 2014 album *Bluffer's Lookout*, the "Celebration of the Life and Music of Larry Lake" event in late November 2013, and the performance at the 2015 book launch for Norma Beecroft's book *Conversations with Post World War II Pioneers of Electronic Music*. With the addition of David Sutherland to the official CEE lineup in 2017, the group's activities have begun to increase, with performances at the Arts & Letters Club and The TRANZAC Club. The CEE sextet gathered for a residency in February 2020 at CMU in Pittsburgh for a series of workshops, a public panel lecture, and a concert.

The shift away from composed works, especially those by non-CEE members, in the quintet/sextet era of the late 1990s and early 2000s has now became even more pronounced. With the exception of a concert featuring John S. Gray's *No Dim Pearls*, none of the CEE's performances has involved the works of outside composers. Indeed, the vast majority of the material the CEE now performs is free group improvisations, as opposed to collectively or individually composed works with titles and notated frameworks. The CEE's improvisational practice, including the role of rehearsal, is discussed in detail in chapter 4. Here, I will mention that the group generally begins each improvisation with a specific "soloist": a CEE member who begins the improvisation and establishes some of the essential parameters for the subsequent group contributions. These "pieces" are named for the person who begins. Thus, the CEE has a series of pieces entitled "Jim Goes First," "Paul Goes First," and so on. No two of these pieces are the same, however.

JOHN KAMEEL FARAH

Pianist and composer John Kameel Farah (b. 1973) was born and raised in Brampton, Ontario. He began piano lessons at the age of eight with a local teacher down the street, then studied with Eric Medhurst at the Royal Conservatory of Music in Toronto. He remembers hearing Glenn Gould's Bach recordings and Wendy Carlos's *Switched on Bach* as a young musician; Bach and electronics became lifelong loves. He initially planned to enrol in Middle Eastern studies, but at the last minute, he switched to music. Many other schools wouldn't allow him to audition so close to the fall semester, but McMaster University in Hamilton, Ontario, permitted him to audition. He transferred the next year to the University of Toronto, where he completed his bachelor of music in composition in 1996. While he fondly recalls hanging out with the jazz students and being immersed in the Toronto music scenes, he wonders if it would have been better to stay at McMaster, where his multi-faceted artistic practice (performer-composer-improviser) may have been better suited to the program.

Farah first performed with the CEE as a guest artist in 2007 and 2008, and his first performance as an official member was in 2009 at the Somewhere There Festival. One of his guest performances was at the Cabbagetown Arts Festival concert on 6 September 2008; by the time the improvisations from that concert were released on the 2013 album *Live in Cabbagetown*, he was a member. Farah characterizes his electronic skills as less developed than those of the other members, or at least less technological. He knows how to use his gear (as "an interface user") but doesn't believe he understands the science behind it in the way his colleagues do. Consequently, he wants to draw on his strength – the piano – without dominating the CEE sound too much. But he explained to me that on some occasions, he does allow himself to, as he phrased it, "go apeshit" as contrast.

Farah refers to his style as "Baroque Middle Eastern cyber punk." He has struggled with using other titles such as composer, improviser, and electronic producer because they lead people to view his creative practice too narrowly. He explained to me that when he began spending a lot of time in Berlin, he didn't brand himself as an improviser or build connections with the Berlin improvisation community: "the price that I paid for that was that people didn't know I was doing free jazz, all of that experimental improvisation" (personal communication, 21 May 2020). He describes himself as a "maximalist kind of composer; in my solo music, there's just a zillion things going on at the time, and it can be semi-virtuosic" (personal communication, 21 May 2020).

GRIEF, CELEBRATION, AND CREATIVITY

This era of the CEE is characterized by three major events. First, Larry Lake's death in 2013; second, the production and release of *Bluffer's Lookout* in 2014; and third, the 2020 residency at CMU, which sparked an increased commitment to co-creating new material together and working towards a new album. The residency at CMU, which involved extensive collaboration with the student experimental group Exploded Ensemble, will also result in a new album.

The CEE members all consider Lake's death an enormous loss, both socially and musically. Farah describes his death as creating a hole in the CEE, explaining that the first rehearsals he attended following Lake's death were striking. Stillwell has a particular affection for Lake, the one who brought him into "the CEE family" (personal communication, 20 May 2020). He emphasizes that the group misses Lake, but that they evoke his memory frequently: "In those ways it doesn't feel so much like he has left us" (personal communication, 20 May 2020). For example, during their February 2020 concert at CMU, the CEE programmed Lake's *Psalm* and closed the concert with an improvisation designed as a meditation on Lake. The CEE toasts to Lake annually on his birthday, and they frequently reminiscence about his humour, musical voice, and important leadership role within the group.

Bluffer's Lookout is the first CEE album created without Larry Lake.[5] On the album's Bandcamp page, the group explains: "It was a difficult time for us as Larry was sick and unable to join us on any of the sessions, however his influence is present in the creation of this music."[6] The album is dedicated to him.

At almost two hours, *Bluffer's Lookout* is the longest of the CEE's albums. It includes some longer pieces, which is typical of the CEE's performance practice and discography: specifically, the first track *7 Below* (19:12) and the last track *IIFTLH* (21:15). Yet this album also has an unusual number of shorter pieces – five of the eleven tracks are under eight minutes – including what would be considered a remarkably short CEE piece, *Star Song* (4:41). With the exception of *Star Song* (performed from 1975 to 1977) and Bolton's *This Is This* (composed and premiered in 2004), none of the album's tracks has been performed in live concert. This album, then, is a documentation more of the CEE's compositional and collaborative approaches outside of real time than of their live improvisational and performance practice. This is the first album to include Bolton, who is not on *Live at Cabbagetown*. As the album was recorded in Stillwell's basement (known as "7 Below"), which does not have a piano, Farah does not perform acoustic piano on this album, but rather uses a Nord Lead 3 synthesizer and laptop (Ableton Live Suite, Reaktor 5, and Absynth); he employs a piano sound at times, including in *Sparse Sunday*, discussed below. Farah does not perform on all tracks, likely due to conflicts between his busy concertizing schedule and the album's recording schedule.

The CEE is collectively credited with composing five of the tracks; of the others, Farah composed two, and Bolton, Jaeger, Montgomery, and Stillwell each composed one. The result, again, is an equitable share of compositional credit and aesthetic leadership. Many of the album's track titles reflect the CEE's humour: *Sparse Sunday* because "It was Sunday and the music was sparse"; *545* because the instructions were to play for five minutes, forty-five seconds (though the track is 7:28); *IIFTLH* because "we're in it for the long haul." But the CEE's attitude towards the music they create is not humorous. They are serious about creating dense, sometimes complex, often weird, electronic sound worlds.

Some of the pieces on *Bluffer's Lookout* involve sounds that are more unusual in the CEE's aesthetic practices, such as the real-world street sound samples of *Street Scenes* and Bolton's voiceover on *This Is This* (and several other voices). This is certainly not to say the CEE never engages with field recordings or recorded voices; Stillwell, in particular, likes to gather and implement such samples occasionally. However, the CEE's sound is dominated by purely electronic music and, with Bolton and Farah, acoustic instruments both plain and processed.

Sparse Sunday, composed by Farah, is a representative example of the CEE's current sound, with the piano – in this case, a piano sound on the synthesizer – contrasting with electronic sounds. It also features Jaeger on laptop using Reaktor, Montgomery on laptop, Bolton on violin with effects, and Stillwell on the Chapman Stick and laptop. The tapping gestures on the Chapman Stick also stick out within the electronic soundscape of *Sparse Sunday*.

The piano is the continuous thread throughout the piece, with various synthesizer, violin, and Chapman Stick layers shifting in and out of the texture. Farah is a virtuosic pianist, but his CEE practice tends to limit the amount of flourishing passagework or quasi-orchestral playing in order to be balanced with his fellow musicians. He explained to me that the piano already stands out in the CEE's sound without needing to bring all of his technical capabilities to bear: "I try to be watchful that my piano playing doesn't take over ... Piano is such a distinct, different sound from everything else. I don't want everything to become piano concertos" (personal communication, 21 May 2020). That being said, he also tries to find a moment in each improvisation to be more virtuosic. In *Sparse Sunday*, Farah remains relatively reserved with his part. He explained to me that in his solo work, he feels like he has to make some profound statement, but that the CEE creates "these giant sound blobs, these giant sound canvases that just evolves endlessly. So it allows me to loosen up" (personal communication, 5 May 2020).

Sparse Sunday is through-composed, with the exception of the opening augmented eighth/minor ninth interval returning in the final minute (though with different pitches). The textural density throughout the piece suggests an arch structure: the piece opens and closes quietly and sparsely, while the middle two and a half minutes (approx. 2:59–5:27) are the most densely textured and cacophonous.

The piece opens with two simultaneous, gently articulated piano notes: B♭3 and B4 (perceived as an augmented eighth). The piano remains alone for the first half minute, continuing with dissonant pitch collections but played softly. Once the first synth drone enters (0:29), a series of other synthesized layers emerge, including a low growl and a knocking gesture that will reappear in various manifestations in the first half of the piece (0:57). The synth layers constantly crescendo and decrescendo as the piano part becomes more varied. Sectional divides are difficult to pin down in this piece, though it clearly has sections that contain specific characteristics. The piano part begins to vary at 1:22, and more variations of knocking sounds join the mix. Overall, the texture remains relatively sparse, allowing the listener to perceive each layer. There are very few sharp attacks in *Sparse Sunday*, so the relatively loud and abrupt Chapman Stick strike at 2:25 is startling. The piano part remains relatively consistent while the synth layers are in constant internal motion.

Despite Bolton's use of the violin on this piece, the listener would be advised not to search in the piece for sounds resembling acoustic violin, as Bolton transforms the violin's timbre through processing. Sounds created through bowing, though, appear at 2:59, and they herald the middle section of the piece, the densest section. The piano, Chapman Stick, and synthesizer engage in a call and response, with each piano articulation answered quickly by an electronic voice. A steady bass pattern emerges briefly (3:26–3:37), resulting in rhythmic tension between its steady pulse and the ametrical articulations surrounding it. The texture to this point has remained relatively sparse, but this gradually changes, beginning with the piano's quickened pace of cluster chords (all still articulated no louder than a mezzo piano/mezzo forte). Around 4:05, the noise level of *Sparse Sunday* picks up; a low growl drone pervades the sound world. The piano adds its own insistent voice through repeated octaves. The Chapman Stick's strikes are more present while the piano briefly steps out of the mix.

Around 5:27, the low growl drone persists, as does the Chapman Stick's tapping. But there is a clear shift in mood here, specifically through new piano material: short descending scalar passages that repeat (at 6:07, Farah descends and ascends on the pattern). The low growl eventually fades (5:48). The piano returns to the opening augmented eighth interval, but here articulated melodically as an ascending octave

(C♯ to C♯) and ascending minor second (to D). Synth layers continue to swirl around the piano. The entire piece is winding down in texture and dynamics, so the articulation at 7:08 jars the listener. The moment is fleeting, however, as the piece continues its descent into silence.

The Chapman Stick features prominently on this album, but ultimately, Stillwell wasn't happy with the instrument. He explained that the Chapman Stick processed through Guitar Rig Pro "just couldn't generate sounds that were weird enough. If you listen to CEE music, we have a lot of weird sounds" (personal communication, 27 January 2016). By his use of "weird" here, I take Stillwell to be referencing the CEE's valuation of timbres that not only deviate from the acoustic sound world but also are surprising – even jarring – in some way.

Stillwell learned about the revival of analog synthesizers and modular synthesis, and he was eager to employ the sounds that he had loved in his youth: the sounds of Pink Floyd and Tangerine Dream. In our conversation on 27 January 2016, he explained that some musicians, what he called "older purists," rejected the Eurorack system for enabling both analog and digital modules. He responded: "I don't really subscribe to that." This rejection of the analog/digital debate is core to the CEE's practice. Montgomery frequently declares: "Ultimately, it all comes back to the music. It doesn't really matter. I always tell students that ... you can make good music with rocks and sticks if you wanted to. If you can make good music, you can make it with rocks and sticks" (personal communication, 26 February 2016).

As Stillwell became more interested in the possibilities of the Eurorack system and acquiring his own modules, he became more involved with the Toronto-based modular synthesizer community. Through this community, Stillwell connected with David Sutherland, who became the CEE's newest member.

DAVID SUTHERLAND

David Sutherland (b. 1952) has been a member of the CEE since 2017. While he took piano lessons as a child, Sutherland describes himself as "not very good at it" (personal communication, 8 June 2020), recalling a resistance to notated music. In 1970, he entered Dawson College to study music ("because I couldn't get into the religion stream"; personal communication, 8 June 2020). He recalls studying piano in his first year and classical saxophone in his second year. While at Dawson, Sutherland also enrolled in the Mosaic alternative arts program led by Morton Rossengarten (visual arts) and Michael Harris (literature). Sutherland completed a three-year degree at Concordia during the 1970s.

Sutherland fondly recalls many experiences with live electronic music in his early adulthood: sitting behind Karlheinz Stockhausen as he diffused one of his quadraphonic pieces (1971); first experimenting with a Synthi AKS (1973);[7] taking an electronic music course at McGill University (1974–75) with Bengt Hambraeus (1928–2000) and alcides lanza (b. 1929) where he worked with Moog, ARP synthesizers, and Hugh Le Caine's instruments. Sutherland didn't enrol in a degree program at McGill, though, noting that "McGill was still very much a classical conservatory in those days" (personal communication, 13 October 2017). In the 1970s, Sutherland performed with MetaMusic, a live electronic ensemble based in Montreal. He tells the story of acting first as a kind of roadie before officially becoming part of the group: "I joined Meta-Music by being the guy that helped them dismantle the studio, assemble it where they were playing, and just sit and listen to the concert and enjoy the music, and then help them take it back and build the studio. So I actually could take the McGill EMS apart and rebuild it, before I actually got in the band" (personal communication, 13 October 2017). Such practical issues of set-up were central to 1970s live electronic music performance practice and continue to be a primary concern. Ever the jokester, Sutherland said to me: "The first lesson in electronics: is it plugged in?" (personal communication, 13 October 2017).

After leaving MetaMusic in early 1978, Sutherland stopped making music beyond singing and playing a bit of guitar for his young children. He worked in computers for thirty years, retiring from the University of Toronto in 2012. As he neared retirement, Sutherland returned to his interest in analog synthesizers. He told me he was thinking: "I'm probably the only person in this city who knows anything about modular synthesizers. I'm just gonna google it." The results of his search demonstrated a vibrant local synthesizer community. He elaborated: "There's a whole world that has evolved in that 40-year period … you discover that that whole thing has not only been revived, it actually has a commercial life!" (personal communication, 13 October 2017). Through his modular synthesizer community, Sutherland met Stillwell. The two jammed and found a musical and social compatibility: "for me, it was just like going back and doing MetaMusic" (personal communication, 13 October 2017).

Stillwell invited Sutherland to jam with the CEE, and following two performances in November 2016 as a guest, Sutherland was officially a member: "the new guy," Sutherland likes to say with a joking stab at his own age. Sutherland recalls his initiation: "It was funny because we did a couple of things, and it was like 'oh, have we told you you're part of the band now?' I said 'No, but it's nice!' And 'yeah, yeah, yeah, we just assumed you knew because you're here now.' So then it was kind of fun" (personal communication, 13 October 2017). Jaeger explained, "we realized immediately he was a kindred spirit" (personal communication, 18 May 2017). Montgomery's CEE records (which he publishes on the ensemble's website) identify 25 March 2017 as the day Sutherland became a member, with his first official concert on 28 March. Sutherland was grateful for the opportunity: "I hadn't done that kind of music in close to forty years ... And it was just like it all came back. Like riding a bicycle. It was easy, just the best thing I'd ever experienced in my life" (public lecture, 26 February 2020).

With the CEE, Sutherland likes to perform on either the Buchla Music Easel or the Synthi AKS. When he performs with the Easel in his home studio, he patches it through a Eurorack Serge Filter, Demora Delay, and an Eventide H9 effects pedal. That set-up is too cumbersome to bring to CEE rehearsals and performances, so Sutherland instead patches the Synthi and Easel to an RME Fireface UC and into Ableton Live. Sutherland's sense of humour emerges when discussing his gear: "How cool do we look? The obvious answer to anyone under 30; we don't look cool at all. Maybe Rose and John pass. But, maybe our gear can have some coolness and lend some credibility to our appearance. Standing on stage with 2 Synthi's significantly raises the cool factor in the electronic music crowd. Throw in a Buchla Easel and you have some serious electro-nerd charisma" (personal communication, 8 June 2020).

The CEE officially became a sextet when Sutherland joined, but as Farah was often performing in Europe and Bolton was busy with her compositional activities, Sutherland was largely filling out a trio into a quartet. The CEE continues to be flexible about each performance lineup depending on people's availability.

Modular Synthesis in the CEE: A Nostalgic Return

In *Strange Sounds* (2001), Timothy Taylor explains the return to electronic analog technology in his chapter "Technostalgia": "some musicians prefer the sounds of these older instruments, and ... older instruments have fewer automated features than today's instruments and thus allow musicians a greater degree of control" (97). Taylor later discusses the physicality (or "muscular activity") of "retro" equipment, which requires kinetic finesse and does not rely only on "mental activity" (110). Taylor paraphrases Moog's argument that "the older equipment invites a physicality, and offers a tactility that are pleasurable and unavailable with most newer instruments having buttons instead of knobs" (110–11).[8]

Stillwell purchased his first Eurorack modules in 2015, thus bringing the CEE back – in part – to its purely analog days. Since then, he says, "I still haven't emerged from the rabbit hole" (personal communication, 20 May 2020). Released first in 1996 with a Doepfer A-100, Eurorack is a compact modular synthesizer format using a 3.5-mm jack (Mishra 2009). It creates a standardization whereby different modules both fit physically into a case and can communicate with each other via colourful patch cables. According to music technology magazine *Sound on Sound* (*SOS*), throughout the 2000s, manufacturers like Make Noise Music, Cwejman, Tiptop Audio, Livewire Electronics, The Harvestman, and Analogue Systems designed Eurorack modules, in addition to Doepfer (Mishra 2009). When Al James wrote about "The Secret World of Modular Synthesizers" four years after Mishra's article (2013), he noted that over eighty manufacturers were using the Eurorack format, resulting in more than 700 modules.

Stillwell expressed the desire for both physicality and unpredictability articulated by Taylor: "For me part of the attraction is having these wonderful sound making devices that are not in the computer. I spend all day on a computer and these devices allow me to get very hands on with my music. I have been vastly more productive as a result" (personal communication, 20 May 2020). With the Eurorack standardization and its inclusion of digital and hybrid modules in the mix with analog ones, Stillwell's modular synthesis practice gains a bit more stability than that found in the 1970s. That being said, Stillwell is still surprised by his gear when, without any seeming change in set-up, a sound he loved the day before will not re-sound the next day.

Stillwell finds the physicality of the actual instrument, and not only his physical interaction with the instrument, inspiring for his practice: "What you do with a particular synthesizer is directly related to the architecture of that synthesizer. Whether it's digital or analog, whether it's software, whether it's hardware, whether it's a sampler, whatever it happens to be. That, at least for me, anyway, feeds into the imagination and what comes out of me" (personal communication, 24 February 2020). For this reason, Stillwell is open to virtual reality modular synthesis, as long it maintains that physicality and architecture.

The Eurorack system is at a relatively accessible price point, especially when compared with the cost of new synthesizers in the 1970s. However, any desire to employ older analog gear has substantial hurdles. Sutherland bought his Synthi AKS new back in the early 1970s for $3,000. Now, to purchase new pins, Sutherland estimated the cost at $20 each: "that's expensive!" (personal communication, 13 October 2017). In February 2020, I witnessed a long discussion within the CEE about older analog gear that members wished to revive, but who faced challenges in finding technicians who could fix them or obtaining the required parts. Sutherland said: "Sometimes you have parts that are 'unobtainium,' like the Synthi. There's a couple of parts in the Synthi which you can't get them; they don't make them anymore, and they haven't made them. So when you're getting older gear, if you end up paying a premium for it and you're rich, you don't mind. But if you're poor, you've got maintenance costs on that. They could really play havoc with your life budget" (personal communication, 24 February 2020).

When the CEE performed at the 2016 Toronto Sound Festival, they were asked to perform on some of the old analog gear. Montgomery performed on the Synthi A and Sutherland on the Synthi AKS, Jaeger performed on the Yamaha CS-40, and Stillwell performed on his Eurorack modular synthesis set-up. Jaeger was particularly excited that the CS-40, a synthesizer that Lake had used frequently, was still working. Furthermore, it had maintained some of the sounds Lake had saved: "We switched it on and found out that of the twenty memories, about 60 per cent of them were still functioning. And so it was like, classic Larry-like sounds, you know, we were all thrilled. It was like having Larry back at the rehearsal" (personal communication, 18 May 2017).

Auner writes that "time seems never to stand still for electro-acoustic music" (2013, 228). The CEE lives this out, not only through changing personnel and technologies but also with changes to its sound. At the start of this chapter, I summarized the "CEE sound," including its relative absence of rhythmic pulse. Ben Neill writes that the divide between pulse-oriented electronic pop music and experimental/classical electronic music had begun to blur by the early twenty-first century, with the specific impact that in experimental circles, "the prejudice [of institutional electronic music] against music with a steady rhythmic pulse is rapidly receding into the past" (2002, 6). Writing over a decade later, Eliot Britton reiterates Neill's binary between "listening oriented, groove-free electronic music of Western electroacoustic/acousmatic origins, [and] ... groove-based electronic music with popular music origins" (2016, 63). He emphasizes some significant genre convergence within electronic music, however. Zareei, Kapur, and Carnegie refer to this convergence as a "hybrid form" because this music "[mixes] polarities: high art and popular, academia and dance, noise and beat" (2013, 464). While many electronic musicians today navigate between and across this aesthetic divide, James Andean (2020) confirms the ongoing rejection of "metered pulse" within what Joanna Demers would call "institutional electroacoustic music" (2010, 3). In the CEE, Stillwell now employs some beat-oriented modules, but he incorporates randomness into the beats to avoid too much of a dance aesthetic. At one rehearsal in September 2015, I was surprised to hear what sounded like dance beats, and I asked Stillwell later if he had made them (because, of course, with electronic music, it can be difficult to assign agency to any particular sound):

> Stillwell: That was Jim [Montgomery]. Surprised the hell out of me.
> Woloshyn: Surprised me!
> Stillwell: Surprised the hell out of me. I was like. "Jim, what are you doing?" Yeah.
> Woloshyn: Is this something that you see could maybe work with the CEE's aesthetic?
> Stillwell: No. No. I say that, but it actually could. (personal communication, 27 January 2016)

Stillwell leaves open the possibility of more beat-oriented material in the CEE's sound, but currently, it still has a minimal presence. Stillwell compares the CEE's sound to the "wild tangents" of Tangerine Dream on their albums *Rubycon* (1975) and *Tangram* (1980): "I loved those. I was really cool with that." He describes those moments as being more ambient: "There isn't a pulse. And they're making sounds that go together. Creating sound space. And when I first heard the CEE and worked with the CEE, that's what I related it to" (personal communication, 27 January 2016). As the CEE moves into its sixth decade, there is no way of knowing exactly what will remain and what will change in the sound spaces it creates.

Conclusion

The CEE is a group with an aesthetic that shifts with changing personnel and technologies, but only within a rather stable set of parameters: non-tonal, ametric, slow-moving timbre- and texture-based music. The group has thrived over five decades because it is not only an ensemble but a community, or as Stillwell describes them, a family. They enjoy being together and making music together.

The social and enjoyment aspects of the CEE's practice, however, do not preclude a seriousness to their study of individual instruments and dedication to live electronic music performance practice. The next chapter examines what "live" means in live electronic music and how norms of Euro-American classical music performance, such as gesture–sound relationships and expectations of virtuosity, manifest in the CEE's practice.

4

The CEE Live

Virtuosity, Perceptibility, and Improvisation

On the same Kresge Theatre stage where Albert Einstein gave a lecture in 1934, the Canadian Electronic Ensemble sextet performs a short improvisation for Carnegie Mellon School of Music students and faculty during their residency at CMU in February 2020. Three large tables span the stage, covered with the CEE's gear, including multiple laptops, synthesizers, and cables. John Kameel Farah is positioned with his usual set-up at one of CMU's grand pianos. The improvisation begins without introduction, including without identifying who is going first (which is now a standard part of their improvisation practice). Hard and soft synthesizer layers build up as sounds emanate from the speakers positioned above the stage. These students are used to seeing acoustic musicians – both solo and ensemble – who rarely require loudspeaker projection for their performances. But the CEE is an electronic ensemble: there is little to nothing to hear without loudspeakers. As each member stares intently at their gear, turning knobs, pressing buttons, and tapping keys, it is nearly impossible to discern which sounds originate from which musician. The exception is Farah's piano playing and some of Rose Bolton's long bow strokes. David Jaeger makes eye contact with his bandmates (other than Farah, who is directly behind him) and gives a little nod, indicating the end of the brief improvisation. The audience applauds because they just witnessed a live performance. But how did this performance align with or challenge how they understand liveness, performance, and skill?

This chapter looks at what is commonly understood as a "live performance" – that is, a performance in which the performance and listeners are in the same space at the same time, producing both temporal and spatial liveness. Because electronic music is mediated through technologies that challenge our conceptions of agency and skill via gesture–sound relationships, audiences may be skeptical that the music is really being created and processed live. When the expected evidence of virtuosity is absent, the audience's imagination "sniffs frantically for other scents of meaning, purpose and virtuosic action" (Overton 2006, 174). To consider how a listener perceives the CEE as "live" and valuable, I draw on alternative notions of virtuosity and Paul Sanden's (2013) typology of liveness. Musical examples from the group's two live albums (*Canadian Electronic Ensemble: Live* and *Live in Cabbagetown*) and first-hand accounts of live performances illustrate how the CEE variously solves, exacerbates, or ignores some of the so-called "barriers" to audience engagement with live electronic music. This chapter deals with issues non-chronologically; however, it focuses on more recent history as experienced during my fieldwork during the last several years.

Defining the "Live" in Live Electronic Music

Live electronic music challenges a long history of gesture–sound relationships exhibited in acoustic instruments. Banging a drum, bowing a string, and even hitting the high notes are seen and understood as results of specific physiological actions. We understand that the exact nature of these actions influences the nature of the perceived sound: banging a drum harder results in a louder sound; moving fingers quickly across a fingerboard results in many fast notes; changes in position of the vocal apparatus produce higher or lower sounds. Listeners to Euro-American classical music – the context in which I place the CEE – understand what a musician is doing with an instrument in order to create sounds, even as they might marvel at the specific talent required to do so.

All instruments, even acoustic instruments like a piano, are inanimate objects. Yet we have been acculturated to interpret acoustic instruments as musical instruments. Electronic technologies, especially those that don't resemble an acoustic instrument (e.g., have no keyboard interface) only become instruments to the audience when a human performance brings it into a musical context. Therefore, the burden is on the electronic musician to communicate that they are not merely a technician but a musical performer (Sanden 2013, 102).

To refer to the CEE as a "live" electronic music ensemble may seem straightforward, but the work of Auslander (2002, 2008), Croft (2007),

Carlson (2004), Emmerson (2007), Smalley (1986, 1996, 1997), and Sanden (2013), among others, demonstrates that "liveness" is a contextual and social concept. Philip Auslander (2002) articulates the crisis for listeners to radio in the 1930s: the source of the broadcast ("live" and in real time or "canned," pre-recorded music) was unknown to the listener. John Croft (2007) builds on Auslander's concept of liveness and applies it to digital music instruments, identifying two types of liveness: 1) procedural, in which sound is produced and manipulated live in real time; 2) aesthetic, in which the sonic output results from corporeal linkages between the human performer and the machine (61). Croft asserts that only aesthetic liveness counts as an actual live performance: "If many perceptibly different inputs generate outputs with no pertinent differences … then the liveness is merely procedural and not aesthetic – pre-recorded sounds would do the job as well or better" (2007, 61).

When the CEE performs a show, they are certainly engaging procedural liveness: there is sound produced and manipulated in real time, though as Jaeger explains, "there were almost always at least some elements that were pre-arranged" (personal communication, 10 June 2016). Yet according to Croft's conception of liveness, the CEE will always struggle to achieve aesthetic liveness – in which a listener perceives cause-and-effect relationships – because the gesture–sound relationship is obscured in much of their creative practice. An audience can see the humans performing and can see their technologies – though with some, such as a laptop, the audience may be given very few clues as to what specifically a performer is using to perform. With laptop performers in particular, Kim Cascone describes this detachment as a violation: "During laptop performances, the standard visual codes disappear into the micro-movements of the performer's hand and wrist motions, leaving the mainstream audience's expectations unfulfilled … the laptop is doing the work, no skill is required or demonstrated, and the artist could just as easily be any one of the audience faking a performance" (2003, 102–3). A hardware synth doesn't have these quotidian associations, and yet similar problems for the audience persist. The synth might employ an arpeggiator, for example, but the many notes moving up and down do not correspond to fast up-and-down physical gestures. The sounds remind us of acoustic performances and the skill they require, but we see no physical traces of that effort and skill.

The keyboard interfaces of the CEE's early quartet era offer the listener a stronger connection to the acoustic instrumental world. When Simon Emmerson articulates the changing relationship between human presence and sound in *Living Electronic Music* (2007), he points to the keyboard as "the first gesture transducer" (135), an interface that mediates and transforms the performer's gesture into a strike of the piano string or an admitting of wind through an organ's pipe. The historical dominance of the keyboard for both performers and composers meant that many of the earliest electronic instruments (e.g., Telharmonium) simply modified the keyboard interface. Nonetheless, even with the presence of keyboard interfaces, the listener can be left confused: the gesture of pressing down a key on the keyboard may not translate directly into a single perceived sound. Each CEE member is also adjusting sliders, turning knobs, and inserting or removing pins or patch cords in real time. Each one of those gestures has a purpose for the performer, but a given gesture may not result in a perceivable change in the sound world in which a listener is immersed.

Despite this breakdown in the gesture–sound relationship, that relationship remains important to many electronic music performers, including Paul Stillwell. Stillwell has been especially vocal about desiring a tactile component to his practice, including the Chapman Stick, which I discussed in chapter 3. He also discusses the physicality of his Eurorack set-up: "Yes, it's technical, but I have to understand that the signal I'm taking out of one device, and plugging into another device, I have to have an idea of what that's gonna do. I don't always! Sometimes I just try it, and see" (personal communication, 27 January 2016). He needs to see the physical connection between one module and another, a connection facilitated by a bright patch cord.

MEDIATING LIVENESS IN ELECTRONIC MUSIC

My analysis of liveness in the CEE's performance practice is largely informed by Paul Sanden's application of "mediatized music," or "a musical experience of any kind in which electronic mediation plays a part" (2013, 8). Sanden approaches electronic mediation as something to be embraced rather than resisted, and he formulates an analytical framework that helps us articulate the persistent forms of liveness in contexts that fall outside of what he calls "traditional liveness" (3).

The CEE's performance practice is not "traditional liveness" because of the centrality of the machine. In this way, the CEE is similar to Cologne's elektronische Musik, about which Sanden declares: "The machine was thus implicated at every level of this music's production, dissemination, and reception, throwing any possible understanding of its liveness severely into question" (2013, 22). For Croft, only aesthetic liveness counts as "live." However, relying on his binary of procedural versus aesthetic liveness is too limiting for the CEE. Sanden's typology permits a more expansive view on liveness, one that celebrates electronic mediation in a way that illuminates the CEE's creative practice. Sanden explains that, in particular, digital technologies since the late 1970s have resulted in "layers of liveness and nonliveness within given works and performances [that] became even more intricately woven" (2013, 23), a reality in the CEE's practice that I explored in chapter 3.

Sanden theorizes seven categories of liveness that any given performance might invoke:

1. temporality: witnessing a performance when it's happening in real time;
2. spatial proximity: being in the physical presence of the performer(s);
3. fidelity: electronic mediation is minimal or obvious in ways that reveal what isn't "cheating";
4. spontaneity: each performance is unique, to both the audience and performer(s);
5. corporeality: expression and perception are embodied, and this embodiment may be perceived even when a visual presence is absent (e.g., in an audio recording);
6. interactivity: there is interaction among performers and between the performer(s) and audience;
7. virtuality: a listener perceives personas in a recording of highly mediatized music through the process of sound recognition.

I will apply these categories (particularly those of spontaneity, corporeality, interactivity, and virtuality) to my analysis of the possibilities and limitations of liveness in the CEE's "live" electronic music practice.

Sanden's categories can apply to both live performances and recordings. The CEE has released two live albums, both with the word "live" in the album titles: *Canadian Electronic Ensemble: Live* (1998) and *Live in Cabbagetown* (2013). The word "live" has a cachet that indicates to the listener that while they will not be experiencing spatial liveness with the performers, they are experiencing a kind of temporal liveness, albeit separated in time from the recorded live performance. One key sonic indicator of a "live" album is the sound of the audience on the recording: cheering and chanting for rock and pop albums, applause for live albums across many genres. As neither of the CEE's live albums includes such indicators, the listener must trust that the title is not a lie. As I will discuss below, the word "live" is in some ways misleading for the album *Live in Cabbagetown*, though all material was created during a live performance. Without that knowledge (or perhaps in spite of it), the listener will believe they are listening to sound shaped through time in exactly the same way as the performers and original audience heard it, and thereby experiencing a kind of live performance practice, or what Sanden would call the liveness of spontaneity: a unique performance, even without temporal or spatial liveness.

Unlike on an album, physical bodies and motions are present in the CEE's live performances; however, we have to rethink the position of the human body in the CEE's electronic performance practice. Kinetic action from human bodies is not the main source of sound with the CEE. For example, a small gesture may produce a loud sound, a single gesture can create several sounds, or a performer may make several gestures of knob turning to achieve a single desired sound: the machines are central. According to Jaeger, "it's really much more like having an instant orchestra" with their gear, in which one instrument can create many things simultaneously (public lecture, 26 February 2020).

The CEE has a striking physical presence, though, with its collection of various electronic tools, from Jaeger's laptop to Stillwell's Eurorack set-up. In my experience observing performances, audiences are clearly more intrigued by the electronic tools with a larger physical presence, with knobs and sliders, than with the laptop. These more eye-catching devices produce what Joseph Auner (2013) identifies as the "technological sublime" in electronic music, applying Leo Marx's concept; for Auner, this encompasses "the visual and performative aspects of a work, which include all the devices, technical assistants, and the overall emotional impact of ... the 'technological sublime'" (227). This impact was certainly part of the CEE's live performances in the 1970s and '80s when the technologies necessitated an abundance of pieces of equipment for each member's set-up. While there was a strong visual impact, this abundance of equipment also meant time-consuming preparation between each piece. Montgomery recalls working with composer Norm Symonds in 1976 to address this down time: "you've gotta help people out, right?" (personal communication, 26 February 2016). Symonds was tasked with providing a narrative as concert host to engage the audience while the CEE set up for the next piece.

The CEE shifted more toward laptops in the 1990s; Jaeger still uses a laptop exclusively, and Jim Montgomery typically uses a laptop and a couple of other pieces. These smaller and more quotidian pieces reduce the technological sublime of the CEE, but Stillwell's relatively massive Eurorack set-up has returned some of the technological sublime to the group's visual presence. I have witnessed this impact on audiences, as Stillwell is often the performer who receives the most audience interaction during intermission and after a concert. This listener interest is tied not only to the increased corporeality of his set-up (which means that a listener maps on more gesture–sound relationships), but also to the visual impressiveness of the set-up itself, especially with flashing lights and colourful patch cords.

The scale of instrument to sound has presented a challenge for audience perception since the CEE's inception in the 1970s. Croft declares: "We expect the sound to have a more or less transparent relation to the properties of the sounding body we see before us" (2007, 61). There are small pieces of gear that can elicit large sounds once patched through a mixer (e.g., SOMA Ether, which transduces electromagnetic waves), and large gear doesn't necessarily produce a loud or large sound. Even back in the 1970s and early 1980s, the CEE would at times be creating relatively small, delicate sounds out of comparatively large and non-delicate gear.

This scale also largely prevents us from perceiving what improviser Vijay Iyer describes as the "audible traces of the human body in improvisational music" (2008, 264). Such audible traces are much more difficult to perceive with the CEE because their music comes through loudspeakers. While the CEE's volume levels vary, the scale remains beyond the audible scale of the human body.

What about the acoustic instruments that are part of the CEE's mediatized performance practice? Sanden explains: "Even subtle electronic manipulations of an acoustic sound in performance ... can also challenge the perceptible connections one usually makes between physical performance gestures and the sounds resulting from those gestures" (2013, 20–1). For example, Bolton performs on her violin, initially an acoustic one and more recently an electric one. She holds an instrument and bow, musical tools familiar to many listeners, depending on the performance context. She bows and plucks – gestures that are familiar. However, because these violin sounds are processed live, the "perceptible connections" are weakened for the listener. Furthermore, Bolton is often testing a sound first while listening to her headphones: this habit of live electronic music performance further weakens perceptible connections. A listener might see Bolton bow her violin without hearing a corresponding sound because Bolton is still adjusting her live processing.

In mediatized performances, sounds that we hear may not be a result of "a performer's physical command of his or her instrument" (Sanden 2013, 26). For some listeners, such a disconnect could feel like "cheating" and thereby keep the performance from exhibiting Sanden's liveness of fidelity for that listener: "A certain ethics of performance, derived from the concept of skill in performance, informs many people's listening aesthetics" (Sanden 2013, 36). Listeners who know a lot about electronic music will perceive skill in a CEE performance differently than a general audience, especially one more immersed in acoustic performance contexts. What the CEE does requires a lot of skill, but this skill doesn't necessarily map on to physical gestures. Moreover, the physical gestures that are involved often don't require a lot of physical effort (at least in comparison to people's assessments of acoustic performance). I have not witnessed audiences interpreting the CEE as "dishonest or inauthentic" (Sanden 2013, 26), but because the "electronic" part of their practice has always been front and centre, listeners must transform their expectations if they are to consider a CEE performance a live performance by skilled musicians. Jaeger explains: "We've become, increasingly, not only used to but also comfortable that there will not be a grasp of how the music is being shaped ... we're expecting the listener to just follow the progression of the music as it unfolds ... they're on a par, or merely on a par with us as the practitioners, in terms of the impossibility to predict what might happen next" (personal communication, 10 June 2016).

I'm interested in exploring Sanden's concept of the liveness of fidelity further in live electronic music. This liveness of fidelity focuses on the perception of limited or non-existent alterations or technological "interference." What can this mean for electronic music? Would there be a base fidelity for modular synthesizers, for example? Would "mistakes" lend a kind of fidelity? Croft argues that imperfections in the relationship between performer action and sonic output are ideal because they create a kind of Barthesian grain, which draws attention to the fragility and fallibility of human and instrumental bodies (2007, 65). Croft's imperfections and Iyer's audible traces both seek the humanness behind the sound practice.

Composers, inventors, performers, and listeners alike have pursued the "humanized" element of electronic music, but what makes technology "humanized"? And, more specifically, what makes the music created with electronic technology "humanized"? Mid-century discourses about ideal electronic music making consistently addressed the lack of "humanized" electronic music, specifically for the studio composer who still needed to "perform" the equipment to achieve a finished work. Hugh Le Caine intentionally designed instruments to address this issue. For Le Caine, "humanizing" electronic music meant offering the composer a real-time performability that mimicked the gestures of the acoustic past while expanding sonic outcomes. In contrast to contemporary equipment, Le Caine's designs integrated the materialities of the instrument, the gestural body, and the resultant sound. In particular, touch sensitivity and coordinated control measures facilitated "nuance-filled expressive performance" (Young 2004) in the studio. Furthermore, the familiar keyboard orientation of his instruments allowed electronic music composers to focus on new sonic territories rather than "contorted ... machine-oriented postures" (Barcelos 2013, 11). Similarly, when, in 1968, composer John Eaton spoke of the "humanization of electronic music," his solution involved "truly sensitive and immediately responsive" electronic instruments, "capable of similarly being performed 'live'" (101). Real-time capabilities have markedly increased since then, so it seems that Eaton's vision has come to fruition. Pierre Schaeffer wanted to bring a sense of the human in performance via corporeality in sound diffusion; using the *pupitre d'espace*, a spatialization control system based on transmitter and receiver coils, the performer would mix the piece live in the performance space, with gestures visible enough and tied plainly enough to sonic results to be discerned by the audience as human agency and creative labour.

By contrast, Cologne elektronische Musik composer Herbert Eimert scoffed at attempts to bring electronic music into the realm of traditional European classical music. He stated: "Electronic concert instruments will always remain a synthetic substitute ... Talk of 'humanised' electronic sound may be left to unimaginative instrument makers" (1958, 1, 9). Writing in 1958, he wasn't yet talking about the synthesizers of the 1960s and '70s, yet I suspect he would have been skeptical of such developments, given their reliance on "traditional" means, namely keyboards.

For those emphasizing the "humanized" in electronic music, a recurring concern is the centrality of the machine and its perceived non-emotionality. Sanden explains: "One of the ongoing challenges of mediatized music has been to create sound and musical gestures that seem 'musical' rather than 'cold and machinelike.' Concerns about machine elements, overwhelming recognizably human elements in music performance ... resonate with a general wariness of technology inside performance studies" (2013, 28–9). The CEE's live performance practice has chosen to prioritize certain elements over others often associated with live musical performance. They don't elaborate or exaggerate physical gestures to draw attention to their human presence or to visualize the sounds. Some listeners may be disengaged – even disappointed – by what seems to them to be a lack of corporeal performativity. The CEE subscribes to a different set of criteria for performativity, namely one that is minimally visual and maximally sonic. They are not concerned with amplifying the "human" or "musical," but they don't believe this makes their music necessarily "cold and machinelike."

So, then, why would listeners be willing "to just follow the progression of the music as it unfolds," as Jaeger puts it? How does a CEE live performance communicate that its liveness is more than procedural? While I will address the liveness of spontaneity in more detail in the section on improvisation, I want to mention certain elements of spontaneity here. While the CEE's practice has always included some relatively predictable technologies, such as soft synths, other aspects are more unpredictable – analog gear, for example. This unpredictability was a part of the CEE's reality during the 1970s and '80s in particular. Montgomery explains: "A lot of the time, when you turned that knob or you pushed that button or you plugged that cable in, you really had no idea what the hell was going to happen. So the craft became responsive" (personal communication, 26 February 2016). Stillwell's return to modular synthesis, with gear that is partly analog, and David Sutherland's use of analog gear mean that the CEE presents a liveness of spontaneity for themselves as individuals and as a group, as well as for the audience. At their performance on 13 October 2017, I witnessed a couple of "false" starts and some synthesizer tuning, both of which demonstrated that everything was not preset and easy to use. Additional examples of this instrumental spontaneity include the individuality of the piano in each space, performed by Farah, and Stillwell's use of the SOMA Ether to pick up the electromagnetic waves of the space. The former's individuality will likely be subtle, while the latter produces sounds that will always be unpredictable and spontaneous, though their mapping of source to sound is likely obscured from the listener.

In live performance, the CEE presents its members as discrete performers, with individual set-ups and individual sounds to contribute to the collective; they do not sample or process each other's sounds. Nonetheless, they prioritize interaction, both with each other and with their respective electronic technologies. Sanden points to musicians who "extended this concept of a mediatized interactive performing ensemble to one in which various technologies could be viewed as performance partners rather than simply as tools or instruments to facilitate this interaction" (2013, 89). The CEE's analog gear is particularly obvious as a performance partner, with its unpredictability and occasional volatility. The "character" of the analog equipment comes through and is embraced by its human partners. Bolton tells the story of trying to repair her Roland SE-02 because of a minor problem: "Taking it back to the store, they wanted to swap the synth I had bought for a new one, and I refused. I felt that there was already some kind of karma formed with the synth (not to mention that i [sic] had programmed it) so I insisted that I keep the one I had bought" (personal communication, 23 June 2020).

Some of the CEE's music, especially during the 1970s and '80s, was composed for a solo acoustic instrumentalist and a fixed tape track, an arrangement also used in the members' non-CEE composing lives. Given the CEE's frequent performances with skilled acoustic performers, it seems obvious that the solo/tape set-up would be a part of a CEE concert as well. This was the case with Lake's *Psalm*, for example (see listening guide). For some, a performance of a piece like *Psalm* would have temporal and spatial liveness but lack liveness of spontaneity or interaction; such listeners would reject that this piece is an example of live *electronic* music. *Psalm* is also a composed piece with written notation, resulting in even less spontaneity from the acoustic performer. Nonetheless, the performer is interacting with the tape part and the space – in real time – and making adjustments. The tape part, while not changing its content, is interacting with the space and the performer's specific approaches in ways that are unique and unrepeatable.

PERFORMER–AUDIENCE RELATIONSHIPS

The CEE's practice maintains the audience–performer binary through spatial separation and Euro-American concert rituals, such as applause after (and not during) each piece. Because of this binary, the interactivity between the audience and the CEE is valued by the group. All members of the CEE remarked to me about the importance of "feeling" the audience and being able to assess their energy and engagement without looking at them. While the CEE sometimes talks about rehearsals and performances being no different from one another, the absence or presence of the audience does matter. And it matters to the listener too: listening to an album (whether "live" or not) denies the listener the opportunity to witness the live negotiation of collaboration.

The CEE has expressed a deep appreciation for its audiences, and yet aspects of their performance practice are in opposition to the interests of the listener. Jaeger explains: "You don't presume the level of their interest, but you do presume that, by remaining in the performance space and taking it all in, that they're at least willing listeners … you're giving them something that no one else on the planet has access to" (personal communication, 10 June 2016). Iyer (2008) asserts that the performer's movement is connected to how a listener perceives musical movement (269). This perceptual habit proves a challenge with live electronic music like the CEE. Montgomery explained to me that an exaggerated gesture doesn't affect the sound; it only looks more impressive, more comprehensible.

In its current practice, the CEE mostly avoids providing exaggerated or sonically inconsequential physical gestures in order to "help out" a visually oriented audience. A liveness of corporeality is less striking in a CEE performance than in the live electronic performance practice of a musician like Pamela Z, who uses gesture controls, resulting in perceptible gesture–sound mappings. In Gina Emerson and Hauke

Egermann's article on audience perception of digital musical instruments, they conclude that listener reception of digitally created music can be positively impacted through "the perceptibility of a causal link" (2017, 364). Emerson and Egermann conclude that "a lack of perceptible gesture–sound causality could thwart performers' attempts at communicating an artistic or expressive goal to spectators and could decrease the perceived instrumentality of the DMI," which has resulted in negative ratings of performances (2017, 366).

According to research like Emerson and Egermann's, the CEE's decision not to prioritize perceptible gesture–sound causalities can have negative consequences, as audiences pay attention to gesture–sound relationships and evaluate performances accordingly. The authors go on to explain that "a clear gesture–sound causality is the foundation for understanding the basic functioning of the instrument, which then underlies such higher-level evaluative concepts as perceived liveness and skill" (2017, 369). The lack of such relationships in the CEE's practice means that audiences are less likely to perceive a CEE performance or performer as virtuosic. Even more fundamental than that, they may be left confused about whether the CEE is any good at all. Rather than considering whether they enjoyed what they heard, listeners to electronic music are often caught up in thinking about the corporeality of liveness.

As Emerson and Egermann conclude, audiences do care about the skill of the performers creating the sounds they perceive. Why are listeners concerned with mapping sound to skill? It is a way for an audience to evaluate a performance. Is this a good electronic ensemble? Is this a good performance? The CEE has accepted that their skills in electronic music are elusive to audiences. Montgomery told me: "They can't see it. They can't see the virtuosity. A lot of it is simply that there's no physiological connection" (personal communication, 26 February 2016). The members of the CEE aren't concerned with whether they are perceived as talented, skilled musicians but rather that they created a meaningful sonic experience for the listener.

CANADIAN ELECTRONIC ENSEMBLE: LIVE (1998)

The group's first live album, *Canadian Electronic Ensemble: Live*, was recorded at the Music Gallery on 8 February 1998, during the CEE's first concert as a sextet after Wilcox became an official member. This is the only album with members Wilcox and Dobinson. The CEE released the album two months later on 5 April 1998, marking the occasion with another performance at the Music Gallery. I will discuss *Caspin's Arrival* in particular to illustrate Sanden's notions of liveness as well as Simon Emmerson's.

Wilcox's viola playing includes an imitation of seagulls (Stillwell's request). There are various synthesizer sounds, varied across register, duration, and timbre. The sound sources for *Caspin's Arrival* are placed variously within the mix: some in the far left (e.g., opening cymbal strikes) and others in the far right (e.g., low bass note at 0:21); others are positioned in the centre or move through the sound world. Such mixing choices create an impression for the listener of motion, and therefore of moving bodies. The sounds in fixed positions delineate the limits of this aural space in which listeners find themselves. Positioning the listener within a space (however virtual) establishes a relationship between them and the sounds encountered. Thus, liveness of corporeality is invoked in this piece, despite not sharing physical space with the original performers. The sounds also have a corporeality, including the abstracted electronic sounds, those that resemble real-world sounds (e.g., fog horn), and the sound of Wilcox's viola, which brings to the listener's mind a clear gesture–sound relationship mediated by the performer's body. Such perceptual imaginations invoke Sanden's liveness of virtuality, allowing a liveness to persist even without temporal or spatial liveness.

Sanden employs Toynbee's concept of the technosphere (2000), which Sanden describes as "a changing technological field, a network of mediatization through which performers communicate with their audiences at varying degrees of distance" (2013, 31). The CEE performs in a technosphere: their performing technologies create varying degrees of distance. As Sanden explains, this "proximity" is not only physical but also conceptual.

Denis Smalley's concept of "gestural surrogacy" further illuminates the CEE's engagement with varying degrees of conceptual proximity. When Smalley discusses the perception of acousmatic music, he argues that humans are culturally conditioned to listen to instruments audiovisually: to see gesture and hear sound, and to conceive of "a chain of activity [that] links a cause to a source" (1997, 111). Smalley explains that when we listen to music without a visual component, "we also decode the human activity behind the spectromorphologies through which we automatically gain a wealth of psycho-physical information" (1997, 111). Smalley defines spectromorphology as "the interaction between sound spectra (*spectro-*) and the ways they change and are shaped through time (*-morphology*)" (1997, 107). This concept can apply to a broad variety of electroacoustic music, chiefly acousmatic music, but also what he calls "live acousmatic music," in which perception of cause and effect is still difficult or impossible even with live electronic music performers visible.

Based on his understanding of perceptual habits, Smalley (1997) articulates a process called "gestural surrogacy" in which a listener becomes increasingly unable to place the sources and causes of sounds. In first-order surrogacy, we hear recorded sounds not intended for musical use, but we can identify the source and the gestural cause of the sound. Second-order surrogacy uses traditional instrumental sounds (either recorded or simulated) in a recognizable form so that the listener can perceive the source and gesture. When the CEE's acoustic instruments are performed in a way that the listener can perceive them as those instruments and can therefore imagine how the sounds are being produced, second-order surrogacy is applicable. This includes elements of the viola's part in *Caspin's Arrival*, but certainly not all. In CEE performances, Farah's piano contributions tend to remain recognizable as piano parts, while Bolton's violin sometimes falls under second-order surrogacy and sometimes is too processed to remain recognizable.

Third-order surrogacy occurs when the listener is unsure about the source and/or cause of a sound, but its sonic qualities (or spectromorphologies) allow us to infer or imagine the kind of gesture that might be required to achieve that sound. With electronic music, such perceptions are often deceiving. A loud sound merely requires turning up the volume knob; it doesn't require a dramatic physical gesture. A staccato sound doesn't necessarily require a quick release of the controller by the performer but rather could be achieved by setting the envelope to have minimal sustain and sharp release.

The final kind of surrogacy is remote surrogacy, in which "source and cause become unknown and unknowable as any human action behind the sound disappears" (1997, 112), though the listener may still perceive gesture. I suggest that in live performances, the CEE typically invokes second-order (if there are acoustic instruments) and third-order surrogacies, with remote surrogacy on occasion. The CEE's albums frequently invoke second-order, third-order, and remote surrogacies as the visual component of human performers and gestures leaves the listener alone with their perceptual experiences, habits, and imaginings. For some listeners and some CEE tracks, liveness of corporeality and virtuality may be perceived.

As I summarized in chapter 1, Simon Emmerson argues in his book *Living Electronic Music* (2007) that the perception of causality is largely up to the listener; thus, liveness is situated within the listener's perception. Liveness is itself, then, a kind of virtuality – something real but not necessarily actual. Emmerson is mostly addressing acousmatic music, but this applies also to live electronic music like the CEE. The listener perceives causal relationships that may be "real" – when the performer has causal agency over the sound – or "imaginary" – when the performer prepares sound material in such a way that the listener believes there must be a real-time trigger. The "actual" of the performer's agency and of how a gesture maps onto a sound is inconsequential. Liveness, then, comes down to perception. Jaeger described this divide in the CEE's practice, saying that audience members "had been witness to performances that were remarkable, but they had no idea why" (personal communication, 10 June 2016). Virtuosity remains a valued criterion in Euro-American classical performance. If audiences are searching for a CEE performer's agency through gesture relationships to sound, then will they perceive anything that resembles virtuosity?

Virtuosity in Live Electronic Music

Given live electronic music's breakdown of the gesture–sound relationship, locating virtuosity in the performances of the CEE remains problematic. This is an excerpt of a conversation I had with Jaeger on the place of virtuosity in the CEE's practice:

> Jaeger: Yes, not only can we be virtuosos, but we can do it at the press of a button. We could preordain our virtuosity. [Laughs]
> Woloshyn: So, it's more like you can *sound* virtuosic rather than ...
> Jaeger: ... actually being [virtuosic]. (personal communication, 10 June 2016)

I think the CEE is virtuosic, though they do not have physical displays of virtuosity, other than moments of flourish from Farah. The group's virtuosity is evident to me in a way it might not be to non-specialist observers, because I have enough knowledge of the skill required to perform with their electronic technologies and other instruments to perceive "skilled and inspired playing."

Adam Overton's definition of conventional notions of virtuosity emphasizes proficiency and the binary between performer and spectator: "The psychological reflex in the spectator is to immediately begin trying to discern the signs of an assumed virtuosity, and for comparison she or he uses either a culturally agreed upon model and/or his or her own self as the model" (2006, 174). Lawrence Kramer similarly emphasizes proficiency, or skill, when he argues that the nineteenth-century virtuoso demonstrated mastery of the instrument and the score by conquering the machine and bringing the musical work (understood as the score) "to life through skilled and inspired playing" (2012, 231). Both skill and expressivity were critical to claims of virtuosity.

What kinds of virtuosities might be witnessed at a live CEE performance? As I discuss above, the problem of virtuosity with the CEE is that sonic segments can resemble passages that would require virtuosity in an acoustic context, when each sound heard would have to be created by an analogous physical gesture (e.g., rapid ascending arpeggios or scales). In this section, I examine the foundations of this concept of virtuosity and how it might impact audience engagement with the CEE. After providing an overview of what I've witnessed at CEE performances, I will discuss in more detail the CEE's performance at the Canadian Music Centre in Toronto on 13 October 2017, focusing specifically on the improvisation "John Goes First."

The CEE is not a showy group. They dress plainly, sometimes in concert black and other times more casually (Stillwell prefers a T-shirt). Other than the relatively brief digression into more deliberate gestural performance components mentioned above, the CEE's gestures are practical rather than expressive, collective coordination and sound activation being the two primary purposes. An example of the former can be observed in the clip of the CEE performing for the *Music of Man* series mentioned in chapter 2: Montgomery provides a sharp cut-off gesture to coordinate the ending of the performance. Similarly, for the live performance of John Gray's *No Dim Pearls* on 4 May 2012, Montgomery conducts a coordinated beginning to this composed piece with an assertive downward gesture; here, no cut-off gesture is necessary at the end because the piece gently fades into silence. These days, the CEE performs only free improvisations, structured only by who goes first. Large physical gestures are even rarer to witness during these concerts.

The CEE has mostly been unconcerned with audience expectations of virtuosity over its fifty years, taking the view that what they do isn't for everyone. The gesture–sound gap may decrease some audience enjoyment, but for the most part, I have witnessed audiences that seem interested and satisfied with a CEE performance. The CEE's challenge is that much of its audience comes from those who typically attend chamber music performances, meaning the genre expectations are quite different. Audiences at the Toronto Sound Festival, by contrast, will have more experience with electronic sound technologies from which to assess and appreciate a CEE performance.

Perceiving virtuosity in a CEE performance achieves a sense of liveness for the audience, as explained by Sanden's concepts of liveness of spontaneity and corporeality. Liveness of spontaneity relies not only on the uniqueness of each performance but also on "a common skill-based understanding of performance" (2013, 37). Sanden describes audience excitement that is incited by "the realization that a performer's skill level does indeed measure up" (2013, 37). Listeners with experience in electronic music and/or free improvisation will be excited by what they hear from the CEE, while listeners more accustomed to common-practice Euro-American classical repertoire may be left confused and underwhelmed.

Almost all of the CEE performances I have attended or seen documentation of have been in designated performance spaces, typically music performance spaces such as the Music Gallery and the Canadian Music Centre's Chalmers Performance Space. Important exceptions include the Glyptoteket's Winter Garden in Copenhagen during the 1979 European tour and the Kirk (St Andrew's Presbyterian Church) in St John's, Newfoundland, during the 2004 Sound Symposium, as well as participation in "happenings" in the early 1970s. More often, however, the CEE performs in spaces dominated by acoustic Euro-American classical music.

Despite the abundance of electronic technologies at their disposal, the CEE in many ways resembles a chamber ensemble. They tend to set up like a chamber ensemble: relatively close (proximity dictated by the amount of gear) in a semi-circle, opened out to the audience. While the CEE members rarely make eye contact during a performance, they typically do so at the beginning and ending of any given piece, whether composed or improvised. Though many of the CEE's technologies are used in other genres, such as electronic dance music, the group's performance practice remains within the realm of Euro-American chamber music, with basic stage lighting (perhaps sometimes a bit darker than an ensemble that needs to read music) and no other visual components. The *Music of Man* clip shows the four original quartet members around a table, each with his own station of monophonic synthesizers, including many keyboard interfaces, and mixers. A 1979 photo from their European tour reflects a similar set-up, albeit with some new equipment: they still work at their individual stations, like a string quartet. With occasional exceptions, this set-up of close but independent work stations persists in their performance practice today.

These details serve to illustrate why audiences at the CEE performances I've observed are evaluating the group on their closest frame of reference: the rituals of Euro-American classical music concerts. Audiences know from the name of the group that the CEE will not perform acoustic instruments (at least not primarily). Yet they are situated in a space and in a concert ritual that prioritizes attentive listening. They will be looking for evidence beyond shared time and space to indicate that this concert is an experience worth having – one that is unique and impressive in some way.

There are excellent live electronic ensembles and mediocre electronic ensembles, but a non-specialist listener has difficulty assessing the electronic musician's skills outside of physical gestures. There are skills that electronic musicians have to create in real time that other electronic musicians cannot do (or haven't yet developed their skills enough to do). These skills are often more conceptual than physical. Composer Owen Green explains: "In electroacoustic musicking – in common with all musicking – whilst we might feel we *know* when we have witnessed something good, it is considerably more difficult to express the reasons for our preferences verbally ... Yet, electroacoustic musicking, particularly at the experimental peripheries, appears to muddy the waters still further with its engagements with modern technologies and sonic forms ... Performances where it's not altogether clear who might be performing what" (2008).

Julio d'Escriván suggests that listeners brought up in the video game and computer age might be more willing to accept what he calls "effortless performances" (2006, 190). This contrasts with "an older generation [that] may tend to require an old-school paradigm of performing virtuosity, where perceived effort and dexterity on behalf of the performer are paramount to the enjoyment of music" (2006, 190). One challenge for live electronic music performance is that audiences are typically unfamiliar with the electronic instruments/equipment, or what familiarity they do have is purely quotidian. Hence the stereotype of the laptop musician checking their email: this is what most people do on their laptops, so it can be hard to imagine anything virtuosic about it. Cascone explains that the problem is that an audience sees "a device more suited to an office cubicle than a stage" (2003, 103). This means that while performing on his laptop, Jaeger may add a flourish of soft synth pitches to the mix, yet the flurry of fingers on his laptop keyboard is interpreted as quotidian rather than virtuosic. In any case, the audience typically cannot see Jaeger's fingers behind his laptop screen.

When Bolton performs her electric violin, the instrument situates her more clearly within the context of acoustic instrumental virtuosity. An audience knows what to look for to conclude that Bolton plays the violin with impressive skill, because a listener relies "more on acculturated notions of virtuosity than on an awareness of the physical characteristics of the instrument" (Croft 2007, 61). Yet, for the most part, Bolton does not fulfill this expectation. The CEE sound is largely atmospheric with slowly changing textures, sometimes contrasted with abrupt moments (Lake's favourite to introduce, according to the current members) or textural densities. Bolton uses the violin to contribute to the CEE's timbral world, which means long bow strokes or brief pizzicato sections. Bolton believes she provides a unique timbre within the group but typically does not take on the role of soloist.[1]

When Farah performs with the CEE, he offers more conventionally virtuosic moments. He intentionally finds moments in an improvisation to add a flourish and momentarily be a kind of soloist. Farah has the skills to perform in a way that would be read as "virtuosic" in the traditional sense, and such an approach is central to his solo career, but this is not the physical gestural presence that he brings to the CEE.

During the group's performance at the Canadian Music Centre on 13 October 2017 (with Farah, Jaeger, Stillwell, and Sutherland in attendance), the CEE implemented a now long-standing strategy for their free improvisations: each player takes a turn starting the improvisation. As the performer on stage left, Farah went first on the fourth and penultimate piece.[2] This improvisation (officially untitled, though it makes sense to call it "John Goes First") is twelve and a half minutes long. In the following analysis, I focus on the role of the piano in this improvisation as a site/sight of possible conventional virtuosity.

Farah opens with a burst of pitches in the upper piano range: seemingly random note selections. His "solo" lasts approximately twenty-two seconds before synth layers begin to join in, including the gentle rhythmic articulations of an electronic mbira sound. Farah has also recorded his opening piano part, and it plays back more softly as Farah switches to chords. This material is also recorded and played back. The piece is still piano-centric ninety seconds in, with the two recorded piano layers supported by electronic layers. About three minutes in, the piano has become largely absent, though Farah brings back some of the recorded chords from earlier in the piece. When the improvisation suddenly quiets down after an increase in intensity and noise, Farah uses this space to introduce his Nord Lead 3. The pitches (octave unisons) provide an aural anchor around which the other musicians add their noise layers. Here, Farah implements his solo practice of introducing layers on the piano or Nord Lead 3, recording them, and then playing them back while introducing new layers. As the synthesizer layers from the other players increase in density, Farah begins to add brief flourishes, mostly scalar passages and ornaments such as trills. He draws out the melodic and harmonic implications of some of the synthesizers' pitch content; this part is situated within an E-flat minor harmony. He decreases the space between each scalar iteration, and soon enough, Farah's command of the piano is plain. The contributions of the other members remain relatively sparse. Though the final three minutes of the improvisation contain a lot of silence or gentle sonic gestures, Farah does not take the opportunity to add more pianistic flourishes. With the exception of some striking synthesizer attacks, the texture remains sparse until the piece fades into complete silence.

In this improvisation, Farah provides a visual glimpse of his skill. Especially with the quickening of the scalar passages, it's easy for me to imagine that audiences would conclude that Farah has corporeal mastery of his instrument. These moments might be too brief to be labelled virtuosic in a conventional classical or acoustic sense, but with his use of live recording and playback, Farah makes visible how technological and aesthetic mastery can be employed as well.

In the nineteenth century, the ubiquity of the piano in middle- and upper-class homes perhaps helped to facilitate the awe in virtuosic displays at the instrument (Vorachek 2000). Kramer points to the massive size of the instrument as part of its perception as a beast to be tamed, a machine to be controlled and overcome (2012, 234). But this perception required a familiarity with the instrument, an awareness of the amateur's limitations, in order to truly appreciate what distinguished the virtuoso from the dilettante. Several similarities persist between mid-nineteenth-century piano virtuosity and live electronic music performance in the late twentieth century. They both involve technology or tools that the performer is intended to conquer – and this conquering must be clear to the audience. Many instances of live electronic performance are also obviously "beyond the power of the amateurs" (Kramer 2012, 233) whose only experiences might consist of presets on mass-produced synthesizers or laptops as a tool for writing papers and emails. In addition, the subtleties and knowledge required to perform with electronic technologies can mislead audiences to believe that an instrument is much easier to "play" than it actually is. The physicalities of the performance itself might not be *impressive*, while the sounds themselves might be considered aesthetically pleasing or *sonically* impressive.

The nature of electronic technologies – namely, that obsolescence is inevitable and updates (e.g., new models) are regular – separates the CEE from acoustic performers, and it also results in an important division among electronic performers. Montgomery has witnessed first-hand the trends and shifts within live electronic performance, and he articulates two paths that musicians take:

> On the one hand there's the impulse towards virtuosity, I guess partially because I come from playing an instrument. The French horn hasn't changed in 150 years, so it's the same instrument. And people who approach that instrument, they're not going to complain about it that it won't make these noises or it won't do that. There's the drive towards mastery of the instrument that you have. But electronic instruments change all the time. It's the nature

of the beast. There's a guy named Thomas Lehn, one of my heroes, who plays synthi [EMS Synthi A]. And he's been playing synthi for thirty years. And he's never played anything else, and he's fantastic! He's really, really good. That's that line.

Then there's the trying to keep up line. There's the Yamaha C40, then there's the Yamaha C60, then there's the Yamaha C80. Every one of them is arguably an improvement on the one that went before. But you have to learn it again. If you're on that track, you're always running to catch up. You're always on the wrong end of the learning curve. But if you don't do that, if you stay on the virtuoso track, that's limiting too. (personal communication, 26 February 2016)

The members of the CEE seem to be navigating a kind of middle road between these two paths. They have not remained with the same gear the whole time they have been performing live electronic music, as I discuss in chapter 3. Yet both Montgomery and Sutherland have returned to instruments with which they had prior familiarity (the Synth A and Synthi AKS, respectively). Jaeger's more recent set-up has remained stable, so he is focused on increasing facility with Reaktor. Stillwell continues to explore new modules and additional gear. The ability to follow the second path and perform with new instruments and updated versions requires technical knowledge; otherwise, a performer will take too long to gain facility for the instrument to be useful in live performance.

When I asked Stillwell what it means to be virtuosic on modular synthesizers, he exclaimed: "I wouldn't consider myself that as I am still learning! … I am not sure that one can ever become a virtuoso at the modular synthesizer as there are simply too many pieces. Each instrument is custom made either for the musician or for a purpose" (personal communication, 8 May 2020). When Stillwell performs, he is constantly adjusting the components on his Eurorack set-up, and he works up a sweat by the end of a performance, yet the gestures remain technical rather than performative or expressive, which could keep his performance from being interpreted as virtuosic. Consider that George Murray referred to Brian Eno as "a technician and an ideas man" rather than "a musician" (Seabrook 2008, 106) when he performed on the EMS Synthi A (which Montgomery performs; Sutherland sometimes performs with an EMS Synthi AKS). Cascone similarly identifies the same kind of "technician" associations with electronic musicians that would certainly apply to Stillwell's Eurorack set-up: "The performer of electronic music hovers over a nest of cables, knobs and blinking lights; electronic circuits filling the space with sound via an 'artificial' process" (2003, 102). This label of "technician" as opposed to "musician" reflects additional theorizing about virtuosity.

Antoine Hennion (2012) and Žarko Cvejić (2016) both articulate positive and negative types of virtuosity. For Hennion, the positive definition positions virtuosity in service of a performance, namely through expressivity. The negative definition considers virtuosity for its own sake, demonstrated through agility and speed. When virtuosic speed is only for show, then it is criticized. In this formulation, a skilled performance could be virtuosic, but without "inspired playing" (Kramer's phrase; 2012, 231), it would remain self-serving, unmusical virtuosity. In Cvejić's analysis, virtuosity must "remain recognisable as that of a human being. A virtuoso had to be perfect, but *humanly* perfect, not *too* perfect, like a machine; he was required, perhaps, to display an almost superhuman level of virtuosity, but still to come across as a human being, not as a machine" (2016, 72). Cvejić discusses the anti-virtuosity criticism of the nineteenth century that positioned virtuosos not as peak human performance but as non-human automata "devoid of all emotion, expression, that is, of *human* presence and content" (2016, 65). Cvejić argues that such criticisms "reveal a more profound anxiety about the presence of the human element in virtuosic music performances that were perceived as simply too virtuosic to issue from a human being, limited and imperfect as we tend to be" (2016, 67–8). Given the gesture–sound breakdown in live electronic music and the foregrounding of machines, the CEE faces an uphill battle in being assessed as exceptional humans performing musically.

Cvejić explains that critics avoided clearly defining "expressivity" out of a desire "to preserve an ineffable human presence, an ineffable human core in musical performance, which could only be expressed *musically*, by means of music, in and through music, and not described, expressed, or communicated in language or by any other means" (2016, 75). As I have discussed above, locating the "human" or "humanized" element in live electronic music has become both more complex and more varied in recent decades. With audiences who vary in familiarity with the CEE's performing technologies, how will they perceive the sounds they hear? Will they hear them as meaningful communication – as *musical*?

Stefan Honisch's work to rethink virtuosity in order to untangle its complicity in anti-disability and the "othering" of disabled bodies opens up additional possibilities when thinking about electronic music virtuosities. Honisch explains: "If musical performance becomes tangible through the expressive play of bodily movement, then widening the range of movements allowed in cultivating the virtuosic body need not perpetuate unimaginative representations of disability as antithetical to virtuosity" (2018, 289). He goes on: "A host of pedagogical and cultural systems have restricted the parameters of the virtuosic body to what the normal body can do, positioning normal bodily ability as the essential corporeal state out of which virtuosities are fashioned" (2018, 289). Rejecting normative standards of corporeality within virtuosity, therefore, creates space for many more musicians to demonstrate "what senses, bodies, and minds can do outside of the boundaries defined by the normal" (2018, 289). While he is focused on addressing anti-disability within music performance, Honisch also offers a way of recognizing how virtuosity exists within the CEE's performance practice.

In the CEE's performances with Farah, the audience's experience remains more closely tied to the classical world of acoustic virtuosity. And yet, at each CEE performance regardless of participants, the individual members and the collective demonstrate their skills in electronic performance – in sound creation and processing as well as in improvisation – that are beyond the skills of the average audience member. The conclusion cannot be that the CEE and other similar ensembles are not virtuosic, or are incapable of virtuosity, simply because there is limited physical effort. If we take virtuosity to mean mastery and exceptional skill, then the CEE is virtuosic. Yet this virtuosity will not be perceived through physical gesture. An audience may not value the CEE's virtuosity because, as Cascone explains, "The more skill (hence authority) the performer can demonstrate, the more value is received by the audience" (2003, 103). However, the CEE reflects an interior mastery – a technical and aesthetic mastery to conceive of and implement sounds. The additional skill required in the CEE's context is collective improvisation. One could be a virtuosic solo electronic musician, but that same musician may not be exceptional at applying technical skill with an attentive ear to contribute to a unique, collaborative sound world.

Improvising Electronic Music

In this section, I consider the CEE's improvisational practice, one that emerges from individual embodied and contextualized practices into a collective expression. I first consider improvisation in its temporal components, based primarily on the work of Vijay Iyer, and explore the temporalities of the CEE's live electronic performance practice and album *Live in Cabbagetown*. I discuss some of the main features of the CEE's improvisational practice, including details from their 2020 collaboration with the Exploded Ensemble. I then situate the CEE's practice within a broader consideration of real-time music-making practices based on George E. Lewis's framework of the Eurological and Afrological. The CEE is not only an improvisational ensemble, although they have increasingly become so over the years. Thus, they do not reject completely the hegemony of the composer status or even of notated music. Nonetheless, over the decades, there are aspects of their improvisational practice that are Afrological in nature: namely, the concepts of personality, freedom, and spontaneity in Lewis's framework.

Vijay Iyer distinguishes between two temporalities: process-oriented "in time" activity, in which time contributes to the structure of the process, and product-oriented or "over time" activity, in which things simply take time (2008). The CEE engages with both temporalities: their predominantly improvised practice involves in-time processes, while over-time processes characterize some of their albums and their earlier focus on composed pieces. In preparing some of their albums, the CEE has embraced the Gouldian "taketwoness" of recording and post-production. The material on some of their albums has never been performed in live performance; these pieces were not designed to be reproduced live. For example, with the exception of *This Is This* (performed in 2004) and *Star Song* (performed in 1975, 1976, and 1977), none of the tracks on the album *Bluffer's Lookout* has been performed live. Some tracks on *Supertrio* (e.g., *Clusters*) also have not been performed live.[3] By contrast, as chapters 2 and 3 demonstrate, other albums document some of the CEE's most performed pieces in each era.

The CEE's practice has always incorporated improvisation to various degrees, from Jaeger and Montgomery's earliest Possibilities Portmanteaux performances to the CEE's current almost completely improvised performances. Joseph Auner's (2013) essay discussing the problem of obsolescence in electronic music – specifically composed pieces that require specific gear or software – underlines the practicality of embracing improvisation as a live electronic ensemble. Like the issue of unpredictability with electronic technologies, obsolescence increases the need to find alternative creative approaches. In addition, Ronald Kuivila explains that because of the particular "temporal behaviour" of electronic music making, "advanced planning is only partially useful, perfect compliance is impossible, and the concepts of contingency and action are essential" (2009, 111). By embracing real-time music making with no expectations of specific gear being used or how the gear will "behave," an ensemble like the CEE can transcend limitations of technology-specific obsolescence and unpredictability.

Central to the CEE's success as an improvisational ensemble is their ability to adjust in real time to the size and make-up of the ensemble (including possible guests) in any given performance, in addition to performance space, audience, and other factors. The CEE members frequently emphasize the importance of listening as the key to a successful improvisation: listening to oneself and listening to each other. Chapter 5 discusses listening ecologies in more detail. While the CEE has had a set membership at any given time, the entire lineup is not always available for performances. In addition, the set of technologies for each individual performance may vary as they incorporate new gear, eliminate other gear, have some gear out of commission, and so on. For example, to travel to their 2020 residency at Carnegie Mellon University (CMU), the members of the CEE had to carefully curate what gear to bring to Pittsburgh based on space limitations (either in the car or in the plane's overhead bins). Jaeger's set-up remained the same, though, because he performs only with a laptop.

Owen Green's analysis of two case studies within what he calls "electroacoustic musicking" is illuminating for my discussion of the CEE. Green's description of Agostino Di Scipio's *Audible Ecosystemic Interface* applies to the unique circumstances shaping each CEE performance: "microphones and loudspeakers are not neutral to proceedings, as both their characteristics and placement within the space are of significant importance to the outcome ... the nature of the space, the situation of the equipment within it, the number of people in the space and even the environmental conditions (humidity, temperature etc.) will contribute to different behaviours" (2008). Green's description of John Bowers's improvisational practice is even more applicable: "the particularities of space, technological failure or limitation, concert programming, social matters (within and beyond the performers) and the types of sonic material brought [to] bear all contributed in various manners to the way in which musicking took place and to the sonorities that resulted" (2008). The contrast between the rehearsal space and performance space alone demonstrates how much the CEE needs to adjust to their surroundings. While Stillwell has good speakers in his basement, the acoustics of the room will contrast highly with the resonance of the Arts & Letters Club, for example. Also, as Stillwell's basement has no piano, Farah plays his other instruments when he rehearses with the CEE. The piano, then, becomes an additional surprise at the concert to which all of the CEE members must adjust.

The performances that immediately pre-date the official formation of the CEE were Montgomery and Jaeger improvising as Possibilities Portmanteaux, and subsequent members have brought various improvisational skills and experiences to the CEE collective. For instance, Stillwell studied jazz trumpet. While he describes the CEE and jazz (at least the jazz with which he is most familiar) as highly contrasting sound worlds, he articulates one feature of jazz that he implements in his CEE practice: "The main thing that carried over was the belief that there really are no wrong notes and that it is how you adapt to what usually only you perceive as a 'mistake' is what is important" (personal communication, 8 May 2020). During her studies at Western, Bolton participated in an experimental free improvisation group with students. She translated those experiences to the CEE context: "It certainly helps to be with a group of people (like the CEE) who know how to listen and know when … to hold back. The CEE are an amazing group of people to improvise with. I have worked with others and definitely the experience of this group is deep" (personal communication, 23 June 2020). Farah considers himself more of an improviser than a composer, so working with the CEE has been an easy extension of his solo practice. Building from his solo improvisational practice, Farah frequently makes suggestions of concepts for approaching a CEE improvisation, whether it's referring to one of his drawings or completing his "one pitch" challenge (in which each performer plays the same pitch but with different timbral explorations). Sutherland is sure to clarify that he didn't study improvisation formally; however, he performed with MetaMusic, which was an improvisational group, and he recalls listening to many different kinds of improvisation (mostly jazz) on recordings and during live shows.

Improvisation frames time in a special kind of way: through what Sanden would call temporal and spatial liveness, the listener and the performer are sharing time (Iyer 2008, 266). Iyer distinguishes between two types of "time sharing": improvised and composed. He argues: "The main source of drama in improvised music is the sheer fact of the shared sense of time: the sense that the improviser is working, creating, generating musical material, in the same time that we are co-performing as listeners. As listeners to any music, we experience a kind of *empathy* for the performer, an awareness of physicality and an understanding of the effort required to create music ... In improvised music empathy extends to an awareness of the performers' coincident physical and mental exertion, of their 'in-the-moment' (i.e., in-time) *process* of creative activity and interactivity" (2008, 267). What Iyer describes here as improvised time sharing is comparable to Sanden's liveness of spontaneity and liveness of corporeality. A listener unacculturated to this kind of music may struggle to hear the sonic interactions and coordination; unlike a chamber ensemble performing written-out music with composed simultaneity, the CEE members rarely gesture simultaneously (whether physically or sonically). Jaeger stated: "All of the components do change simultaneously, you know, but only by accident" (personal communication, 10 June 2016).

With electronic music improvisation, there is always the chance that both types of "time sharing" will be present. As I discussed earlier in this chapter, sound elements (if not timbres, then at least action chains) may be pre-composed. A degree of pre-composition is necessary for an ensemble like the CEE, for whom the sound world experienced is the most important. For example, some sounds, like field recordings gathered by Stillwell, need to be recorded outside of the performance time. Furthermore, computer-assisted improvisation has been part of the CEE's practice: "We could pre-compose material to be used in live performance. And we could compose it in a way that there were actual live performance variables around a fixed structure, like a musical soundscreen" (David Jaeger, personal communication, 10 June 2016).

The CEE album *Live in Cabbagetown* (recorded in 2008 and released in 2013) is the only album in the group's discography that consists entirely of free improvisations, as well as one of only two live albums, the other being *Canadian Electronic Ensemble: Live* (1998). This album was recorded on 6 September 2008, at the Cabbagetown Arts Festival, a neighbourhood festival in Toronto.[4] The album includes four improvisations, the first three of which are a little less than fourteen minutes each, while the last is about seven minutes long. In 2008, the CEE was officially a quintet, with Bolton, Jaeger, Lake, Montgomery, and Stillwell. However, the lineup of individual concerts didn't always include all five members, given people's busy schedules, and often included guests. In this case, Lake, Montgomery, and Stillwell were the CEE members performing, with soon-to-be member Farah appearing as a guest artist.

The Cabbagetown performance strikes me for its abundance of trumpet playing, contributed by Lake, such as on *Improvisation #4*, with the trumpet's longer tones balancing the keyboard's more active parts during this specific piece. The entire album is also keyboard-centric, with Farah offering busy atonal passagework throughout the album on his synth, as there was no piano. There are also a number of speech samples incorporated by Stillwell (including one from the Berlin airport), an approach I haven't witnessed as much in the following decade of CEE performances.

I would describe each improvisation as through-composed. That term from the formal analysis of notated European classical music is in some ways nonsensical when applied to a free improvisation. Yet it captures, I argue, a characteristic of the CEE's improvisations that Iyer calls "temporal situatedness" (2008, 267): improvised musical forms are modular, smaller units rather than large-scale hierarchies. For example, I perceive *Improvisation #4* in six smaller units (see listening guides for further discussion). Describing these CEE improvisations in formal terms like binary, sonata, or rondo forms makes little sense. These improvisations don't contain what we might call motives or themes that are presented, transformed, and re-presented in a structural way based on tonal regimes. Perhaps because of the practicalities of beginning and ending a free improvisation, I could argue that there is some kind of arch form, if only in overall energy profile and not in content (e.g., motivic recall). But even that is not always the case, with some improvisations opening quite densely and loud and then ending with a gradual fade out.

When listening to this album, I find myself in different zones: each zone could be focused on a particular timbre, or it could be distinguished by a comparatively dense or sparse texture. It can be difficult to pinpoint precisely when I perceive a shift from one zone to the next: this experience makes sense given the collective music making of CEE improvisations, in which decisions are constantly being made and responded to in real time with little or no advanced notice before a sound joins the mix. Abrupt changes may occur, but only accidentally.

This album is identified as "live," and all of its material was indeed recorded during a live performance. However, there is also an "over time" component, though not one of "taketwoness." Stillwell edited out some of the material that he characterized as "wandering," which he explained occurred when they "hang out on a vibe a little bit too long" (personal communication, 8 July 2020). He cross-faded sections that bookended any cuts with the goal that he himself would not notice any edits. Can we say that this is a live album, then, when the listener is not hearing the CEE's performance exactly as it progressed in time? Some listeners might feel deceived – a violation of the liveness of fidelity – and yet the album still presents a liveness of corporeality and virtuality. There remains a liveness of spontaneity for the listener, as Lewis argues that even in recordings of improvisation, which we might think are now fixed and lack spontaneity, "the listener also improvises, posing alternative paths, experiencing immediacy as part of the listening experience" (2002, 233).

IMPROVISATION IN COLLABORATION

Valuing the skills and perspectives of all musicians involved is at the core of the CEE's collective music-making practice. The major collaborative relationships between the CEE and other performers each came about after a period of intense workshopping. For example, to prepare for the twentieth-anniversary MEGAJAM concerts in 1992, the eighteen musicians (including the three members of the CEE trio) had a one-week residency, which, according to the album's liner notes, "allowed the large group to form a cohesive whole" (2000). The Supertrio collaboration in the 1990s included its three-week residency at the Banff Centre (discussed in chapter 3). Stillwell, Montgomery, and Bolton speak often of their collaboration with dancer Lina Cruz during a week-long residency at the Music Gallery in June of 2000. Stillwell recalls that Cruz began the week with predetermined choreography, but over the week of working with the CEE as they improvised, Cruz gradually abandoned the predetermined material until the final performance: "she let go completely and everything was just on fire. And that was really a truly wonderful collaboration. All the lines of communication were open: the communications visually from Lina with us, her responding to what we did, us responding to what she did. All of that kind of stuff happened. And that made for a really wonderful collaboration" (public lecture,

26 February 2020). The collaboration with the Exploded Ensemble at CMU also involved several hours of rehearsal and experimentation before the public concert on 27 February.

For a primarily improvisational group, what is the purpose of rehearsals? How do rehearsals differ from performances? I posed these questions to the members of the CEE. For Sutherland, they aren't that different. In his view, improvisation is like a meditation practice: every time you meditate, you are doing the practice. Rehearsals and performances, then, are both the practice. He believes, though, that the "rehearsal process is getting people tuned in" (class lecture, 24 February 2020). Stillwell described this "tuning in" as opening the lines of communication. Group improvisation highlights the importance of listening because, as Linson and Clarke explain, performers "afford one another opportunities for future actions" (2017, 64). Listening is an essential act of readiness, and this readiness is subjective to the divergent perspectives of each individual, encompassing not only their particular cognitive, perceptual, and motor skill capabilities and tendencies but also their embodied creative practice, which is tied to their chosen performance technologies.

When the CEE began its collaborations with CMU's Exploded Ensemble students, the first step at rehearsals was listening to each other. Each ensemble performed a short improvisation in order for the rest of the musicians to "tune in" to that group's style and sound palette. During this particular semester, Exploded Ensemble included many more acoustic instruments than the CEE typically performs with (including clarinet, harp, and double bass), as well as a vocalist (which is rare for the CEE, though not unheard of, with one example being their collaboration with Janice Jackson in 2004). Because this collaboration was bringing together two ensembles (for a total of eighteen musicians), these rehearsals involved more specific prompts than the typical "who goes first" of CEE rehearsals and performances. For example, in one improvisation, only a quartet of musicians was playing at any given time, with the quartet shifting at regular intervals around the "circle." This collaboration also took advantage of specific skills within the two ensembles, most notably with visuals. Student Jeena Yin produced live manipulations of Farah's drawings as the moving score for this combined collective. This process of combining visuals and sound (which is typical in an Exploded Ensemble performance but rare for the CEE) was deemed so successful by all the performers that they also included it in the live performance.

While the other members articulated to me that in many ways they approach both rehearsal and live performance similarly, Farah and Bolton offered two distinctions. Farah views rehearsals as an opportunity to suggest new ideas and to articulate strategies for improvement, as opposed to criticizing others' musical decisions. Bolton explained:

> I am probably equally as risk taking in the performance as in rehearsal. Taking a risk in a live setting is more worth it than in rehearsal, because the stakes are higher, and "failure" only means that it turned out not how you hoped, but the fact is something happened that was not predicted, and that enriches the performance. It is hard to take a risk in a rehearsal, because it is lower stakes. However, the kind of risk I reserve for rehearsal is trying out new tech. Certain combinations of equipment or software, etc. So sometimes in rehearsals, i [sic] may be "beta testing" certain plugins or setups, and I don't want to do that in performance. (personal communication, 23 June 2020)

Thus, rehearsals are the time to experiment with what Andy Keep calls instrumentalizing, which "seeks to discover the performability, intrinsic sonic palette and possibilities for sonic manipulation of objects" (2009, 113). While other improvisational practices may seek to improvise the process of instrumentalizing during live performance (e.g., sound making with found objects in the performance space), this is not the CEE's practice.

Group music making is a complex system, as "at any given moment there is a multiplicity of choices, each of which branches into a further multiplicity of choices, and so on" (Cook 2018, 321), even when a score is part of the performance. To watch the CEE perform is to observe a collection of musicians deeply concentrating on what they are doing. Whenever they perform, their creativity comes from the social, interactive, collaborative, and collective aspects of music making; "intentionality occurs at the level of the group and is dispersed across the players" (Cook 2018, 26). This complex system includes the broader histories of electronic and experimental music, improvisation, and new music in Canada, which can be illuminated by George E. Lewis's analysis of racialized notions of real-time music making and his framework of the Afrological and Eurological.

Drawing on sociologist Alfred Schutz's work on collective music making, which emphasizes its social aspect, Lewis clarifies: "Improvisation engages local agency, history, contingency, memory, identity, and embodiment. In this way, an improvised music can directly address issues surrounding the practice of everyday life itself" (2011, 461). Because this improvised music is a collective effort, "the focus of musical discourse suddenly shifts from the individual, autonomous creator to the collective – the individual as a part of global humanity" (2002, 234).

Lewis speaks of "the possibility of internalizing alternative value systems" (2002, 234) inherent in performing improvised music. He frames his discussion of improvisation by articulating two perspectives on real-time music making: Afrological and Eurological. These two concepts are not meant to be ethnically or racially essentialist, as if all (and only) Black musicians engage in Afrological real-time music making and all white musicians engage in Eurological real-time music making. Lewis is reckoning with the "historically emergent rather than ethnically essential" (2002, 217) contexts that led to the development of each musical belief system and its associated behaviours. What Lewis, then, sees in the practices of "improvised music" groups like the Association for the Advancement of Creative Musicians (AACM), European "free" improvisers, and the "downtown (New York) school" (2002, 236) is a "welcoming of agency, social necessity, personality, and difference, as well as its strong relationship to popular folk cultures" (2002, 234).

The CEE primarily inherited a Eurological approach to improvisation due to the founding members' music education within formalized Euro-American university music training. Many of its later members had also gone through similar programs before joining the ensemble. These courses of study emphasize notated music written by composers and engage minimally (if at all) with musics from so-called "popular" (including jazz) or non-Western contexts. As I argued in chapters 2 and 3, the CEE has always had to include some element of improvisation even in composed and notated works because of the unpredictability of their electronic gear. Such instances align more with the Eurological perspective on improvisation, as there are still rules constructed by a composer that specify "culturally ad hoc systems of specified musical behavior options" (Lewis 2002, 239). Furthermore, the CEE emerged from a trajectory of studio-based, institutional electronic music that has dismissed "known" or idiomatic styles in favour of sound worlds without history or memory – that is, without reference. (Think of Schaeffer's "reduced listening," in which a sound object with origins in the real world is listened to as a sound in itself, without any attempt to identify its source or meaning.)

Yet, despite strong ties to the Eurological value system of real-time music making, in some key aspects, the CEE's practice has come to more closely resemble the Afrological perspective. This shift in value system seems to be due to the group's emphasis on interpersonal connections and presence (as opposed to only musical connections), the welcoming of newer members with more diverse musical experiences, and a shift away from composed music to improvising almost all of their performances. The result is a real-time creative practice that reflects Lewis's concepts of personality, freedom, and spontaneity in the Afrological value system.

Lewis summarizes how the Eurological and Afrological forms define spontaneity differently, the former based in Cageian indeterminacy. The criticism from within Eurological music is that improvisation (by which they mean jazz improvisation) is idiomatic, as "one plays what one knows" (Lukas Foss quoted in Cope 1993, 127; Lewis 2002, 230), whereas Cageian indeterminacy, by contrast, results in completely unpredictable and unique experiences (at least according to its advocates). This charge of insufficient spontaneity is tied to differing notions of freedom. In Eurological forms, the freedom is from rules, while the Afrological seeks freedom through discipline and self-control. The CEE's practice is more aligned with the Afrological in this aspect. The members tend not to try out completely new gear or software in a performance, but instead take the time to learn and practise those tools before implementing them. Similar to the Afrological improvisers Lewis discusses (2002, 238), the CEE also emphasizes technical knowledge (in this case, of their electronic instruments and the physics behind them). For example, Jaeger continues to perform on his laptop with Reaktor, and he desires to deepen his knowledge of the software. Farah wishes to expand his toolbox for live sound processing, but he is still primarily a pianist, and his contributions to the CEE reflect his years of discipline in learning the instrument.

In its creative practice, the CEE also rejects the notion that "true" spontaneity cannot result from history or memory, as demonstrated by their inclusion of pre-composed components within improvisations.

Furthermore, I have attended rehearsals where the group generated material that was subsequently recalled during a live performance. There is also the story I told in chapter 3 of the CEE pulling out Lake's old synthesizer and finding many of his sounds intact. They brought into their performance the history and memory of the ensemble and of Lake as an individual performer. With sounds, titles, and stories, the CEE frequently references its own history, and this is a valued part of their practice. Their shared history as musicians and friends is as important as any potential future experiences.

The personalities of individual CEE members are embraced and encouraged in their collective musical practice, and the significance of personality for the group is both social and musical. As members have explained, the CEE has performed with many great musicians, some of whom were considered as potential new members. But the ability of a prospective member to function well as an individual within the collective has been a deciding factor: they need to connect with the CEE's way of coexisting as humans and musicians. Sonically, personality manifests timbrally and texturally as well as through the musical influences from which they each draw. For example, Bolton's experiences with Celtic fiddling and Farah's interest in Middle Eastern music influence the material they contribute to the collective sound. While the distinctive instrumental sources of Farah's and Bolton's sounds clearly mark who created them, the origins of many of the other sounds in the mix are unknown – even to the CEE members. Bolton explains: "When we're improvising together, sometimes it's not clear who's doing what. So it's just purely what you're hearing, not knowing who it is" (public lecture, 26 February 2020). When multiple synth sounds are emitted from loudspeakers and not directly from the musicians, is the individual lost in the collective? Losing the individual is not the CEE's aim; rather, it's an outcome of their chosen medium. With their improvisational practice of taking turns with who starts, the CEE prioritizes the individual voice and leadership within the collective. Recalling the CEE during Lake's tenure, Bolton stated: "Larry always liked to lay down an amazing thick bass pad. So Larry had a definite input into the shape or arc a piece or [improv] would take" (personal communication, 23 June 2020). Many of the CEE members have a clear conception of their role in the group and what they would like to contribute to any given improvisation or to an entire concert. For example, Farah always aims to "go big" a couple of times in a concert, but he consciously holds back from dominating the soundscape too much.

When the CEE rehearsed with the Exploded Ensemble, the personality of each student performer was valued and highlighted through specific improvisation strategies. For example, one improvisation had only four performers at any given time, slowly rotating around the room like a clock as one musician faded out and another one faded in every thirty seconds. This allowed the large room of performers to listen with concentration to specific individuals and for each musician to be perceived and appreciated for their own instrument and style.

Ultimately, it should also be noted that the CEE's practice shares one further similarity with the Eurological value system of real-time music making: an exnomination of race and, to a lesser extent, gender, as I will discuss in greater depth in chapter 6. The ensemble's personnel has been almost entirely white and male across its five decades, reflecting the unmarked systemic whiteness and patriarchy in Canada's broader new-music community. This larger sphere encompasses electronic and experimental music communities; improvisational communities; and institutions of Euro-American classical music like the University of Toronto, the Canadian Music Centre, and CBC Radio. Thus, discussion of the CEE's improvisational practice creates an opportunity to name the value systems within university music programs, funding bodies, presenting organizations, and so on. In chapter 6, I discuss how these institutions reflect and reinforce gender and racial inequalities, as evidenced by performance and recording opportunities and competition results. I consider the CEE as a site of privilege within the Canadian new music scene, but also point to important efforts the group and its members have made to counter inequalities.

Conclusion

Attend a CEE performance, and you will experience temporal and spatial liveness. The listener is likely to assume that the musicians are performing live: spontaneous and interactive. Yet the mystery and mystique of their instruments leaves the listener with questions about their skill and the level of spontaneity and interactivity. With performances these days introduced as "Dave Goes First" or "Rose Goes

First," the audience is provided with evidence that there is some kind of interaction. And the listener can track human agency to sound, at least for the opening seconds until another player joins in. However, that listener may never know what aspects of perceived liveness are actual as opposed to merely real (i.e., perceived). Sanden's conclusion reminds us of the listener in these considerations of "live" electronic music: "The perception of an interactive liveness between musician and machine does not depend on the *actual* existence of dialogues between performers and technologies. Rather, it rests on these musicians' exploring the *illusion* of such dialogues; put another way, it rests on the *virtual* existence of such dialogues" (2013, 109). The CEE employs real-time collective music making through skilled and expressive implementation of their electronic technologies. Whether a listener hears and values this is a matter of perception.

The process of listening to the CEE is essential to its musicking. This listening begins with the CEE members themselves, and then, through live performances and recordings, it extends to other listeners. Chapter 5 examines how listeners act as musicking agents while also being guided by institutional spatial sound ecologies and listening strategies.

5

CEE Listening Spaces

Embodied, Embedded, and Virtual Contexts

Listening Encounters

Christopher Small's concept of "musicking" pushes back on conceptions of music that maintain *thingness* over process. His definition rejects the emphasis on composed works notated in scores, welcomes in more actors than one that considers only composers and performers, and emphasizes contextual factors of any musicking experience: "*To music is to take part, in any capacity, in a musical performance, whether by performing, by listening, by rehearsing or practicing, by providing material for performance (what is called composing), or by dancing*" (1998, 9; italics in original). In the previous chapter, my discussion of the Canadian Electronic Ensemble's improvisational practice similarly affirms process and rejects a fixed notion of the musical "work." Yet this framework still prioritizes the ensemble members as performers over other relationalities that cannot fully capture the CEE musicking experience. Furthermore, discussing audience perception only in terms of virtuosity misses other key aspects of their listening approaches and contexts. Chapter 5 therefore analyzes the CEE's various listening spaces, positioning the members themselves as the first listeners (a musicking strategy central to their performance practice). Nothing illustrated the CEE's approach as first listeners more clearly to me than their collaboration with the Exploded Ensemble. During their first rehearsal, each ensemble improvised alone to allow the other to listen to their sonic and relational tendencies. The ensembles also experimented together with different improvisational prompts that invited careful listening to shifting timbres and textures. While the public concert was a highlight for all involved, the hours spent in rehearsal were what established a deep bond between the musicians, with engaged conversations about gear and favourite electronic musicians/composers.

This chapter begins by relating listening strategies inherited by the CEE through their training in university music programs in the United States and Canada, as well as through personal and professional relationships with key figures. In contextualizing the CEE's practice within listening strategies espoused by R. Murray Schafer, Glenn Gould, Hildegard Westerkamp, and John Cage, I also offer a critique of how the spatial ecologies of the CEE's performance history promote what xwélméxw (Stó:lō) scholar Dylan Robinson (2020) describes as fixed listening as opposed to flexible, agile listening.

Small's book was groundbreaking for the field of musicology in its challenge to the use of "music" to mean "works of music in the Western tradition" (1998, 3), and his work is foundational for Robinson's critique of musicology and sound studies in how it re-centres encounter and relationalities. Small writes: "We begin to see a musical performance as an encounter between human beings that takes place through the medium of sounds organized in specific ways" (1998, 10). Thingness over process is a common ontological characteristic of Western thinking, which has been called out in particular by ethnomusicologists (e.g., Robinson 2020; Diamond 2019; and Levine and Robinson 2019). Indigenous scholars in various fields have long pushed back on the dominance of Western thinking in the arts, including music.

Robinson's work extends Small's by way of positioning normative listening within settler colonialism. Through Robinson's framework, I will be critiquing normative listening modes in Canada and the United States that fall into the category of what he calls "hungry listening" (2020) – a teleological, single-sense listening – and deny broader relationalities and other-than-aesthetic listening approaches, such as affective or responsive listening. Joanna Demers (2010) emphasizes institutional electronic music's strong link to Pierre Schaeffer's "reduced listening" ("écoute réduite"), which requires a single-sense listening that minimizes the role of the body. Robinson's critique has resonances with Demers's, but he also points to the colonial foundations of the fixed listening reinforced in Western music education and concert performance. Analyzing the CEE's listening strategies thereby presents an opportunity to further address settler colonial sonic legacies in Canada by acknowledging the broader context of institutional regimes of listening and venues that resist non-fixed listening. I consider how Robinson's work in particular can push for more open and flexible interpretations. If listening is an encounter, who is welcomed and who is excluded (explicitly or implicitly)? What kinds of encounters are acknowledged? That is, what listening approaches and values are legible in the CEE's listening spaces?

This chapter discusses chronologically the CEE's rehearsal, recording, and performance spaces in Toronto, including the Music Gallery, The TRANZAC, and the Arts & Letters Club (illustrated by a discussion of a 2012 performance of *No Dim Pearls*). While the CEE retains significant creative and listening agency, much of the spatial sound ecologies of the group and listening relationalities they foster are determined by broader institutional processes. I then discuss the virtual listening spaces of radio and recording (including streaming) as intimate listening experiences. I illustrate my particular experience of intimacy with Rose Bolton's *This Is This*, which includes the recorded voices of the members of the CEE and some of their family members. In a brief postlude, I discuss a recent project of the CEE called "Pass the Track." Necessitated by COVID-19 pandemic restrictions, Pass the Track positions CEE members in listening relationships to each other that differ from typical collective improvisations.

Because "music's primary meanings are not individual at all but social" (Small 1998, 8), this chapter considers space – both physical and virtual – as the sites for creating social meaning around and within the CEE's musicking. Small writes: "The act of musicking establishes in the place where it is happening a set of *relationships*, and it is in those *relationships* that the meaning of the act lies" (1998, 13; italics in original). While the CEE is a live electronic ensemble, the group's discography is experienced by individuals as collections of fixed media works. My discussion of virtual spaces draws on existing work that centres the listening experience and relationality within electroacoustic/electronic music, such as the construction and perception of intimacy.

John Cage the Listener

Media scholar Kate Lacey notes: "While it is possible to be trained in the arts of public speaking and, in various ways, media literacy, it is rare to find the equivalent opportunities to hone the arts of public listening (in contrast to the legion of books about listening in interpersonal situations)" (2013, 190). While Lacey may be correct about the imbalance of these two perspectives in training and published books, there are key figures in sound studies, composition, and musicology who have been devoted to this work, specifically Pauline Oliveros, John Cage, R. Murray Schafer, Hildegard Westerkamp, and Dylan Robinson (though his work is not so much about "honing the arts of public listening" as it is a critique of the limiting normativity of what he has termed "hungry listening"). The CEE members are the group's first listeners, and the ideas about listening they have inherited from Cage and others shape not only their creative practice and the sonic results but the spaces in which they music and the normative listening behaviours engrained therein.

As David Cecchetto and Jeremy Strachan explain (2015), John Cage's strong influence on modernist and experimental music extended from the United States to Canada. The CEE's founding members were all initially trained in the United States, making their early encounters with Cage all the more likely, but Cage has become canon in twentieth- and twenty-first-century music studies at Canadian institutions as well. Cage also visited the Toronto area several times, reinforcing his influence on contemporary Canadian music. I articulate three major influences that Cage has had on the CEE as an experimental electronic ensemble, all of which centre the act of listening: 1) instrumentalization; 2) electronic sound sources; 3) spaces as co-performers.

One of Cage's stated goals was to embrace all sounds as music. Thus, to Cage, noise becomes music if one pays attention to it. In his essay "The Future of Music," he declared: "Wherever we are, what we hear is mostly noise. When we ignore it, it disturbs us. When we listen to it, we find it fascinating" (1973, 3). Chapter 4 discusses this process of instrumentalization in which seemingly non-musical objects become musical objects through performative intention; Ann Southam's *Natural Resources* (see chapter 6) relies on such instrumentalization of acoustic hardware objects. Indeed, it is the act of listening that shifts the ontology of the sound from noise to music. The CEE's earliest live performances also exhibit a kind of instrumentalization of electronic tools intended for studio use. Many tools are part of a longer history of repurposing electronic devices for creative sonic purposes as well as turning some gear into live instruments as opposed to compositional tools. While performing live, CEE members will often instrumentalize first into headphones, exploring settings until they arrive at a satisfying sound that they bring up in the mix.

While Cage is not solely responsible for an interest in electronic sound sources in the United States, his embrace of the phonograph, radio, and other electronic devices was part of experimental music's expansion of timbre and studio-based curiosity. His pieces challenged the listener accustomed to Euro-American classical music by de-emphasizing or excluding musical parameters typically associated with that repertoire, namely pitch and pitch-based hierarchies expressed harmonically and arranged through small- and large-scale structures. The CEE's music is similar in this way. Their embrace of the "weird" is typically concerned with timbres and textures. I am reminded of the October 2017 performance at the Canadian Music Centre in which the CEE performed an improvisation based on one of Farah's ideas: to select a single pitch as the basis for the entire work, with each performer iterating that pitch on their instrument, producing vastly different timbres between them, sometimes as a single note and sometimes in a cluster of sounds.[1] While this improvisation centred pitch much more than the CEE typically does while improvising, it did not function at all to shape small- or large-scale structures; the pitch served only as a constant to better highlight the timbral variety within the group.

Each member of the CEE is on a continual quest to explore the timbral possibilities of their existing gear and to seek out new gear. Sometimes instruments and tools are abandoned because they are timbrally unsatisfying. Although it typically de-emphasizes pitch and pitch-based hierarchies, the CEE's music is not without structure on both small and large scales. Some formal elements are apparent to live listeners during improvisations, namely, an overall arch form that begins and ends with relatively low density and the gradual layering of textures, with whoever "goes first" being joined by each member as they desire.

Cage's infamous *4'33"* not only challenged the idea that silence exists, demonstrating rather that there is always sound, whether notated by a composer or not, but also highlighted audience members and performance spaces as sound makers. Alvin Lucier pushed this idea further by exploring the sound – namely, resonant frequencies – of specific spaces through playback and recording in *I am sitting in a room*. The CEE sometimes similarly listens to their performance spaces. Stillwell in particular likes to find the resonant frequencies of each space and then incorporate them into the group's performances. As I discussed in chapter 4, Stillwell also uses the SOMA Ether to transduce the electromagnetic waves of any given space.

In all three Cageian influences outlined above, Cage de-emphasizes the composer's intention and declares rather that "music" only becomes possible through the act of listening. In his essay "Experimental Music," Cage reflected: "And what is the purpose of writing music? One is, of course, not dealing with purposes but dealing with sounds" (1973, 12). Earlier in the same essay, Cage explains that he initially disliked the phrase "experimental music" because a composer has already made the plan for the work, and the performers have rehearsed. However, when he shifted his perspective to that of a listener, the word "experimental" made sense to him: "What has happened is that I have become a listener and the music has become something to hear" (7).

Thus, the CEE inherited from Cage ideas about listening that challenge certain hierarchies of Euro-American classical music. Because of this influence, the CEE's improvisational practice reflects some of the values of Eurological real-time music making. Joanna Demers (2010) characterizes Cage's ideas about noise in particular as still relying on "musical listening." Surely, it is only through fixed listening that an object is instrumentalized or a space's sounds become part of a composition. While Demers credits Cage's influence on expanding notions of musical sound, she also clarifies that experimental electronic music demands more than "musical listening," which she describes as listening that focuses on "discrete beginnings and endings and development ... predictable forms, instrumental timbres, and structures" (151). As an alternative approach, Demers invokes the phrase "aesthetic listening," which "heeds intermittent moments of a work without searching for a trajectory that unites such moments" (151). Demers here is accounting for how music like EDM "permits and encourages attention to many simultaneous occurrences" (152), such as someone's own movement or the behaviour and appearance of dancers around them. The CEE's performance spaces – predominantly theatres and concert venues – do not encourage this kind of "aesthetic listening," nor does their performance practice, which separates performers and audience spatially and through lighting. Indeed, the ritual of a CEE performance is one in which the spotlight on the stage closes off listening possibilities. In such a performance context, which I discuss in chapter 4, "listeners are expected to pay full attention to the music and ignore almost everything else around them" (Demers 2010, 152). Despite the human performers on the stage, the CEE's sound world of primarily electronic sounds emanating from loudspeakers is rather similar to acousmatic concerts. Acousmatic listening facilitates Schaeffer's reduced listening (écoute réduite), "bypassing external associations to focus on a sound's inherent qualities" (Demers 2010, 172). Robinson critiques the darkened room in particular for "[lessening] our perception of spatial subjectivity itself" (2020, 97). Thus, the CEE's performance spaces, such a key part of their history, are often hosting a performance practice that minimizes their spatial subjectivity. To be clear, to perform otherwise would require the CEE to reject the standard practices of many of these spaces, violating the expectations of both hosts and listeners, such as the clear separation of audience and performer, a seated and quiet audience (until applause after the completion of a piece or improvisation), and lowered lights above the audience to further minimize attention to their corporeal presence.

Nonetheless, because the CEE's version of experimental electronic music encourages "momentary attention that does not necessarily demand hearing larger-scale patterns or growth" (Demers 2010, 152), it finds resonance with the electronic music Demers associates with her concept of "aesthetic listening" (which is distinct from Robinson's use of the same term) and creates possibilities for flexible listening. The performance approaches of the CEE and the listening approaches of their audiences may close or open such possibilities.

Listening In/To Canada

The influence of Cage's ideas about listening, noise, sound, and experimentalism is undeniable for a musician in North America trained in a formalized music program on Euro-American classical music. For many musicians trained and working in Canada, additional voices have been particularly influential: R. Murray Schafer and Hildegard Westerkamp, two of the many celebrated Canadian composers with whom the CEE has personal and professional connections. Schafer, working out of Simon Fraser University starting in the 1960s, was groundbreaking in the Canadian experimental music scene with his notion of the soundscape, his site-specific compositions, and his World Soundscape Project (WSP), which launched the field of acoustic ecology. His writings outline a specific ethic of listening and sound making: relying on a simplistic binary between beautiful sounds and noise, he calls on composers to improve the world's soundscape by adding more beautiful sounds, rather than destroying it through noise. Schafer explains in detail his ideas about soundscape and soundscape design in his book *The Soundscape: Our Sonic Environment and the Tuning of the World* (1977).

Many of the CEE's younger Canadian members would have studied Schafer in their music programs. Schafer himself rarely included electronic sounds in his music, preferring in-person encounters with acoustic sounds. He coined the term "schizophonia" to describe recording acoustic sounds and thereby disconnecting the sound from its source; his word choice connotes his negative view of recorded sound. However, Schafer has had a strong influence on electronic and electroacoustic composers because of his embrace of sounds that are not conventionally understood as "music." The CEE's sound certainly deviates from Schafer's personal aesthetic, yet the members share his desire to enhance each soundscape through their musicking.

The founding members, in particular David Jaeger and Larry Lake, had personal interactions with Schafer that left a strong impression on their ideas about music, sound, and space. Jaeger (2019b) tells the story of his CBC colleague John Reeves requesting financial support from his and Lake's radio program *Two New Hours* for a recording of Schafer's *Music for Wilderness Lake* (1979), for twelve trombones around the lake at dawn and dusk. Jaeger agreed, and the music was recorded and mixed into a popular short film about the piece with the same title. *Two New Hours* then recorded parts of *And Wolf Shall Inherit the Moon*, the *Epilogue* to Schafer's twelve-part *Patria Cycle*. This 1995 recording at Wildcat Lake was broadcast in 1996 and later released on Centrediscs. Jaeger and the *Two New Hours* team continued its involvement in preserving and sharing Schafer's creative goals when the program recorded his "environmental opera" *Princess of the Stars* in 1997. Again, Jaeger was immersed in Schafer's sound world for a week while they recorded several performances of the opera on Wildcat Lake in the Haliburton Forest.

German-born composer Hildegard Westerkamp has also had a significant influence on Canadian composition and sound studies, and her participation in the WSP influenced the development of her creative practice and an ethics of composition. All of Westerkamp's electroacoustic works incorporate the environment in its context (McCartney 2006; see also Steenhuisen 2009), that is, with only moderate processing so that the original "real" sounds remain recognizable. For Westerkamp as a soundscape composer, this aesthetic approach to sounds, namely maintaining their recognizability, stems from an ethical stance that developed in her work with the World Soundscape Project and later with acoustic ecology. Through the WSP, Westerkamp became passionate about "issues of environmental listening and active engagement with our soundscapes" (Westerkamp 2002, 51). She insists that acoustic ecology, or soundscape studies, as "the study of the interrelationship between sound, nature, and society" (52), was first initiated by composers and musicians: "We are the ones that make listening and working with sound and music our profession ... If we – who are specialists in listening and sound-making – are not concerned about the acoustic environment, then who will be?" (52). From her acoustic ecological standpoint, soundscape composition must deepen both the awareness and understanding of "relationships between living beings and the soundscape" (52).

From Schafer and Westerkamp, the CEE has inherited an approach to spatial ecologies and listening that remains "hungry," seeing all sound sources as resources to mine for aesthetic purposes. In the case of these two influential composers, Indigenous knowledge, histories, and cosmologies are absent from the relationships acknowledged and constructed within their works, such as Westerkamp's *Beneath the Forest Floor*. Robinson critiques works like Schafer's *Music for Wilderness Lake* as "representational landscape compositions" that "resolutely depict (re-sound) the landscape in contrast to Indigenous cosmologies ... that think of song as being 'for' the land, rather than 'about' it" (2020, 189). The CEE composes from specific relationships to land and place, and this should not be surprising because we all bring our positionalities and relationalities to our creative practices. For example, the Supertrio collaboration was influenced by their time immersed in the sights and sounds of Banff, and the ensemble's rehearsal studios are immortalized through work titles. And yet, we as listeners to the CEE can bring additional – even conflicting – relationships to land and place as we listen. Regarding *Supertrio*, one might listen through a recognition of Indigenous sovereignty and treaty obligations (Banff being in Treaty 7 territory). Or listening through Toronto spaces may bring up experiences of gentrification, anti-Blackness in certain neighbourhoods, or lack of safety in certain spaces for women and/or feminine-presenting bodies. Ultimately, the CEE's output represents a relationship to place that is shaped by sonic ecologists like Schafer and Westerkamp, and that reflects their own experiences moving through such spaces. Yet Robinson challenges us to hear these relationships not as objective and inevitable but as subjective – both to the CEE as creators and us as listeners – and flexible. We can acknowledge and even appreciate those limitations that are unavoidable, and then respond by listening through and beyond, based on our own experiences and positionalities.

The CEE's relationship to each other while performing embraces each one's sonic positionality and the background and interests they present. This acceptance and responsiveness remind me of Westerkamp's views on listening. When Westerkamp speaks of listening, she is often talking about listening on a soundwalk or immersed in some kind of natural, acoustic soundscape. Nonetheless, her description of "true receptive listening" in a 2015 keynote talk aligns with what I've witnessed in the CEE, and what I think is necessary for a group of variable size, with variable gear over decades, to persist. Westerkamp explains: "If we open our ears to this experience of sound unfolding as a continuous now it inevitably includes an opening to surprises, to the unexpected, to the difficult and uncomfortable, to noise or potential discomforts with silence. It means staying with the sound for a time no matter what reactions it may elicit in us" (2015). The members of the CEE are open to the sounds that the other members create, taking each one in and responding in kind, even if they may not love every sound created by a bandmate. The listening and response are more important than an aesthetically pleasing moment. But as they continue to listen, build trust, and learn about each other, they find those moments of connection and aesthetic satisfaction more frequently. As I've discussed elsewhere in this book, the CEE's improvisations are typically slow-moving, without sudden shifts. This is because it is a listening-based practice. They must experience "sound unfolding as a continuous now" and "[stay] with the sound for a time" (2015).

Westerkamp describes the kind of listening outlined above as disruptive because "it asserts change inside us over time, and as a result eventually in the soundscape, in our community with others, in society at large." The overarching requirement for achieving this kind of listening is "an inner place of non-threat, support, and safety" (2015). This is the kind of situation that the CEE aims to create for its members and has successfully created for decades, which has enabled the group to survive and new members to be welcomed in.

Andra McCartney refers to Westerkamp's aesthetic goal of "knowing one's place," which she explains as "trying to understand as much as possible about the social, political, ecological and acoustic aspects of a location before creating a piece based on sounds recorded in that place" (2006, 34). This desire is possibly a significant factor in her frequent choice to use sounds from her own home soundscapes – Vancouver, the Canadian West Coast, and northern Germany. Her intention to "know" the place and to respect the sounds' self-expressions impacts the final product. Westerkamp considers listening to be "a continual and gentle process of opening" (2015). This idea of continual process resonates with the role of listening (both metaphorically and literally) within the CEE. The long-term process of building trust and familiarity has been central to the CEE's success and longevity. The familiarity within the CEE is not only between its human members but also with long-term rehearsal and performance spaces.

Spatial Sonic Ecologies in Toronto: CEE Rehearsal and Performance Spaces

As I discussed in chapter 4, the CEE approaches rehearsals and performances similarly. While they acknowledge and appreciate the energy of a live audience, their collective creative process does not significantly change between rehearsals and performances. Over the group's decades of activity, rehearsals have been essential for bonding the members musically and socially. They also speak fondly of their rehearsal spaces over the years.

With the group's origins as University of Toronto students, the CEE's first rehearsal spaces were at the university. By the mid-1970s, the CEE was able to rent a rehearsal/studio space in a friend's building: this studio is known as Davies. They then moved to the Camden studio, followed by Artscape, a not-for-profit organization that facilitates affordable spaces for artists and cultural organizations, among others. At the time, the CEE had grant funding to support the rental and maintenance of a studio space. When they lost that funding in the mid-2000s, they decided to shut down the studio. Home recording gear was more affordable at this point, so they did not require a designated acoustic space to record. Stillwell explains: "We can record pretty much anywhere" (personal communication, 25 February 2020).

Following the group's hiatus through most of 2005 and all of 2006, the CEE shifted to rehearsing in members' houses: in Lake's basement and dining room and once in Stillwell's old basement. When I asked about quality sound systems, everyone reassured me that Lake had a good home sound system. Stillwell declared: "We both had the audiophile sickness" (personal communication, 25 February 2020). The CEE's current rehearsal space is Stillwell's basement, which they have nicknamed "7 Below." Stillwell assured me that he also has an excellent home sound system with speakers that he built with his father (personal communication, 25 February 2020). Stillwell's house is located near the Scarborough Bluffs, in which there are some beautiful lookout points.

These studio names will ring familiar to those who know the CEE's discography: the ensemble has pieces named *Davies*, *Camden*, and *7 Below*, and an album entitled *Bluffer's Lookout* (2014).[2] These pieces are not programmatic depictions of the studios after which they are named; rather, the names are used to document and honour these moments of CEE history.

Davies (1974) appears on the 1990 album *Catbird Seat*. It is written for accordion and live electronics, with the accordion the main feature throughout. The CEE premiered it in 1979 with Canadian accordionist Joseph Macerollo as the featured guest; Macerollo commissioned the work with a grant from the Ontario Arts Council. The CEE performed the piece at the Holland Festival on 8 June 1985, with Dutch accordionist Astrid in 't Veld. In 1986, Jaeger composed *Shadow Box* for accordionist Joseph Petric, who then performed *Davies* with the CEE in the late 1980s and 1990s, including on *Catbird Seat*.[3] The liner note does not reveal the title's reference to the ensemble's studio; rather, it discusses only the compositional process, in which each CEE member composed his own section of the work based on the following instruction: "The accordion was to be processed electronically throughout the work, and it was to be the featured solo instrument throughout." Then, the CEE members assembled the discrete parts into one continuous piece.

7 Below is the opening track on *Bluffer's Lookout*. This album's brief liner note acknowledges their current studio space without explicitly connecting it to the title of the piece or the album: "A nice long composition dedicated to the comfy confines of our basement recording studio in Scarborough." The piece includes Bolton on violin and effects, Jaeger on laptop, Jim Montgomery on laptop, and Stillwell on Chapman Stick and laptop. (John Kameel Farah did not take part in this piece, as his extensive travels meant he was not able to participate in every piece on the album.)

The CEE's performance history is also a documentation of spaces in Toronto, an issue close to the heart of Toronto-based musicians as gentrification (and more recently, the COVID-19 pandemic) has closed performance spaces that musicians of various genres rely upon for financial, social, and artistic survival. Some of the CEE's performance spaces highlight long-standing organizations or institutions that have been able to secure space for decades (e.g., the University of Toronto). Some have needed to change spaces over the years (e.g., Music Gallery), a reality that reflects not only changing organizational needs but also shifts in Toronto's real estate. Other spaces are rented by individuals or organizations who do not have their own designated space in Toronto. The CEE's relationship to performances in Toronto is a single case among countless others that reveal how Toronto's creative communities and reputation as a cultural city rely on access to performance spaces (Finch 2015; Ross 2016; Ross 2017; Dovercourt 2020).

During the early quartet days and into the trio era, the University of Toronto was an important venue, and one easily accessible to students. Throughout the 1970s and early 1980s, the CEE performed at several different theatre venues, including Theatre Upstairs, Theatre Downstairs, the Winchester Street Theatre, and St Lawrence Hall. The early-1980s theatrical productions *Nightbloom* and *Eye of the Beholder* were both performed at Comus Music Theatre, a venue that hosted many additional CEE performances. In the trio era, the group also performed at the Church of the Holy Trinity as part of CBC's Free Noon Hour Concert Series and at the du Maurier Theatre Centre, which opened in 1986 at the Toronto Harbourfront.

The most important venue for the CEE in terms of consistency and longevity is the Music Gallery. The organization itself has lived in a few different spaces in Toronto. The CEE began performing there in 1976 and continued through the quintet/sextet/quintet era of the late 1990s and early 2000s, when the Music Gallery provided a regular home for the CEE's concert series. The CEE also had single concerts at the brewpub C'est What, a long-standing feature in the St Lawrence Market area, and Factory Theatre Studio, a one-hundred-seat studio in Toronto's Fashion District. In the late 2000s, the CEE performed at the Arts & Letters Club for the first time, and The TRANZAC became an important venue for the CEE since the earliest concerts featuring John Kameel Farah, then a special guest rather than a member. Located in the Annex neighbourhood of Toronto, The TRANZAC has been an important venue for Toronto-based musicians of diverse genres, with its three different rental spaces accommodating different audience sizes and sound needs. As a not-for-profit organization dedicated to offering its space for community arts, it has affordable rental fees.

In the CEE's most recent era (with the addition of Farah and David Sutherland), the group has continued to perform at The TRANZAC. In 2012, the Canadian Music Centre head office (the Chalmers House) renovated its building in Toronto and created a small but flexible space called the Chalmers Performance Space that can be rented for performance, recording, workshops, and special events. The CEE has performed in this new space, including to launch *Bluffer's Lookout* (17 July 2014) and to perform at the launch of Norma Beecroft's book *Conversations with Post World War II Pioneers of Electronic Music* (26 September 2015). The Arts & Letters Club became the CEE's most important venue throughout the 2010s. Jaeger praises its acoustics: "I imagine there are moments when [the CEE] feels absolutely orchestral, like in the Arts & Letters Club. It's a lovely, big space. It's not big but it's high, and there's volume. There's room" (personal communication, 10 June 2016). While concerts there achieve a more casual feel before and after performances, with alcohol available in the lounge adjacent to the Great Hall and attendees milling about and approaching the musicians, the CEE's actual performances rely on conventional concert hall rituals of a quiet, focused audience, all facing the musicians at the front of the room.

Lake's last performance with the CEE was on 4 May 2012, at the Arts & Letters Club. The CEE premiered *No Dim Pearls* by their friend John S. Gray (b. 1953), who had composed a piece for them in 2004 entitled *Three Old Friends*. In the video, we can see the group is set up along a long table, facing out to the audience.[4] Montgomery sits on the left end of the table (from the audience's perspective), with Jaeger, Lake, Stillwell, and Bolton along the back side from left to right. In discussions about rehearsal spaces, Stillwell has underlined that electronic music sounds great through headphones, so the acoustic space isn't as important. In this live performance, though, there is an acoustic element that cannot be completely perceived through headphones. Both Lake and Bolton are playing acoustic instruments, trumpet and violin, respectively. (This performance occurred before Bolton purchased an electric violin.) While both instruments are miked and processed, because their sounds are produced acoustically, acoustic trails of the instruments hit the ears of listeners in addition to any sounds picked up and/or processed and transduced through the speakers. The acoustic feedback regarding timbre and intonation is also an important part of the listening process for Lake and Bolton as performers.

As I discussed in chapter 4, when the CEE performs, they exhibit few physical signs of collaboration, such as eye contact or expressive gestures, yet despite long stretches of seeming non-coordination, they are always listening to each other. In this performance, Montgomery must provide two clear conducting gestures – one at the beginning (1:50) and another two-thirds of the way through the piece (7:31) – in order to achieve the composer's instructions of coordination in those moments. Montgomery's opening gesture also starts a large clock that provides a running time for the musicians to coordinate with their individual score instructions.

Through the dimmed lighting, spatial placement of the ensemble at the front, and the musicians' concentrated faces, this performance indicates to audience members what kind of listening is appropriate: fixed attention with little to no corporeal response (until the applause at the piece's conclusion). In this performance, one section in particular sticks out to me and makes me wonder about what responsive or affective listening could look or feel like at a CEE performance. Starting at 5:54, there is a synthesized drum kit pattern. As I discussed in chapter 3, steady pulses are relatively rare in the CEE's sound, though not completely absent. When they do occur, they are typically electronic beats, making the use of a drum kit sample stand out. This drum kit pattern invites the listener into a groove, which is reinforced through the trumpet's and violin's long tones. If the CEE was performing in a club rather than a concert space, this is where I imagine the bodies of the audience would shift from a general responsive sway to motions coordinated with the pulse. But because the CEE is performing at the Arts & Letters Club, the performance space and audience expectations mean that the audience is prepared to use only their ears to listen carefully and to minimize engagement of their bodies.[5] Soon the drumbeat seems to invite a cacophony of textures that unsettle the listener's sense of groove. While the beat remains constant for two minutes, it's increasingly difficult to "lock into it" as a listener, even more so when Jaeger and Montgomery play rapid high-pitched sounds and echoey water droplets that do not synchronize at all with the beat.

This performance of *No Dim Pearls* at the Arts & Letters Club reflects the more recent relationship the CEE has established with this membership-based organization in downtown Toronto. Such patronage has been essential across the ensemble's many decades. The CEE has been hosted by many different arts organizations, such as Somewhere There, AMBiENT PiNG, the Toronto Sound Festival, Nuit Blanche, Spillage Festival, and Cabbagetown Arts Festival, in addition to the CEE's own events like MEGAJAM and series like Guitar Boogie. None of these presenting organizations have their own performance spaces. Thus, they rely on the availability and affordability of spaces in Toronto, both for-profit, like the brewpub C'est What, and not-for-profit, like The TRANZAC. As I discuss in more detail in chapter 6, the CEE's access to many of these spaces has also been afforded to them because their existing institutional connections privilege them over others who did not study at the University of Toronto, work for the CBC or the Music Gallery, or have extensive networks within the city's main cultural institutions.

Virtual Listening Ecologies: Intimacy over Radio and Recording

The listening spaces created by the CEE are not contained to the physical places in which they create their music (e.g., concert space). Their music has been broadcast on CBC Radio, which reaches the ears of individual Canadians in their cars and homes via loudspeakers, or, these days, via headphones through streaming to computers and smartphones. Their albums are perceived through home stereo systems or headphones. In this section, I discuss how both radio and recording construct intimacy. Through the example of Bolton's *This Is This*, I also examine how an electronic composer can create a virtual space and how intimacy is constructed through recorded voices.

Recording changed our relationship to listening because we could now play something back at any moment, repeating it as many times as we desired, and always hearing what Lacey calls "the self-same sounds" (2013, 12).[6] While the listener will never be exactly the same with each repeated listening, the sounds on the recording remain the "self-same." In Eric F. Clarke's analysis of the recording's impact on listening, he contrasts music's past, which relied on what Paul Sanden identifies as spatial and temporal liveness, with today's environment in which, to quote critic Nicholas Spice, "music is everywhere, streaming through the interstices between the lumpy materials of life, filling the gaps in the continuum of human activity and contact, silting up in vast unchartable archives" (quoted in Clarke 2007, 47). Though Spice's comment was published in 1995, Clarke illustrates its continued applicability in his analysis of new listening platforms and resulting listening ecologies.

The history of the CEE is also a history of recording, at least since the 1970s. The CEE's first albums were LPs, followed by CDs. Since 2013, the CEE has released their albums on Bandcamp, a website that allows listeners to stream or purchase downloads of the albums. In 2019, the CEE also re-released its debut album from 1977 on Bandcamp, simultaneous to a CD release by Artoffact Records. This history of recording media aligns with what Lacey calls a "'craze' for miniaturization ... with the availability of mobile devices small and flexible enough to allow a personalized soundscape to be carried along as the user weaves through public and private spaces. These devices give the listener the impression of control, overlaying the ambient sonic environment with an intimate soundscape of their own choosing" (2013, 12).

Regardless of where it occurs – even in public alongside other people all listening to whatever is played through loudspeakers – listening is a personal experience (Lacey 2013, 17). Clarke (2007) claims that the repeatability of recordings results in one hearing in the exact same way, echoing Hans Keller, who declared recordings "anti-musical" (1990, 22); yet such a charge denies the agency of humans whose act of musicking is listening. Improvisation scholars in particular, such as George E. Lewis and Ajay Heble, accentuate the listener's agency in crafting a new path with each listening, even to the same recording, or "self-same sounds."

The CEE's online presence networks the group and its listeners in innovative ways, from Bandcamp statistics (streaming and purchase numbers) to social media interactions. Lacey sees two sides to this newer digital reality: "On the one hand, this means that listening is a practice that is increasingly surveilled and increasingly open to measurement and commodification. On the other hand, it is also a sign of a persistent desire to create and partake in forms of collective listening to mediated music, sound and speech, albeit in virtual space" (2013, 155). Sharing sounds online through new digital platforms has been an important part of the CEE's story since long before the group's presence on social media or Bandcamp. As I discuss in chapter 3, Stillwell first encountered Lake on CompuServe, to which Stillwell was posting some of his music. Because of that networked connection, Lake invited Stillwell to compose for the CEE, followed soon after by an offer of membership.

Lacey contrasts the listening facilitated by recording – in which "a multitude of listeners ... experience identical recordings in separate locations" and outside of coordinated time (2013, 125) – with public radio. Because radio is experienced simultaneously by an unknown, unseen number of listeners, "new imagined communities" (125) are possible out of what John Durham Peters calls "a diaspora of simultaneous intimacies" (1997, 14). This sense of connection and the formation of a new imagined community is certainly true for *Two New Hours*, Jaeger and Lake's CBC Radio show, which I discuss in greater detail in chapter 6. While a lot of radio listening has been deemed passive (Berland 1990), this is not the case for the *Two New Hours* audience, who intentionally gathered each Sunday evening. The program was not for the casual or distracted listener.

Because of Canada's diverse population and vast geography with large distances between cities, the radio was seen as a medium to unify the nation and was often paralleled to the railroad. Jody Berland credits radio with "unique capacities to map our symbolic and social environment" (1990, 191). While this impact of ending social isolation was more striking on remote Canadian listeners in radio's earlier days (the 1920s and 1930s), the importance of radio as a connection has persisted for the CEE's community. Given that the ensemble's performance history has been concentrated in Toronto, the reach of recordings and radio broadcasts across the country has been essential in building the CEE's audience and fostering a virtual community.

Radio has also been described as an intimate medium, which helps to explain why laws and policies have aimed to "protect" listeners from certain subject materials and sounds (Kuffert, 2016, 37). Glenn Gould believed that radio could achieve this kind of intimacy with the listener despite physical separation. His *Solitude Trilogy* (1967–77), for instance, lacks a voiced interviewer, which places the voices in direct conversation with the listener, rather than the listener simply overhearing someone else's conversation.

Transportable recording equipment erases the boundary between public and private spaces in electroacoustic music. The soundscape of nature found outdoors generally signifies a public space with free and easy access – depending, of course, on which specific natural environment one wishes to explore. Alternatively, the sounds of the home (e.g., conversations with friends and family, sharing life stories, or engaging in sexual acts) signify a private space, where intimacy is a privilege granted or earned. Social conventions – and sometimes government regulation (Blatterer et al. 2010; McKeon 2005) – keep these activities in the private sphere.

In the work of soundscape composers like Westerkamp, the blurring of public and private becomes essential for creative expression. The composer can manipulate the sonic material, shifting once-private sharings towards public space. The sounds become public through listening, either through live diffusion or on recordings. Yet, they retain the referential significance of the private sphere. The intimacy of the private sounds is often foregrounded through techniques such as close microphone placement, which creates a "dry" voice that expresses directly and clearly to the listener.

Sounds can also extend from public to private. While the specific locations in which real-world sounds are recorded may have meaning to the recordist (who may also be the composer), that specificity is likely to be lost for most listeners. However, general spaces (e.g., grocery store, waterfall, train station) can be related to each listener's personal life and private memory. The CEE's music has included sampled real-world sounds, but only rarely. Nonetheless, their electronic sound worlds can also vividly inspire a listener's personal memory, with timbres and gestures reminiscent of real-world experiences (recall Sanden's "virtuality" and Smalley's gestural surrogacies in chapter 4).

Soundscape elements shift to private spaces through private listening contexts (i.e., the home stereo and personal listening devices). Nicola Dibben's work (2009) on intimacy in the recorded medium insists that intimacy is intrinsic on some level to all fixed-medium works that are designed to be, or can be, experienced in private space, at home or through headphones. Voices heard, even of crowds, seem to be inside one's head when heard through headphones, and extraneous noises are shut out to allow a more intensified, detailed listening experience (Stern 2003). The sounds of nature fill the private space, creating an intimacy perhaps only rarely experienced in the original public space.

Glenn Gould famously retreated from the live concert hall to the studio because he believed that the studio facilitated idealized performance. Gould experimented with different microphone placements and, most notably, splicing different takes together not only to eliminate mistakes but also to combine interpretations according to his imagination (Gould 1966, 53). Gould, like the CEE, integrated the roles of composer, performer, listener, and manager (or record engineer) through his studio work. The listener to recordings by Gould or the CEE doesn't know who has done what. Gould believed this situation to be ideal, as it creates a "zero-to-one relationship" between listener and artist (Gould 1990, 318). As Barry Mauer explains: "The communion he sought was between listener and sound, not listener and performer, listener and composer, or listener and other audience members" (2010, 104).

In chapter 4, I discussed the importance of virtuosity for audiences of live music. By contrast, Gould believed that virtuosity drew too much attention to the performer and away from the music, whereas with recordings, as Mauer writes, "the new listener chooses a recording by a performer who lets the music speak for itself. Ideally, the performer disappears and all that remains is the listener and the music" (2010, 104). In some ways, the CEE achieves this same kind of disappearance in their live performances as well, as the group has minimal body movements and their virtuosity mostly does not have the typical physical manifestations of acoustic Euro-American classical music.

Gould desired a new kind of listening context and a new kind of listener. He affirmed recordings in particular as giving more agency to the listener: the listener can stop and start the recording, play back or skip a particular section, change the volume and adjust the mix, and shift their position in relation to the speakers (Mauer 2010, 102). Gould writes: "The listener is able to indulge preferences and, through the electronic modifications with which he endows the listening experience, impose his own personality upon the work. As he does so, he transforms that work, and his relation to it, from an artistic to an environmental experience" (1966, 59). Gould's dream was for the listener to have playback devices that would enable them to splice together their ideal version.

Rose Bolton's 2004 composition *This Is This* manifests some of Gould's ideas regarding recording and new listening. *This Is This* is one of only a few CEE pieces that features the recorded voice. In the version recorded for *Bluffer's Lookout* (2014), the voices include Bolton, Jaeger, Montgomery, and Stillwell, in addition to Jaeger's wife Sally and Stillwell's wife Lynn Chan. Bolton identifies the text sources in the album notes: "In this version of the piece, news and stories of interest from the 1913 Toronto World are being read over excerpts of a sermon about happiness and misery, written by John Donne."[7]

The piece contains two primary sound sources: voices reading various passages, principally from the news, and synthesizer pitches that create varying densities of texture. Based on the synthesizer layers and the number and type of voices, I group *This Is This* into five sections, with two sections further subdivided (see table 5.1).

The piece opens with a consonant synthesizer interval (C-E, then A added to create a minor triad), and within seconds, a woman's voice begins speaking: "They say that the world is made of sea and land as though they were equal. But we know that there is more sea in the western than in the eastern hemisphere." The voice has a slight reverb on it, but my ears feel close to her voice because the microphone has picked up subtle mouth sounds as she speaks and the voice's volume remains above that of the synthesizers. Gently whispering voices are barely audible in the left and right channels, and the discrete synthesizer pitches crescendo and decrescendo. I know that this is the voice of Rose Bolton: the composer. I imagine that someone without that knowledge would have a different interpretation from mine. In this case, this knowledge has two impacts on my interpretation: first, that the composer has decided to speak these opening words herself suggests to me that they are some kind of overarching philosophy for the work (this is only my interpretation rather than Bolton's acknowledged intention); second, my understanding of Bolton's personality as gentle and relatively soft-spoken reinforces how I interpret the mood of this opening section (0:00–2:03). With two minutes of only this one woman's voice, an unfamiliar listener may predict that this will be the only voice for the entire piece. Thus, when a new voice enters at 2:04, it is striking.

Section B (2:04–4:11) is characterized by the entrance of three new voices, including those of two men. The vocal layers become contrapuntal. The new woman's voice and first man's voice are telling the same story of a destructive wave, but they are separated temporally and spatially: woman in the left channel and man in the centre. A second man's voice enters with a new story (2:51), another distressing report about a natural disaster in northern Hondo, Japan. The dreariness of the stories is amplified by the increasing synthesizer layers that surge in both

Table 5.1 Formal outline and description of *This Is This*.

Timing	Section	Description	Voice source
0:00–2:03	A	• consonant synthesizer pitches at a medium volume • sound of woman's voice gently narrating about the earth and universe, and then about happiness and misery • soft whispers from a woman's voice in the left and then right channels	Rose Bolton
2:04–4:09	B1 (2:04–3:56)	• additional voices added to the mix: first a woman (left channel) and then a man (centre), both reading the same story about a destructive wave • new man's voice enters (2:51; centre) with a story about hundreds dying in northern Hondo • synthesized sounds surge across the mix in both directions • only the woman's voice remains (3:23)	Sally Jaeger Paul Stillwell David Jaeger
	B2 (3:57–4:09)	• second man's voice returns, with a news story about destruction in Hokkaido • the woman's voice is reduced to a whisper • a man's voice begins to tell a new story about a school closing (4:06)	David Jaeger Paul Stillwell
4:10–4:57	C	• as the previous stories continue, a woman's voice (left) relatively low in the mix tells the story of someone in solitary confinement • the synthesizer texture reduces • a new man's voice (4:21; centre) enters at relatively loud volume simultaneous to a woman's whisper (right, with increasing reverb): "thou shalt subdue the earth" • the Hokkaido story returns (4:40); synthesizers entirely absent (4:41)	Rose Bolton David Jaeger Jim Montgomery
4:58–6:57	D	• synthesizers re-enter, louder than in the previous sections • the stories at the end of section C continue • a new story about a farmer (5:25), read by a man • women's whispers in both left and right channel; exact words are difficult to discern • a new woman's voice enters with a story about tonic treatment (5:47) • woman's voice tells a story about a violent prisoner (6:25) • final statement from a man about school being cancelled (6:48)	Paul Stillwell Lynn Chan Rose Bolton
6:58–10:06	E1 (6:58–8:06)	• only women's voices remain: one story about gold (centre), another about nerves and blood (left), and a third about a procession to a cemetery (right); see figure 5.1 • reduced texture and volume of synthesizers; surges in volume and density (7:48–)	Rose Bolton Lynn Chan Sally Jaeger
	E2 (8:07–9:02)	• only one woman's voice remains • the synthesizer layers drown out the voice, until the voice (centre) fades and stops (ca 8:42) • woman's voice in left channel returns (8:38–9:02) but is too quiet in the mix to discern words	Rose Bolton Unknown woman (too quiet to identify)
	E3 (9:03–10:06)	• synthesizers remain alone, with pitches in increased dissonance with each other, darker timbres, and lower ranges (see figure 5.2) • arrives on a quiet G major triad as the synthesizers fade into silence	

Figure 5.1 Channel placement of voices: Bolton's voice in both L and R (perceived as centre), Chan's voice in L, and Jaeger's voice in R (6:58–7:36).

dynamics and spatialization across the mix in both directions, seeming to depict the waves of destruction in the stories. Soon, the woman's voice alone remains (3:23). The three voices in this first part of Section B are Sally Jaeger, Paul Stillwell, and David Jaeger – again, I know all of these people and can easily recognize their voices. Sally Jaeger is herself a professional storyteller, so she seems particularly suited to this role of narrator. The entrance of a man's voice again (David Jaeger) is striking, but to my ears, this is not a new section but perhaps a subsection of Section B. The overall sound remains consistent, and no new voices have been added yet. The woman's voice – which I assume is still Sally Jaeger – has been reduced to a whisper, leaving the focus on the story of Hokkaido. A man's voice (Stillwell) begins to tell a new story about a school closing (4:07).

The shift from Section B to C is imprecise. The entrance of a new story at 4:06 could sound to some ears like a new section, but in my outline, I delay the new section a few seconds until there is a textural shift in the synthesizer parts (4:10) and a new voice and story. The man's story acts as a brief transition between Sections B and C. The Hokkaido story continues (Jaeger) as the first voice returns (Bolton), this time with a story about a prisoner in solitary confinement. The synthesizer textures have been greatly reduced, leaving the voices more exposed. A new man's voice enters with an unsettling opening phrase: "When great calamities such as this arise" (4:21). This new voice is Jim Montgomery. I'm not sure how quickly someone who doesn't know Montgomery would notice, but this section is the only time his voice is present in the piece, which gives his words even more weight, in my interpretation. Just as Montgomery

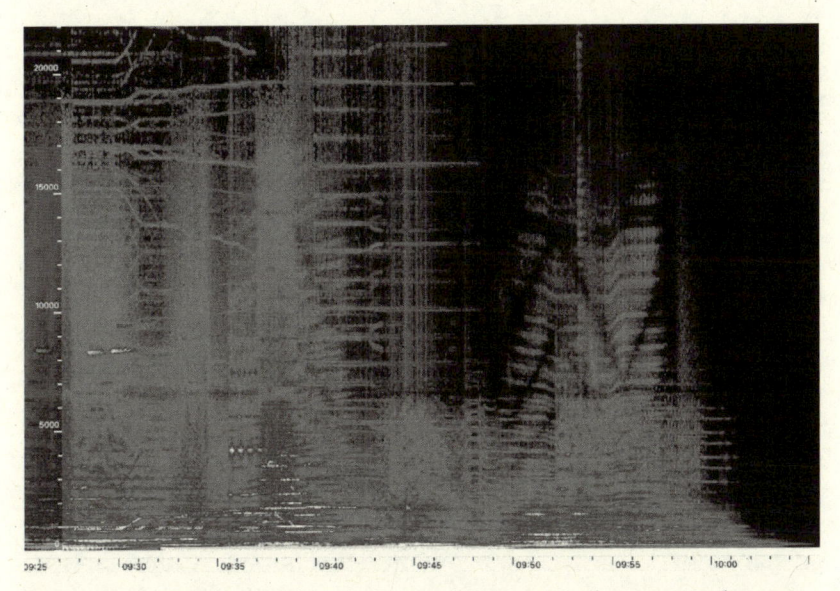

Figure 5.2 Spectrogram of synthesizer-only Section E3 showing simultaneous, moving layers across a broad frequency range until fade out (9:30–10:06).

finishes stating "Thou shalt subdue the earth," the voice (Jaeger) telling the story of Hokkaido re-enters (4:40), followed almost immediately by the synthesizers dropping out entirely. The woman's voice (Bolton) has been reduced to whispers with heavy reverb in both the left and right channels. This vocal staging is a contradiction, as whispers are spoken in close proximity but reverb connotes large spaces and distance.

When the synthesizers re-enter at a louder dynamic level than in previous sections (4:58), I hear this as the beginning of a new section, (Section D, 4:58–6:57), even as the stories from the end of Section C continue. The contrapuntal storytelling expands as a new story about a farmer is read by a man's voice (Stillwell). Beneath this story, women's whispers with indiscernible words are present in both the left and right channels. I suspect the voice is Bolton's, but it's too difficult to confirm. A new voice and a new story enter (5:47), this one about a tonic treatment. This is the one voice I do not know well, but by process of elimination from the voice credits, I can conclude that this is Lynn Chan. The levity of a story about tonic treatments is contrasted by a story about a violent prisoner, read by another woman's voice (Bolton). Beneath all of these vocal layers, the synthesizers continue to surge discrete pitches in and out of the mix, in the low, mid, and high range, with different timbres. The section ends with a man's voice (Stillwell) reading a story about a school cancellation (6:48).

The final section, Section E (6:58–10:06), is the longest; I divide it into three subsections, but I hear it as one long section because of the presence of only women's voices until subsection E3. The three women's voices are placed variously in the mix (left, centre, and right) to help delineate the contrapuntal lines in the listener's ears.

The spoken texts in this section are no longer as bleak as the previous stories of death, destruction, and violence. These women speak about gold, a now-outdated understanding of nerves and blood, and a procession to a cemetery. The synthesizer layers reduce their textures and volume, allowing us to hear the different voices clearly. Particularly at 7:48, though, the synthesizer sounds surge more dramatically in volume and density, creating more competition with the voices for attention. In subsection E2, only one voice remains (Bolton, centre). The synthesizer layers continue to compete with the voice, soon enough drowning out the voice until it fades and stops (ca 8:42). As this voice is fading out, a woman's voice in the left channel returns (8:38–9:02), but its volume in the mix is too low for me to discern any words or to identify the vocal source. When this unknown voice finally fades out completely, the synthesizers are left alone in subsection E3. The pitches are increasingly dissonant in relation to each other. The lower register expands and somber timbres increase. It seems like *This Is This* will end in a dreary mood, but in the final moments, the synthesizers arrive on a quiet G major triad as they all fade into silence.

As I've already discussed throughout the description above, my knowledge of the people whose voices were recorded for *This Is This* makes my experience of the piece much more personal, which points to how widely interpretations of any piece of music can vary. In addition, it means I likely focus more on the identity of the vocal sources than on other sonic elements. The piece feels more intimate to me because I know these people – and it likely made the piece more personal for Bolton too, as she treated the recorded voices of her friends and bandmates.

Because I know each vocal source and their gender identities, I suspect that I have suggested a more gender-essentialized interpretation than other listeners. Gender is performed through the voice, but register and timbre do not map on narrowly to gender identity. A listener with no knowledge of the individuals recorded for this work may have different gender interpretations of the voices, or may not think in those terms at all. In addition, the intimacy of the voices as experienced through headphones and enhanced by certain vocal staging (e.g., close microphone placement, whispers) may inspire more queer and/or sensual experiences of the work (Woloshyn 2017), whereas my friendship with these individuals means I cannot disentangle my platonic associations with them as people when I hear their voices. The same familiarity that enhances the idea of social intimacy in my listening may foreclose other potential interpretations or experiences.

The simultaneous vocal layers of *This Is This* recall Glenn Gould's concept of "contrapuntal radio," which he implemented most famously in his radio documentary *The Idea of North* (1967). In this documentary and the two others of his *Solitude Trilogy* (1967–77), two or more voices are heard simultaneously. Such vocal counterpoint puts atypical demands on the talk-radio listener, as now the listener may shift awareness between the two voices, unable to process completely each word and phrase of each speaker at once. But a listener may also potentially perceive relationships (e.g., convergence or divergence) between the voices, similar to contrapuntal music in which the musical lines are independent but also dialogic. According to Kevin McNeilly, "Gould the musician/composer/producer is foremost a proactive listener; for him, listening is a means of participating, directly, crucially, in the multiple streams of human presence in the world" (1996, n.p.).

The CEE has always made sure that concerts and recordings balance the compositional voices of its individual members. On *Bluffer's Lookout*, *This Is This* is Bolton's compositional contribution. It stands out in the CEE's output for its inclusion of recorded voices. In other ways, though, the piece aligns with the CEE's social and sonic influences. *This Is This* invites many listening possibilities, depending on one's connection to the many different recorded voices and their vocal staging. Listening at home on a stereo or with headphones does not make either Robinson's fixed or Demers's aesthetic listening inevitable. One might listen to *This Is This* and other CEE tracks sitting motionless in the dark, alone or with others instructed not to talk during the piece. Alternatively, one has the freedom to make listening part of other activities or to embrace one's body (and those of other listeners) as part of the listening process.

Listening beyond Regimes

This chapter has demonstrated that even the seemingly counter-institutional listening approaches of Cage, Schafer, and Westerkamp establish their own listening regimes based on Western ontologies of music. The CEE has inherited these approaches and they exhibit a hungry listening that relies on "'fixed listening' strategies that are part of a larger reorientation toward Western categorizations of single-sense engagement" (Robinson 2020, 40). Robinson explains that while teleological, fixed listening can be appropriate, it becomes harmful when it remains the unmarked norm and excludes other ways of listening and expressing these other listening values.

In its history, the CEE has performed in ways that allow for more spatial subjectivities and responsive listening, particularly when in non-conventional concert spaces. In conventional theatre and concert spaces, though, the CEE is positioned within spatial ecologies that compel fixed listening and aesthetic contemplation rather than responsive or affective listening. However, it also falls on us as listeners to develop self-reflexive listening and embrace "the affective feel, timbre, touch, and texture of sound" (Robinson 2020, 38) in defiance of the spatial ecologies in which we find ourselves. In private listening encounters with the CEE, express the intimacy of your musicking through "new temporalities of wonder" (Robinson 2020, 53), or perhaps, like Gould, embrace ecstatic listening. Mauer explains: "Photographs of Gould listening to his recordings in the studio show him dancing in ecstasy, enraptured by the sound, communing in solitude even though others were watching him. Gould reveals to us that his ecstasy can be ours" (2010, 106).

In this chapter, I have emphasized the role of listener in the CEE's musicking, both with the CEE members as listeners and with those listening to their music in physical and virtual spaces. My discussions of inherited listening regimes and performance spaces in Toronto both point to institutional power in establishing and upholding musicking norms for the CEE. In chapter 6, I examine the institutional context in more depth, focusing on interpersonal connections, institutional access and privilege, and institutional patterns of exclusion that have impacted the CEE's career and those of its individual members across the decades.

Postlude: Listening through a Pandemic

The CEE experienced a renewed energy following their 2020 residency at Carnegie Mellon University. They were eager to perform live together while Farah was in Toronto and to record new music. Indeed, they performed at a monthly Frequency Freaks concert on 7 March (minus Bolton, who was out of the country). However, in only a few short days, the threat of COVID-19 in Toronto and beyond brought gatherings, live music, and travel to a halt.

Jaeger recounts in a September 2020 feature for *The WholeNote* magazine the origins of a remote collaboration process the CEE initiated as the pandemic isolation of the spring continued. It seems to have started with Farah, who is quoted in the essay: "I felt unable to make solo music because of the stress and isolation of the COVID-19 pandemic, which left me feeling very little creative inspiration. I thought maybe the answer would be instead to be creative in a collaboration, so I asked Paul Stillwell to send me some electronic sounds to work with. He sent me a beautiful synth drone and I added piano over it" (quoted in Jaeger 2020). Farah was so encouraged by this type of collaboration – outside of shared time and space – that the track was then passed along to the remaining members of the CEE, who each added a part. They have now completed six "Pass the Tracks," with each track initiated by a different member of the CEE, and they plan to release all of the tracks as an album. At the date of this writing, two tracks have been released on YouTube with visuals by Stillwell (under the pseudonym Intrepita).

The Pass the Track project positions listening differently than in the CEE's typical creative practice, and it affirms their roles as listener first and performer second even more due to the rupture of time and space in the CEE's improvisational practice. As I discuss in chapter 4, the CEE's collective improvisation occurs in real time, with simultaneous (though typically not coordinated) layers and of-the-moment responses to other members' contributions. With Pass the Track, each CEE member listens alone (likely with headphones) to the entire piece. While the sounds they hear emerged from the improvised contributions of the recorded CEE members, listening to it in this way – in its entirely, probably a few times – gives the next member more time to think about and prepare a sonic response. While the next recorded layer may be "improvised" (as opposed to notated), it is not emerging from an unpredictable interaction with the other recorded parts. In chapter 4, I mentioned Stillwell editing *Live from Cabbagetown*, an album that claims liveness due to its recording of a live performance, though the tracks were edited to achieve a more ideal trajectory. With Pass the Track, no such post-production editing is required because each member passes along only a layer with which they are completely happy. That being said, Stillwell still edits the material once all the tracks are together to create an ideal interpretation of the combined performances.

Because the CEE performs collective improvisation and the electronic sounds emerge from the speakers rather than from the technology that created the sounds (e.g., laptop), sometimes they do not know which sounds have come from which member, a situation I mention in chapter 4. With Pass the Track, especially earlier in the process for each one, CEE members have access to a sonic intimacy typically withheld from them in their live performances and rehearsals. While they have absolutely built an intimacy over the decades of playing together, and their improvisational game of "[name] Goes First" allows each member to shine, it has still been limited by the eventual dense counterpoint of multiple musicians. With the Pass the Track process, they can trace completely the musical thoughts and outcomes of a single CEE musician, and then respond in kind. This kind of listening clarity becomes increasingly difficult, if not impossible, by the time a track has arrived at the fourth, fifth, and sixth CEE member, but each member has an opportunity to be early in the rotation.

Montgomery (2020) outlines the order for each track as follows:

PtT-1: Paul, John, Jim, Rose, David J, David S
PtT-2: Jim, David S, Rose, David J, John, Paul
PtT-3: David S, Rose, David J, John, Paul, Jim
PtT-4: Rose, Paul, John, Jim, David S, David J
PtT-5: John, David J, Paul, David S, Jim, Rose
PtT-6: David J, Jim, David S, Paul, Rose, John

This means that, for example, Bolton has the opportunity to listen to Stillwell, Farah, and Montgomery (PtT-1), Montgomery and Sutherland (PtT-2), and just Sutherland (PtT-3). The difference, though, between the CEE members as listeners and the rest of us as listeners is that they are eventually required to respond with their own recorded layers, while we are only able to hear the final result.

Pass the Track grew out of a unique situation but was quickly embraced by the CEE as a project that felt at once in line with their creative practice but also completely new. Until the CEE is able to gather in person again, we can't know how this project may impact how they listen and respond to each other when spatial and temporal liveness return.

6

A CEE Musical Network

Supporting Musical Life in Canada and Beyond

Listen to any story from David Jaeger or Jim Montgomery, and it quickly becomes clear that they seem to know everyone in the English-speaking (and many in the French-speaking) Canadian contemporary concert music world over the last few decades. Beyond Canada as well, with stories about Cage, Boulez, and Lutosławski, among many others. Both as individuals and as a group with the Canadian Electronic Ensemble (CEE), they are hubs within vast musical networks. The larger institutional contexts of the CEE's education and employment have run parallel to and intersected with the ensemble's activities for decades.

Like chapter 2, which contextualized the CEE's early days as students within the institutional history of the University of Toronto, this chapter examines broader institutional networks of both the ensemble and its individual members, namely CBC Radio, the Music Gallery, and the Canadian Music Center (CMC). Here, I discuss some of the CEE's commissions, which reflect relationships fostered primarily through these larger networks, with a particular focus on *Consequences for 5* by Norma Beecroft (b. 1934) and *Natural Resources* by Ann Southam (1937–2010). This chapter also highlights musicians with whom the CEE collaborated in performances and recordings, or whom the CEE presented in concert. While the CEE creates its own musicking ecology, the networks examined in this chapter emerge from broader social contexts (Born 2011). The University of Toronto, the CBC, and presenting organizations like the Music Gallery remain predominantly white and male spaces. Thus, throughout my discussion of these institutions and the CEE's relationship to them, I critique their gendered and racialized aspects, as well as the issue of class privilege.

The individual and group activities of the CEE and its members have sometimes sought to specifically counter these inequalities, yet have also reinforced them in many ways, however unintentionally. The members of the CEE have been generous to me and to so many others, and they have intentionally amplified women composers and musicians. Nonetheless, the ensemble is also complicit in supporting and creating exclusionary networks whose participants and beneficiaries are primarily white, cis male, and class privileged. This problem far exceeds the scale of the CEE as a single ensemble: vastly more institutional power – and, thus, responsibility – lies with the CBC, the CMC, and funding agencies like the Canada Council for the Arts (CCA) and the Ontario Council for the Arts (OAC). Drawing on my fieldwork in 2017, I highlight one initiative of CEE member Rose Bolton to counter gender inequality: her EQ program supported by the CMC (2016–2018), which aimed to intervene in electronic music's gender disparity.

I begin with the CBC, as a national organization and one that employed three of the original four CEE members. It became the main networking hub for David Jaeger, Larry Lake, and, to a lesser extent, David Grimes, fostering decades' worth of relationships and opportunities that frequently intersected with CEE activities.

The Canadian Broadcasting Corporation (CBC) as Nation Builder and Career Maker

EARLY YEARS AT THE CBC: LAKE AND JAEGER

Larry Lake was the first CEE member hired in CBC Radio's music department, in the position of music producer. It was through this professional opportunity that he met Karen Kieser (1948–2002), hiring her to host *Themes and Variations*. Starting in 1976, Kieser regularly performed with the CEE, including on the 1979 European tour. Only a few months after that tour, Lake and Kieser were married.

David Jaeger joined the CBC Radio music department in 1973, producing shows like *Music of Today* (then hosted by Norma Beecroft) on the CBC-FM network. He has many fond memories of these early years with the CBC, such as meeting Pierre Boulez in London during the 1975 BBC Radio symposium on broadcasting contemporary music (Jaeger 2016a) and producing the ten hour-long episodes for Glenn Gould's *Arnold Schoenberg: The Man Who Changed Music* in 1974, which resulted in a close friendship with Gould until his death in 1982 (Jaeger 2015c). Jaeger's participation in commissioning new Canadian works also began in this period, initially producing broadcasts of works commissioned by John Peter Lee Roberts, the head of music at that time. Jaeger estimates that Roberts commissioned about 150 works during his tenure from 1965 to 1975 (Jaeger 2018), and this priority influenced Jaeger's vision within the CEE and at the CBC for the next thirty-five years.

The CBC Radio music department that Lake and Jaeger joined already enacted disparities in race, gender, and class. For example, Radio Canada International (RCI) collaborated with RCA Victor to produce a seventeen-volume series entitled *Music and Musicians of Canada* for the 1967 centennial. Jeremy Strachan notes its visibility in the United States and its considerable sales (77,000 copies sold within a year) as signs of its success (2020, 215). This collection is revealing in its dominance of white performers and composers, and, furthermore, of the enormous gender divide. Of the fifty pieces performed across the series, six (12 per cent) were composed by women. Indeed, the series records pieces by only four different women composers: Norma Beecroft, Barbara Pentland (one piece on each of Vols. III and XI), Sophie-Carmen Eckhardt-Grammatté (two pieces on vol. XII), and Jean Coulthard. By contrast, the series features thirty-five different male composers, or almost 90 per cent of the composed material.[1] The gender inequality of the performers is also striking, and it further reflects the gendered history of instrumental and vocal performance: of the seven women among the thirty-eight named performers, only four performed as instrumentalists, making up around 10 per cent of the total performers.[2]

The CBC has been mandated to both reflect and create Canadian national identity, making it "a place where Canada gets made and remade" (Cormack and Cosgrave 2013, 18). Such nation-building efforts were particularly pronounced and well funded during the 1960s (Berland 2009; Strachan 2020). The Canada made and remade in the music programming was largely white and male.

Similarly, the *Musical Portraits* series (1976–1987), which was sponsored by the Composers, Authors and Publishers Association of Canada (CAPAC), supported by the CBC music department, and distributed by the CMC, is almost entirely white, and women make up only 11 per cent of the featured composers. The *Musical Portraits* series also features names included in many CEE concerts (with the ensemble either performing or presenting): Sergio Barroso, Paul Dolden, Tim Brady, Marjan Mozetich, Marcelle Deschênes, Serge Arcuri, Peter Paul Koprowski, Walter Buczynski, Alex Pauk, Harry Freedman, and Norma Beecroft (who also produced the series). Such a crossover of names demonstrates how these networks that originated and were bolstered within the CBC and CMC in particular became the CEE's main source of connections.

Jaeger's work with the CBC had him interacting with the biggest names of contemporary Canadian concert music, like Harry Freedman, co-founder and one-time president of the Canadian League of Composers (CLC; 1951–), or Harry Somers (1925–1999), who is also part of the story that connects Jaeger to Toronto's New Music Concerts (NMC) and its founders Robert Aitken and Norma Beecroft.[3] Since its formation in 1971, New Music Concerts has been dedicated to performances of contemporary classical music by both international and Canadian composers, including commissioning new works. When Jaeger joined the CBC Radio music department, one of his first opportunities to record for broadcast was New Music Concerts' performance of Somers's *Zen, Yeats and Emily Dickinson* (1975). A few years later, when Lake and Jaeger's *Two New Hours* was on the air, NMC's performances would regularly provide material for their weekly radio program.

COMMISSIONING NORMA BEECROFT: CONSIDERATIONS AND CONSEQUENCES

Jaeger's access to New Music Concerts helped build the CEE's relationship with Norma Beecroft, a celebrated Canadian electronic composer, producer, and broadcaster. Her presence highlights the gender disparity in electronic music, as she was frequently the only woman in those spaces, such as at the University of Toronto Electronic Music Studio (UTEMS). In 2018, she published a print version of her book *Conversations with Post World War II Pioneers of Electronic Music*, which features remarkable interviews with the most recognizable names in concertized electronic music: Pierre Schaeffer, Iannis Xenakis, John

Cage, Karlheinz Stockhausen, and Luciano Berio, among many more. As I noted in my review of the 2015 electronic version, it is striking that no women are interviewed, yet "this is hardly surprising given the project's provenance in the late 1970s, as women electronic/electroacoustic composers still continue to fight against the gender bias in the twice male-dominated space of electronic music (composition + technology)" (Woloshyn 2016, 103). While Beecroft's impressive intimacy with electronic music comes through in her interviews, her own creative contributions to electronic music remain absent. To characterize Beecroft's presence, especially in the 1970s and '80s, as tokenistic is not to detract from her own agency and skills but rather to critique institutions that attempt to distract from pervasive gender inequalities by pointing to a single woman's success as evidence of the impossibility of gender-based exclusion.

The CEE members and Beecroft have a long history. Beecroft's 1975 *Piece for Bob* (for Aitken) utilized the University of Toronto digital sound synthesis system, which Jaeger helped to install (personal communication, 6 August 2020). It was this piece that the CEE took as its inspiration for "Incipit Norma" when the ensemble performed at Beecroft's book launch in 2015. In addition, in the first *Musical Portraits* series that Beecroft produced, there is an album for each member of the young CEE quartet, with each album featuring music performed by the CEE. Then, in 1977, with support from the Canada Council for the Arts, the CEE commissioned Beecroft to compose them a piece. The result was *Consequences for 5*, dedicated to Kieser and the CEE (for a total of five performers). The CEE members doubled on brass while also performing on synthesizers with changing settings on the Echoplex (a tape delay that includes volume, sustain, and delay time controls). *Consequences for 5* is an elaborate work consisting of Sequences I through IV and Interludes I through III, with each section drawing on particular temporal, rhythmic, registral, textural, and pitch-based elements. In the listening guides, I discuss this work in detail.

This piece was included on Beecroft's 1982 album in the series *Anthology of Canadian Music*. On this recording, though, the brass parts are performed by other performers because of the difficulty of managing both the live electronics and brass simultaneously. Regardless of this revision, *Consequences for 5* reflects both Beecroft's compositional creativity with mixed media and her high estimation of the CEE's skills.

NEW OPPORTUNITIES FOR JAEGER AT THE CBC

Beecroft's *Consequences for 5* was composed and premiered in 1977. That same year was significant for Jaeger's growing career at the CBC: he took on a new role with the International Rostrum of Composers (IRC) and proposed a new radio show, *Two New Hours* (2NH). The IRC is a mechanism for national broadcasting networks to exchange programming. The European Broadcasting Union (EBU; 1950–) distributes to its full and associate members the works presented annually by delegates. Jaeger recalls that CBC Radio was increasingly interested in broadcasting new Canadian concert music (Jaeger 2015b). His proposal for 2NH was bolstered by the CBC's participation in the IRC. Jaeger explained to me: "This was the time when planning for the creation of *Two New Hours* had begun, and we knew there would be a great need for significant international content. I was thus attending in order to become aware of the sources of this type of content, and to establish lines of communication to my fellow producers, as well as a 'supply chain' as it were, for obtaining a steady source of content" (personal communication, 6 August 2020). His proposal for *Two New Hours* was approved, and it first broadcast on 1 January 1978. 2NH replaced the one-hour weekly program *Music of Today* (1964–77), which had relied on pre-existing LP recordings. In Strachan's analysis of Roberts's contributions at the CBC, he articulates a change in the early 1970s: the Meggs-Ward Report (1970) pushed the CBC to create more news programming and "[cautioned] against a continuation of the CBC's role as a de facto state patron of art and culture" (2020, 221). Strachan describes a charge of elitism against "art music (both conventional and avant-garde)" (2020, 221). Yet he points to *Music of Today* and *Two New Hours* as two programs that continued the CBC's support of this so-called "elitist" contemporary composition. 2NH was given a modest budget to record premieres and commission and then record new works, all to be broadcast across Canada, thus defining for decades Canadian contemporary concert music. What might seem like discrete activities were actually consolidating Jaeger's connections within contemporary and experimental concert music spheres, connections that have weaved themselves in and out of the CEE's activities across the decades.

The new networks at Jaeger's disposal were also predominately white and male. Take, for example, the IRC's annual competition, which has two categories: "general" and "under 30." Some of the most recognized names in contemporary Euro-American classical concert music have won this award, including Luciano Berio, Witold Lutosławski, Krzysztof Penderecki, Benjamin Britten, Luigi Nono, Tōru Takemitsu, György Ligeti, George Crumb, Henryk Górecki, Louis Andriessen, and Thomas Adès: all men and, with the exception of Takemitsu, white European or European-descended men. Of the more than 130 composers who have won the IRC's annual competition, only about 10 per cent have been women. Perhaps, then, it is all the more remarkable that of Canada's four winners in this competition, one (25 per cent) was a woman. These four Canadians all won in the "under 30" category: Steven Gellman, *Mythos II* (1970 IRC); Chris Paul Harman, *Iridescence* (1991 IRC); Brian Current, *For the time being* (2001 IRC); and Abigail Richardson, *dissolve* (2004 IRC). Yet the broader history of the competition reveals that the IRC network has been male-dominated; thus, the relationships with the CBC and the broadcast materials to which Jaeger and 2NH had access were reinforcing gender inequality within contemporary concert music.

Another source of programming for the new weekly radio program was New Music Concerts. NMC's programming reveals the broader problem of gender equity in contemporary Euro-American classical music, though the organization has frequently performed music by Beecroft, Alexina Louie, Barbara Pentland, and Ann Southam in decades past.[4] The names of these four women have come up in many of the institutions this chapter discusses; such repetition speaks not only to the success and acclaim of these specific women composers but also to the problem of limiting diversity (in this case of women composers) to a small number of individuals. NMC was crucial to the CEE's early connections, and that influence reveals itself in the programming of 2NH and in the CEE's guest performers and commissioned composers in the 1970s and '80s.

2NH was on the air from 1978 until its cancellation in March 2007. When it began, it involved three of the four original CEE members: Jaeger, Lake, and Grimes. Jaeger served as producer and later executive producer. Lake was originally a music consultant, writing material to be presented on air; Jaeger recalls that Lake "drafted each and every script for the hosts" (personal communication, 3 August 2020). Lake became host himself in 1996 and remained in that position until the show's end. Grimes, who composed the show's theme song, was also involved as a co-host from 1978 to 1986, alongside Warren Davis. Jaeger recalls: "David had the so-called 'gift of the gab' and with Larry writing backgrounders for him, he was supported by a knowledgeable, even inspired team. Our team chemistry was great!" (personal communication, 3 August 2020).

The big names of contemporary Canadian music were key to 2NH's early activities, namely through the commissioning of composers like Beecroft, Brian Cherney, Schafer, and Weinzweig (the CEE's composition teacher from the University of Toronto) (Jaeger 2018). For the first broadcast on 1 January 1978, Jaeger featured *Voiceplay* composed and performed by Harry Somers, a piece that Jaeger had previously recorded; it was also the last work aired on the final show of *Two New Hours* twenty-nine years later.

The 2NH team worked with many Canadian composers who also show up in the CEE's presenting and performing activities. For example, in 1978, 2NH recorded for broadcast Mozetich's modernist piece *Disturbances*, which Jaeger then chose to submit to the IRC. As a result, *Disturbances* received airplay around the world. 2NH then commissioned Mozetich in 1979 for a piece in his new tonal style; the result was *Dance of the Blind*, which 2NH recorded and broadcast in 1980. In 1981, the CEE commissioned him, and the result was *In the Garden*. Jaeger recalls: "[Mozetich] responded to our commission with a virtuosic display for electronic keyboards. The CEE members decided to digitally sequence the entire score, for both ease and accuracy of performance. The work became a core composition in the CEE's repertoire, and was performed frequently on tour" (2019a).

As 2NH expanded its programming of new Canadian concert music, individuals in its network were also key to the CEE's performing and presenting. For example, the CEE programmed music by Alex Pauk in 1979 and 1980. Pauk founded Esprit Contemporain in 1983 (now Esprit Orchestra), an orchestra dedicated to contemporary music. This new ensemble enabled 2NH to record and broadcast new orchestra works, which had previously been prevented by both budget constraints and disdain within pre-existing major orchestras for contemporary concert repertoire. Esprit Contemporain gained a global audience in 1984 when it premiered Brian Cherney's *Into the Distant Stillness …* (1984) and Pauk's own *Mirage* (1984) at the International Society for Contemporary Music (ISCM) World Music Days hosted in Toronto and Montreal.

Roxanne Snider's article on the immense event highlights works by both Canadian and international composers, and interviews Jaeger because CBC Radio and *Two New Hours* broadcast most of the Toronto concerts (1984, 59).

The Winnipeg Symphony Orchestra's New Music Festival inaugurated a new era for 2NH from its beginnings in 1992, as its organizers asked 2NH to broadcast music from the festival.[5] Thus began 2NH's tradition of broadcasting live from the festival each Sunday night of its run, in addition to CBC Radio Music broadcasting many more of the festival's concerts. The performers and composers involved are names that also appear in the musical networks of the CEE and CBC Radio. For example, the inaugural 2NH broadcast from the festival was pianist Christina Petrowska Quilico performing music by mostly Canadian composers like Steve Gellman, Peter Paul Koprowski, and Ann Southam, all associated with the CEE: Petrowska Quilico performed with the CEE frequently starting in the late 1980s, including a track on *Catbird Seat* (1990); Gellman composed *Universe Symphony* (1985) for orchestra and live electronics, which the CEE performed across the country; the CEE performed Koprowski's piece *Quotations* (1978); and Southam's connection to the CEE is discussed below.

With Jaeger and Lake at the helm, 2NH curated contemporary Canadian concert music for the nation.[6] In addition to the IRC competition winners, 2NH also broadcast winners of the National Radio Competition for Young Composers and the Karen Kieser Prize. Both competitions point to the overrepresentation of white and male composers in the sphere of contemporary concert composition in Canada.

The National Radio Competition for Young Composers began in 1973 through Roberts's leadership at the CBC and the support of the Canada Council for the Arts. David Grimes placed third with *Increscents* in the 1975–76 cycle. The CBC recorded and broadcast the winning compositions. Because Jaeger took over administration of the competition in 1975, it seems natural that he would link it to 2NH: after 1978, the winners were broadcast on the Sunday night program. During the first ten cycles of the CBC/Radio-Canada National Competition for Young Composers (1973–90), no women composers won. Of the final five cycles, four women placed in the competition, and three of them won the Grand Prize: in 1994, Kelly Marie Murphy won first prize in the string quartet category, and Melissa Hui placed first in the chamber music category and was the Grand Prize Winner; in 1999, Ana Sokolović won first prize in the chamber music category and was the Grand Prize winner; in 2003 (the competition's final year), Analia Ludgar won first prize in the chamber music category and won the Grand Prize. Of the ninety winners from 1973 to 2003, only 4 per cent are women; women, however, make up just over a quarter of the Grand Prize winners (a prize not awarded each cycle). The competition winners are predominantly white.

As I mentioned in chapter 2, the Karen Kieser Prize began in 2002 in memory of Kieser. It continues to be awarded annually to a graduate student in composition at the University of Toronto. From the prize's inaugural year until the show ended, 2NH recorded and broadcast the winning pieces. Despite being a more recent initiative, the Karen Kieser Prize indicates that gender inequity persists within the composition world. Of the twenty winners between 2002 and 2020, only seven (or 35 per cent) were women. A mere 20 per cent were ethnically non-white, and no winners were Black or Indigenous. These numbers are certainly an improvement by comparison, but they still highlight the gender and racial inequalities in formalized contemporary music spheres like the University of Toronto.

Jaeger argues that with its commissioning activities and the National Radio Competition for Young Composers, "CBC Radio had positioned itself at the very centre of contemporary musical creation in Canada" (2015b), and he views 2NH as a key factor in reinforcing CBC Radio's leadership position during its tenure. In his stories, told to me in person and published in a series of essays in *The Whole Note*, Jaeger has articulated the importance of relationships and connections in "making it" in the contemporary Canadian classical music world. Jaeger views himself as a piece within a larger network of relationships that can establish and solidify the careers of composers. Indeed, he played a big role in deciding which pieces would be brought to the annual IRC competition for consideration. In addition, Jaeger estimates that through *Two New Hours*, he commissioned approximately 250 new compositions by Canadian composers (2018), and that "the show had grown to an audience share of four percent as measured by the Bureau of Broadcast Management (BBM)" (2018).

Jaeger's status within the international community of contemporary concert music was reinforced when he was elected the first non-European president of the IRC, a position he held from 2002 to 2008.[7] Jaeger explains that he thought this decision "signalled that Canadian music, and of course CBC Radio as its producer, was garnering an increasing amount of respect from the international delegation participating in the IRC. The investment that we at CBC Radio Music had made in Canadian music was recognized by our sister public broadcasters around the world, who showed an intense curiosity about new Canadian repertoire" (Jaeger 2016b). When I asked Jaeger to say more about what he noticed across his first twenty-five years with IRC, he responded:

> I witnessed the gradual rise of interest in Canadian music on the part of my international colleagues. At first, it was clear to me that nobody in the public [radio's] new music community knew anything at all about Canadian music. In fact, they knew so little about Canadian composers and repertoire, there almost seemed to be sort of a 'mystique' about it … how was it that these intelligent people were bringing such interesting works about which we know nothing … ? But gradually, as our submissions began to win accolades, and to consistently score high in the voting, there was a noticeable shift in the respect paid to our composers and our productions. (personal communication, 6 August 2020)

Jaeger characterizes 2NH's cancellation as "a devastating blow for the entire Canadian new music community" (personal communication, 3 August 2020). He sees the gap as an ongoing problem:

> The focused approach of a dedicated program on the national network was irreplaceable. Additionally, the imported concerts and content from the European Broadcasting Union (EBU) also disappeared. The result of this was that we lost the contextualizing that had come in the past from our inclusion of these global factors in 2NH programming. It has been a complete disaster, and has thrown Canadian music back into the cauldron of obscurity it had occupied previously. Various single initiatives continue to be tried, but there's no coordinated, focused source of high-quality programming. Even the CMC, which makes valiant efforts in addressing the void of significant Canadian new works, has had limited effect to redress the loss. (personal communication, 3 August 2020)

When Jaeger speaks here of "Canadian music," he is speaking specifically about contemporary concert music. According to Colin Eatock, the Canadian League of Composers also saw the cancellation of 2NH "as an attack on contemporary music," by which they meant "new music that, in its aesthetic goals, creative methods or historical lineage, is somehow connected to Western classical-music traditions" (2008, 266).

Compared to this time of declining institutional activity in the late 2000s, the early 1980s were a prodigious time for the CBC, CMC, and the CEE, with funding available to support two major recording projects with the CEE. These projects reflect opportunities afforded to the CEE because of their deep connections to major music institutions in Toronto.

Recording the CEE:
The Electronic Messiah and Centrediscs

Thus far in this chapter, I have examined Jaeger's and Lake's work with the music department at CBC Radio and demonstrated how the CBC as a hub afforded them access to various networks of contemporary classical concert music institutions like the IRC and New Music Concerts. Many individuals in these networks participated in the CEE's own network of performers and composers that the ensemble programmed and presented over the decades, with Lake acting as artistic director.[8] This next part of the chapter highlights two stories that demonstrate opportunities afforded to the CEE through interpersonal connections in other institutions: first, the Canadian Music Centre's Centrediscs label and a self-titled CEE album; second, the CBC and *The Electronic Messiah*.

John Peter Lee Roberts was head of the CBC music department when Jaeger and Lake joined in the early 1970s. Roberts was embedded in multiple intersecting networks advocating for Canadian music, including the Canadian Music Council and the Canadian Music Centre (CMC). He served as president of the CMC (1971–73) and then executive director (1977–81).[9] Part of Roberts's vision for supporting Canadian composers and increasing their visibility was to establish a record label "dedicated to showcasing the talent of Canadian composers" that would "become Canada's foremost label of contemporary concert music" (Canadian Music Centre, n.d.). The first Centrediscs album, released in 1981, was none other than the Canadian Electronic Ensemble, with the quartet's second self-titled LP.

Perusing the names in the CMC's Centrediscs catalogue reinforces my argument that many of the same names have received the privilege of access and promotion through multiple platforms: CBC Radio, CMC, and also the CEE. As such, the catalogue features mostly men, mostly of European descent; despite more recent efforts to diversify, the catalogue is also almost exclusively Euro-American classical music. Names like the Elmer Iseler Singers (multiple albums), Ann Southam (multiple albums), Walter Buczynski, Robert Aitken, Rivka Golani, William Aide, David Mott, Beverley Johnston, Jean Piché, Serge Arcuri, Steve Tittle, Christos Hatzis, Lawrence Cherney, Barbara Pritchard, Christina Petrowska Quilico, Harry Freedman, Marjan Mozetich, and Tim Brady: these composers and performers circulated through CBC Radio music programming and commissions (including 2NH), on Centrediscs, and on CEE concerts, with the CEE functioning as performers and presenters. CEE members are further highlighted as individual composers on Centrediscs. Four of Jaeger's compositions have been featured on Centrediscs albums: *Favour* is included on Golani's 1983 album *Viola Nouveau*, *Shadow Box* (performed by Joseph Petric) on the 1988 album of the same name, *Lyrics for Solo Marimba* on Beverley Johnston's 1992 album *Alternate Currents*, and *Fool's Paradise* on Golani's 1992 album *Prouesse*. Many of these pieces were also featured on CEE concerts to balance CEE ensemble pieces with guest performances. Lake's *Psalm* (performed by Lawrence Cherney) is also included on *Shadow Box*.

As another form of gatekeeping, all repertoire recorded on Centrediscs must be written by CMC Associate Composers, which requires a paid registration fee (currently $125) and used to require a master's degree in composition. Though Associate Composers do not need to compose music that uses conventional Western notated scores, notated musics remain normative within the culture of the CMC and its networks. The CMC National branch has, however, supported initiatives like Rose Bolton's EQ program (discussed at the end of this chapter) in order to address persistent gender inequality in contemporary music.

As further evidence of the insular nature of contemporary Canadian music networks, Centrediscs relies on technical support from CBC Radio Music. Jason Van Eyk explains: "CBC Radio Music has been a long-standing partner in Centrediscs, providing licenced access to existing, unreleased archival recordings, as well as to technical facilities and staff for each record, up to and including the master tape" (2013). In return, the CBC had first broadcasting rights, which Jaeger programmed on 2NH during the show's tenure.

One of the CEE's most distinctive opportunities in the 1980s – if not across their entire history – is *The Electronic Messiah* (1982). *The Electronic Messiah* is the most successful album to which the CEE ever contributed, yet you won't find the name "Canadian Electronic Ensemble" credited on the actual album. What you will find is the name "Synthescope" Digital Synthesizer Ensemble and those of the four CEE members. *The Electronic Messiah* was a for-profit venture that was outside of the CEE not-for-profit organization, and the project seemed – at least at first – not to align with the experimentalist priorities of the CEE. Therefore, a new entity was created to perform on *The Electronic Messiah*, a nine-track LP featuring the professional choir the Elmer Iseler Singers[10] and the "Synthescope" Digital Synthesizer Ensemble. *The Electronic Messiah* features a number of favourite choruses from Handel's celebrated oratorio *Messiah*, including "For Unto Us a Child Is Born," "Glory to God," "Hallelujah," and the final "Amen."[11]

When I asked Jaeger how this project came to be, he explained that the idea originated with Robert Sunter (b. 1931), head of the CBC Radio Music department from 1976 to 1982. According to Jaeger, Sunter's own musical predilections lay in opera, but he was deliberate in supporting ventures outside of the opera realm (personal communication, 1 August 2020). In addition, Sunter knew about Jaeger's activities with the CEE, and he concluded that this might be a good opportunity to produce an album along the same line as Wendy Carlos's *Switched-On Bach* (1968), the first in a series of successful commercial releases that included *The Well-Tempered Synthesizer* (1969), *Switched-On Bach II* (1973), and *Switched-On Brandenburgs* (1980).

The next step was to earn Iseler's agreement. The CEE members produced a demo track of "And the Glory of the Lord," which satisfied Iseler. In creating the album, the CEE worked directly only with Iseler, who spent a few hours with them, specifying his desired tempi for the selected choruses. The CEE used the Roland MC-4 MicroComposer to sequence the foundational material of each chorus according to Iseler's tempi, then built up the arrangements from there. The group relied on the relatively new Roland Jupiter 8 – purchased with their fee for this project – for the vast majority of their sounds.

Both Jaeger and Montgomery told me stories about Iseler and the issue of tempi. Montgomery recalls wanting to demonstrate to Iseler what the Roland sequencer could achieve in terms of tempo flexibility, choosing a rather unmusical contrast between slow and fast tempi to make his point. Montgomery explains that Iseler was offended, giving him the impression that Iseler took this demonstration as Montgomery's own interpretive agenda (personal communication, 27 July 2020). In the end, Iseler was thrilled by the tempo flexibility. As Jaeger recalled to me, Iseler had encountered resistance to his tempi from instrumentalists and singers in the past, especially with "All We Like Sheep," which he preferred at a fast pace. With *The Electronic Messiah*, Iseler had absolute discretion in this regard, and he thus realized some of his *Messiah* dreams with this album.

The chorus "All We Like Sheep" already sticks out in tone in the oratorio, following the minor-mode chorus "Surely He Hath Borne Our Griefs" and the minor-mode fugue "And With His Stripes." When the buoyant major-mode chorus "All We Like Sheep" begins in any *Messiah* performance, the shift in tone is striking. *The Electronic Messiah*, which includes all three choruses, pushes this contrast further with its brisk tempo and almost magical electronic accompaniment.

Across decades of acclaimed *Messiah* recordings, "All We Like Sheep" has been performed at an allegretto tempo – moderately fast (100–116 beats per minute, or bpm).[12] Because of the tempo precision of the Synthescope accompaniment, Iseler chose his ideal tempo for each chorus: in this case, 128 bpm. Jaeger explained to me that Iseler imagined "All We Like Sheep" to be like a scherzo. From the opening eighth notes of the synthesizer bass line, this chorus takes off like a rocket. For listeners familiar with the oratorio, and especially anyone who has sung it, this tempo might also elicit some anxiety about how the singers will vocalize the sixteenth-note passagework, which is difficult at any tempo.

The "magical" synthesizer parts are relatively subdued in the opening passages of "All We Like Sheep." While the bass line is perceptibly not acoustic, its constant presence normalizes its timbre to my ears. The opening antiphonal dialogue between the homorhythmic chorus and the "orchestra" reveals only slightly the kind of electronic sparkle the rest of the chorus will present. The instrumental parts (in this case, the synthesizers) double many of the vocal lines. Throughout the chorus, this

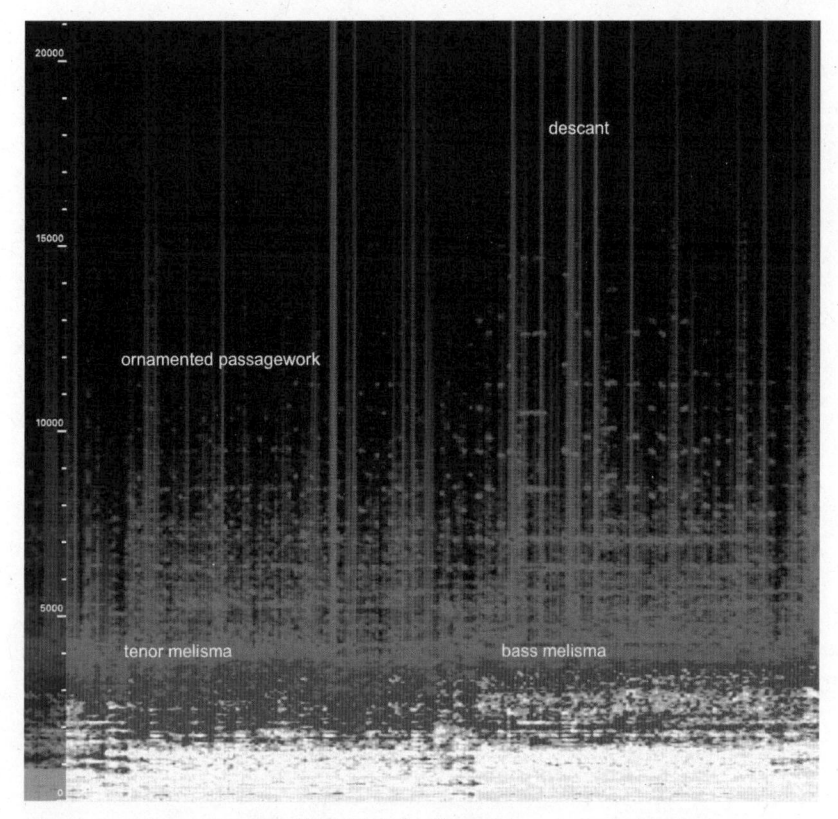

Figure 6.1 Spectrogram of "All We Like Sheep" (mm. 42–5) showing ornamented passagework and descant in synthesizer accompaniment.

doubling remains subtle, with the electronic timbres barely audible. The impact of this subtlety is that the more explicit synthesizer contributions are rather surprising. For example, after the choir's first full declaration of the chorus's text and the return of a homorhythmic texture in m. 17, the "orchestra" response (mm. 18–19) in the synthesizers has an arpeggio effect that adds a series of rapid, high pitches in an exuberant flurry. Almost immediately, the synthesizers return to their subtle doubling, allowing the choral parts to be the focus. Soon, though, the synthesizers emerge as showstoppers, with a descant (mm. 29–30), additional runs (m. 32), ornamented passagework (mm. 42–3), and another descant (mm. 44–5) (see figure 6.1), all musical decisions made through consultation with Dennis Farrell, whom they hired as a consultant on Baroque performance practice. Jaeger described the result: "It's like a party" (personal communication, 1 August 2020).

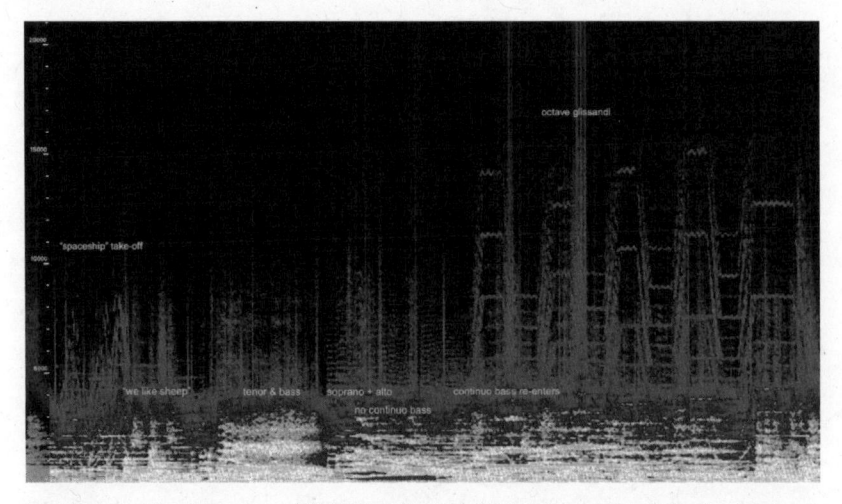

Figure 6.2 Spectrogram of "All We Like Sheep" (mm. 54–64) with electronic flourishes.

The Synthescope's fun electronic additions to the chorus do not end there. For the final homorhythmic "all we like sheep," we hear what sounds like a spaceship blasting off into outer space (m. 54): *Messiah* has gone interstellar (see figure 6.2). The synthesizers join the choir in building momentum through the ascending stepwise sequence with octave leaps (mm. 60–4): we hear the same pitches as the soprano line but in a higher range and with glissando between the octaves (see figure 6.2). A C pedal (m. 64) is the final articulation in this section of electronic fireworks. For the remainder of the chorus, the synthesizers are restrained to the notated parts. The dynamic levels of the synthesizers are high in the final homorhythmic phrase and in the closing adagio section: they do not add any additional flurries of notes, but they take full advantage of their timbres to signal a shift to heaviness in comparison to the light and almost rollicking performance of the chorus.

Both Montgomery and Jaeger recall approaching this project like other big CEE projects, including collectively composed works and large-scale projects like *Nightbloom*: they divided up the material, and each member was responsible for a portion of it. They also both recall that any initial resistance to this commercial project, which could be seen as a rejection of their artistic values, disappeared once they were involved in the actual arranging. For example, Jaeger recalls Lake having a lot of fun arranging the Overture (personal communication, 1 August 2020).

The CEE musicians did not interact with the choir directly. Rather, once the accompaniment tracks were complete and transferred to the CBC Radio mobile van, the van drove to St Anne's Anglican Church, where the choir was set up to record. By the time this project was in its final stages, Sunter was no longer head, having been replaced by Harold Redekopp. The initial recording of the choir did not meet Redekopp's satisfaction, who preferred a warmer and more resonant choral sound, so he secured the funds to hire the choir to re-record the material (Jaeger, personal communication, 1 August 2020).

Despite early hesitation about participating in the project, Jaeger and Montgomery both fondly share memories from the experience and laugh about the "Synthescope" credit. Jaeger explained to me that the "anti-purist thing" of *The Electronic Messiah* attracted attention (personal communication, 1 August 2020). The sales indicate this was good attention. Iseler's biographer Walter Pitman explains that when the Elmer Iseler Singers were going to premiere this electronic re-visioning live at Expo '86, the reactions were mixed: "*Electronic Messiah* ... horrified some conservative choral enthusiasts but delighted many who saw this as another example of Elmer's courage" (2008, 166). While *The Electronic Messiah* may seem like only a quirky anecdote in CEE history, it emphasizes the group's connections to institutional power and money that create opportunities for some musicians and leave others out.

Supporting Canadian Music: The CEE's Commissions

Across its first fifty years, the CEE has commissioned over thirty works by thirty different composers (see table 6.1). This chapter has already discussed Beecroft's commission in detail and mentioned some of the other composers commissioned. One of the CEE's most successful commissions is also one of its most surprising: *Natural Resources* (1981).

When the CEE commissioned Ann Southam (1937–2010) to compose them a piece, such a request could hardly be surprising, given Southam's involvement in new music, including teaching electronic music at the Royal Conservatory of Music in Toronto. Her compositions in the 1970s included works for acoustic performing forces (piano and chamber music), but at the time of the CEE's commission, she had also composed a number of electronic pieces, such as *Boat, River, Moon* (1972; included

Table 6.1 List of composers and musical works commissioned by the CEE.

Composer	Title	Notes
Allik, Kristi	RIDDIM for tape and three synthesizers (1984)	For electronic tape, Roland JPB, Yamaha CS 40-M, Vocoder-Korg, digital delay and flanger
Barroso, Sergio	Charangas Delirantes (1993)	Funding support from the Canada Council for the Arts; version for solo keyboard and tape performed by Barroso on his 1996 album Délirantes
Bauer, Robert	Greenwood Station (1978)	For four synthesizers and prepared tape
Beecroft, Norma	Consequences for 5 (1977)	
Bussière, Michael	Hypothesis of Memory (1987)	
Buczynski, Walter	In Paradisum	First performed in 1980
Carpenter, Patrick	Ladyfinger Triptych	First performed in 1978
Celona, John	Networks	First performed in 1995
Ciamaga, Gustav	Ars Nova (1976)	For synthesizers, tape, and narrators
Degazio, Bruno	On Growth and Form (1988)	
Deschênes, Marcelle	deUS irae (1985)	
Farrell, Dennis	Convivium (1983)	Funding support from the Ontario Arts Council
Frykberg, Susan	Waxing Your Cloth (1981)	
Hannan, Peter	System I (1988)	
Hatzis, Christos	Nadir (1988)	Funding support from the Ontario Arts Council
Healey, Derek	Wood, Op. 51 (1978)	For soprano or shakuhachi and four synthesizers
Kasemets, Udo	David & David & Larry & James	First performed in 1977
Keane, David	Dithyramb (1978)	For four synthesizers and prepared tape; funding support from the Ontario Arts Council
Koprowski, Peter Paul	Quotations (1978)	
Mozetich, Marjan	In the Garden (1983)	For three keyboard synthesizers and tape
Pauk, Alex	Touch Piece	First performed in 1979
Pauk, Alex	Dance Climb	First performed in 1980
Piché, Jean	Avant, pendant, et après	First performed in 1977
Shin, Ann	Many Words for Home	First performed in 1988
Smith, Randall	Continental Rift (1995)	Funding support from the Canada Council for the Arts
Southam, Ann	Natural Resources (1981)	
Steven, Donald	Wired (1981)	Optional tape part
Symonds, Norman	Quintet for Clarinet and Synthesizers (1977)	Included on James Campbell's 1978 LP Transcription

Composer	Title	Notes
Thrower, John	*Synthemaphon*	First performed in 1983
Tittle, Steve	*Blues Division* (1978)	For trumpet, horn, trombone, electronically prepared piano, optional percussion, prepared tape, and electronics and amplification equipment
Tittle, Steve	*Standing in the Light*	First performed in 1987; recording by Upstream Ensemble on *Open Waters* (1992)
Young, Gayle	*Usque ad mare* (1981)	Funding support from the Ontario Arts Council

on the 1980 album *Electronic Music by Canadian Composers*, volume I), *Walls and Passageways* (1974), *The Reprieve* (1975), and *Seastill* (1979), the last three of which are included on the 1999 album *Seastill: The Electroacoustic World of Ann Southam*.

Jaeger writes about meeting Southam in 1973 at a CEE performance. At that time, the group knew about her private studio and her many electronic works; then, in 1975, she self-released her fifty-minute piece *The Reprieve*. Jaeger explains: "The members of the CEE took note of this and we eventually approached Ann with the offer of a commission to create a new work for the ensemble" (2015a), with the support of the Ontario Arts Council. So, in 1981, Southam composed *Natural Resources,* or *What to Do till the Power Comes On.* The contents of this piece were unexpected to the CEE, as Jaeger and Montgomery recounted in conversation with me:

> Jaeger: We were all completely surprised. No one was not surprised by Ann's piece.
> Montgomery: When she delivered it, there was some expression that she was putting us on.
> Jaeger: Or putting us down.
> Montgomery: It wasn't until we actually met with her that we could tell that she was serious ... Once we had met with her and figured out she was actually serious about it, then our approach to the piece became much more friendly. (personal communication, 25 February 2020)[13]

Natural Resources is a bold composition for an electronic ensemble because it's not written for any electronic resources, but rather wooden dowels and various metal objects one can procure at a hardware store.[14]

Southam provided the CEE with the objects required to perform this piece, but any ensemble can assemble their own set based on her instructions. Southam's score describes the work as a "sound game for 4 players" (1981, 1), though she later explains in the score that the piece can be performed by as few as two performers or more than four. Southam's stated goal for the piece is to organize found sound (i.e., wood and metal objects) into musical patterns. The contrasts between metal and wood sounds and between sound and silence are organizing principles of Southam's instructions.

Southam's score is sixteen pages of written instructions, with the only conventional notation illustrating rhythmic patterns in 4/8 (or 2/4), 3/8 (or 6/8), and 2/8 (or 1/8); she also includes some pictures to illustrate the layout of the three "instruments," each consisting of five positions that the sound objects will occupy in various ways during the piece. Only three of the four performers play the instruments, with the fourth performer tasked with placing and removing the sound objects according to Southam's instructions.[15]

The three "instruments" begin and end with no sound objects. Players one, two, and three begin tapping each of the five positions, from left to right and back. Player four places metal objects one by one into any one of the five positions, making sure to add one to each instrument until all five positions are filled with metal objects. Player four then replaces all of the metal objects with wooden dowels, one by one, and then removes one object from each instrument. This pattern of switching between all wood or all metal objects and removing one object from each instrument continues until there are no remaining objects. Players one, two, and three are instructed to feel their rhythms in particular metres based on the number of objects remaining in their instruments. Southam offers two possibilities for extending the game, as well as an option for adding occasional off-beats.

This is a piece about timbre and rhythm, one that, if performed at a fast tempo, would be both impressive and entertaining for the audience. The CEE performed the piece a few times between 1982 and 1992. They featured it during their 1985 Holland tour, where percussionists Renee Jonker and Peppie Wiersma were guests.[16]

Evan Ware (2011) explains that during the 1980s, Southam shifted from electronic music to acoustic instruments only. Jaeger similarly remarked: "The underlying message was that she was bidding farewell to electronic music. In the late 1970s and early 1980s Ann's focus shifted to creating works she called 'made by hand for hands'" (2015a), or what Ware refers to as "an interest in the physicality of performing" (2011). Indeed, in the same year as *Natural Resources*, Southam composed *Glass Houses*, a set of fifteen piano pieces inspired by Philip Glass's minimalism and East Coast Canadian fiddle music in the style of the CBC television show *Don Messer's Jubilee* (1959–69). *Glass Houses* signalled Southam's new interest in minimalist-like motives and repetition that requires the pianist to memorize left-hand motives of unusual length (e.g., thirteen notes) below right-hand lyrical motives, all at a dizzying tempo – at least in the hands of Christina Petrowska Quilico.

This chapter has discussed two commissions by women composers, yet the CEE's programming, including commissions and performance as well as producing, is dominated by white men.[17] While it is important to highlight the presence of women as composers in the CEE's history, we must also recognize that Beecroft and Southam do not represent the norm for the ensemble's commissions, and that pointing to the success of individual women in male-dominated spheres can be used to distract from persistent inequities within those organizations and networks. The CEE's collaborations with performers have been more equitable in terms of gender, with several women performing regularly with the ensemble – Christina Petrowska Quilico, Rivka Golani, Karen Kieser – and others performing less frequently, such as Billie Bridgman (1979 tour), Beverley Johnston, and Gayle Young. Here too, however, a gendered divide is evident: while men have been guest performers on both electronic and acoustic instruments, the women have mostly performed on acoustic instruments or as vocalists, falling within gendered norms that position the feminine as performance and "natural" (i.e., acoustic) sound, as opposed to the masculine as composition and electronic sound (Bosma 2006).

The Music Gallery: A Home for the CEE's Electronic Musicking

There are many visions for what a contemporary music community should look like and how it should function. The Music Gallery in Toronto began with its own clear vision. The Music Gallery was founded in 1976 by the Canadian Creative Music Collective (CCMC), which formed in Toronto two years earlier as a "free music orchestra" ("CCMC" 2013). The Music Gallery has been a musician-run experimental organization for decades now in Toronto, and it has been a crucial platform for collaboration, performance, and recording for both local and visiting musicians.

The CEE already had a long-standing relationship with the Music Gallery by the time Montgomery became artistic director in 1987, a position he held until 2005. The CEE had recorded its first album, the self-titled 1977 album, on Music Gallery Edition, the organization's rather brief but productive record label (1977–81). CEE performances during the Music Gallery's first decade include the inaugural album release concert on 11 February 1978, with several guest improvisers, the First Annual Electronic Music Festival in January 1979, and New Trends in Electronic Music in 1985.

In our conversation (27 July 2020), Montgomery recalled the organization having six categories of contemporary experimental real-time arts: contemporary concert music, improvised music, multimedia works, dance, non-Western musics (he dislikes the phrase "World Music"), and performance art. Montgomery credits his work with Robert Aitken of New Music Concerts with developing his skills in arts administration. He also recalls a competitive atmosphere in the 1970s and early 1980s, one he wished to reject. Instead, he wanted to find ways for people to come together to do what he termed "unpopular music" (personal communication, 27 July 2020). He saw this kind of community at work at the Music Gallery: "I didn't want to transform it, just nourish it and augment it. I succeeded, to a degree" (personal communication, 25 July 2020).

The beginning of Montgomery's tenure at the Music Gallery was also the beginning of the CEE's regular appearances: the group performed and presented series each year until 2004, thanks to external funding. The previous homes for the CEE's series were St Lawrence Hall, Theatre Upstairs, Theatre Downstairs, COMUS Theatre, and Winchester Street Theatre.

For their first Music Gallery series from 29 April to 3 May 1987, the CEE presented CEElectric Spring, with six concerts featuring Canadian and international composers and Canadian musicians. Included in this busy series was the first of six Guitar Boogie concerts (1987–95) that celebrated new repertoire featuring the electric guitar. With six to eight series concerts each year, it's difficult to summarize everything that the CEE achieved as presenter/producers at the Music Gallery. Some standout events include presenting Japanese musician Yas-Kaz (24 June 1991), the Berlin Improvising Composers' Ensemble (30 October 1993), a concert of works by Bernard Parmegiani (20 February 1993), and a concert of works by Tim Brady (19 March 1994).

Under Montgomery's leadership, the Music Gallery secured its space at 179 Richmond Street West (1991–2000). As he was leading a relatively small organization, Montgomery had to contribute to tasks beyond typical AD duties. He told me about how refurbishing the space required an emergency exit opening to the alley. As an act of thoughtfulness to anyone coming in or out of that doorway, there was a short, covered passage. Due to the building's placement within the entertainment district, this covered exit became a favourite place for drunken revellers to relieve themselves of various bodily fluids. Each morning upon his arrival, Montgomery would mop that area clean. During our phone conversation on the topic, Montgomery laughed recalling one time when theatre producer David Mirvish (founder of Mirvish Productions), who was supportive of the Music Gallery's activities, was scheduled for a meeting there: "He comes up, and I'm out there with my rubber boots and a mop and a bucket and bleach [laugh]. He walks down the alley, and he says: 'Wow! I always knew there was a difference between for profit and not-for-profit artistic directors' [laugh]" (personal communication, 27 July 2020).

While the CEE already had a relationship with the Music Gallery before 1987, having a member as the artistic director strengthened that relationship and ensured certain opportunities. It meant that Montgomery presented artists through the Music Gallery who would become CEE collaborators, such as Trio Collectif. It also meant that young musicians like Rose Bolton and John Kameel Farah – who were eager to be close to exciting new music but needed jobs – were employed by the Music Gallery, came to know Montgomery, and were invited to be guests with and then members of the CEE. These extensive networks of relationships and connections require institutions like the Music Gallery to facilitate.

As Silvia Gherardi and Barbara Poggio explain, organizations are "gendering agents": "they are not merely contexts or settings for gendered identities ... [I]nstitutions, and not only individuals, are gendered, and gender is a central control mechanism in organizations and constitutive of organizing" (2007, 15). The CBC in particular has reinforced leadership as a male domain. Even the Music Gallery did not have a woman in a position of leadership until Dewi Minden (executive director, 2007–10). Since then, the Music Gallery's leadership has seen a significant shift from its male-dominated past. Monica Pearce served as executive director (2013–18), with Kayla McGee replacing her until June 2020. David Dacks served as artistic director (2012–20) before moving to executive director (2020–). Sanjeet Takhar was named artistic director in 2020.

Organizations are also racializing agents. Given Canada's history regarding racialized communities, the whiteness of the country's new music institutions should not be surprising. Whiteness is a structure that affords power and privilege, such as through the legal protection of property rights (Harris 1993). Whiteness relies on a racialized "other," which is historically contingent and changing, and can be conferred fully or only partially to various ethnic groups (such as through the "model minority" stereotype) (Tuck and Yang 2012, 18). As Barbara Applebaum explains in her article "Critical Whiteness Studies," "white people have an investment in whiteness, which can obscure how white people, even with the best of intentions, are complicit in sustaining a racially unjust system" (2016). White people gain race-based privilege within white supremacy, but white individuals may divest themselves of whiteness (Lipsitz 2006). Thus, while whiteness is not the same as white people, the ubiquity of white individuals, particularly in positions of power, acts as a normalizing agent for whiteness. Canada's racialization of whiteness is based on its specific national racial regimes (Garner 2007), including whiteness as property and citizenship, pervasive anti-Blackness, official multiculturalism,[18] and anti-Indigeneity (e.g., the Indian Act).

The racializing hierarchies within Canadian cultural institutions, then, will manifest in the industry in various ways, including genre divisions. Jaeger explained to me that one of the goals of *The Signal* (2007–17), the daily music show that absorbed much of 2NH's budget, was to include more pop/indie music under the broad category of contemporary music (personal communication, 3 August 2020). Despite genre functioning with flexibility and contradictions, and with changes over time (such as the obsolete "race records"), genre still holds power in the imagination of music industry participants, from listeners to performers and producers (Brackett 2016). The programming change at *The Signal* reflects how genre can be coded for classist and racialized patterns of exclusion; in this case, "contemporary music" had previously excluded pop and indie music despite the seeming openness of the word "contemporary." David Dacks, the Music Gallery's former artistic director and current executive director, explained in an interview: "The music industry is far less diverse than its artists, and the industry's priorities are less diverse as a result" (Sheikh 2016). A panel held at the Music Gallery in November 2015 entitled "Music: Racism, Power and Privilege 101" wrestled with some of this legacy of past and ongoing inequities. Even this event evidenced deep-seated resentment within the different segments of contemporary music in Toronto – resentment about cultural appropriation, a lack of racial diversity in positions of power, and racialized structures of exclusion within funding bodies that favour indie-rock, among other concerns. The stories shared at the event highlighted how broader systems of racialization and socio-economic inequality are replicated in the music industry (Gillis 2015). By leaving whiteness unmarked as normative and embracing colour-blind rhetoric, many organizations, including the Music Gallery, can believe that racism either does not exist or is not the responsibility of its white members.

The CEE and the Music Gallery are only two nodes in the complex networks of music making in Canada, with institutions like the Canada Council for the Arts (CCA) and the Ontario Council for the Arts (OAC) maintaining significant power in amplifying or silencing certain creative voices. The CEE and the Music Gallery themselves have relied upon funding bodies like the CCA and the OAC to support their touring, recording, presenting, producing, and performing. Yet it is important to acknowledge the power that the CEE and its members have held in various contexts to uphold or reject institutional patterns of exclusion and privilege, patterns that have long seen white men as both gatekeepers and beneficiaries of existing inequitable systems.

Rose Bolton's EQ: Building Community for Women in Electronic Music

Rose Bolton is well accustomed to being the only woman in the room within composition and electronic contexts, two spheres that have historically been male-dominated and considered "masculine," leading to the exclusion or marginalization of women (Bosma 2006; McCartney

2006). Andra McCartney's ethnography revealed that many female electroacoustic composers use alternative metaphors for technology and how they engage with it (1994; 1995; 1996). Their language contrasts with the masculine language of electroacoustic music – the metaphors, images, and myths – found in magazines, textbooks, and software jargon. McCartney concludes that women electronic musicians create bounded spaces within which to find reprieve from the male-dominated sphere and often implement alternative strategies and metaphors for their aesthetic practices.

As McCartney outlines, these stereotypical assumptions are reinforced in electronic music discourse. Electronic music practitioner and researcher Tara Rodgers admits "[defaulting] to stereotypical assumptions about gender, audio, and computer technologies" (2010, 1). Rodgers explains that women are positioned "outside the scope of study" (2010, 11) or tokenized as exceptions (2010, 11–12). Metaphors for labour, audio technologies, spaces, and sound practices still frequently rely on a masculine-feminine binary (Rodgers 2010, 12–16), resulting in "the universalizing male claims to creation that have thus far characterized dominant discourses in electronic music" (Rodgers 2010, 15).

Despite women's ubiquitous participation in electronic music, women electronic artists continue to be marginalized and dismissed in electronic music circles because "a patrilineal history of electronic music production is normative, and ideologies of sound production circulate unmarked for a particular politics of gender" (Rodgers 2010, 15). Bolton told a story about attending an electronic music gathering in which the men in attendance, who were similar in age to her, assumed she needed more help than them and that she in turn had little help to offer them (public lecture, 26 February 2020). By contrast, Bolton explained to me that she feels comfortable with the CEE: she feels like a respected equal (personal communication, 7 January 2016). In another conversation, Bolton explained that she thought the generational difference between her and Jaeger, Lake, and Montgomery helped avoid some of the condescension she experienced in other spaces from her generational peers. Because the CEE's founding members were older than her, she looked to them as mentors (public lecture, 26 February 2020).

The university and UTEMS have been male-dominated spaces, so it's unsurprising that the CEE has consisted of mostly male members. But in the broader electronic music community, specifically in Toronto, Bolton wanted to experience alternative spaces of learning, sharing, and production. EQ: Women in Electronic Music is a project initiated by Bolton with the support and coordination of the Canadian Music Centre–Ontario branch and its then director, Matthew Fava.[19] As stated on the program's logo, EQ's mission is "mentorship and community building for women in electronic music."[20] It is an alternative strategy within electronic music, in the same vein as what McCartney and Rodgers note in their research. Bolton ran three iterations of EQ (2016–18) with a total of nineteen participants.[21] While she currently has no plans to run EQ again, given its significant time commitment and her desire to advance her own compositional projects, she hopes the project will continue. I discuss it here to examine Bolton's own gendered relationship to electronic music, including within the CEE, and what interventions can be made to address inequities in the field.

Each EQ iteration included both one-on-one mentoring sessions with Bolton and group workshops. Bolton also hosted guest group facilitators, such as Pursuit Grooves and Laura Dickens. Bolton aimed to dismantle hierarchies that position some as experts and others as learners. Rather, she emphasized that each musician is continually "in process" – including herself – and encouraged peer feedback during group sessions.

EQ was not genre exclusive in the ways typically found in dominant narratives of electronic music. Applicants had to demonstrate only that "electronics and sound play prominent roles in [their] present work." Some participants were strongly oriented to a pop aesthetic, while others were more experimental; some identified as performers, while others considered themselves composers. Such diversity of sound practices runs counter to many electronic music historiographies that dismiss electronic genres perceived as overly influenced by popular musics, such as DJ culture.

I interviewed participants in EQ's second year and observed individual and group sessions. Many of them mentioned being one of few women in their classes in composition or electronic music. For example, Vilde explained that the women in her music technology class at the University of Toronto tended to be quiet and hold back from participating. She knew that EQ, by contrast, "would be a safe space to dare to ask stupid questions" (personal communication, 20 April 2017). Julia described it similarly: "It definitely was appealing to kind of explore new territory with a safe environment. I'm kind of a shy person, so it's always nice to have that support from other people" (personal communication, 20 April 2017).

Some spoke of feeling minimized as women in other creative contexts, such as within their bands or in the recording studio. For example, Vilde joined EQ to expand her capabilities in solo performance. Her duo combines electronics, voice, and guitar, and she finds a lot of creative satisfaction with the duo medium. However, she also wants to be able to create full electronic textures around her voice in solo performance. I asked her why she was so determined to perform solo when she enjoys her duo work. This was her response:

> Because I know I can do it. My personal aesthetic might be a little different from my duo's aesthetic, and people don't know I can do it. They always assume it's him that's doing everything. That's an irritating notion. We recently released a single, and it was played on a radio station in Norway. And he introduced us that my partner did the electronics and I wrote the lyrics: that is what he said, and it was annoying to me because I'm a co-producer. (personal communication, 20 April 2017)

The legacy of such gendered spaces in composition and technology pushes women to create alternative gendered spaces, but ones in which they occupy all roles. Christine described a powerful feeling when she arrived to the first group workshop: "When we showed up and took out our laptops and controllers and interfaces, and everyone was setting up, I was like 'this is rad.' It was an empowering feeling" (personal communication, 18 May 2017). Christine went on to describe a typical gendered divide in technologically focused creative spaces and how EQ challenges it:

> A lot of the conversations I have with guys about making music are more technical, whereas with women it's often more what has inspired the music and where it is coming from – spiritual, emotional, psychological. So to flip that around – to be with women but talking about the technical element – was a good feeling. Because I knew that if we needed to, we could flip it again and talk about our psychological inspiration for whatever we're working on. But it's almost like that's unsaid: "Yeah, yeah, we know about that. But we're doing this as well." (personal communication, 18 May 2017)

EQ was a valued initiative for both Bolton and the women who participated. Bolton reflected: "I feel that the three years I ran EQ were very successful in its goal, which was to cultivate community and support among women electronic music creators" (personal communication, 10 August 2020). While the EQ program is currently not running, in-person and virtual communication and collaboration persist. Many participants mentioned the private Facebook group that continues the knowledge sharing of face-to-face group sessions and builds relationships across groups and between EQ iterations. Nicole articulated a strong sense of community through both the face-to-face and online contexts: "We have that Facebook group. There's something really nice about having that kind of group that you can belong to, or that you can bounce ideas off of, and we can all support one another" (personal communication, 20 April 2017).

While such women-only spaces do have value as interventions within electronic music, some research has found that "women's close circles are detrimental for their careers" (Lutter 2015, 230) because the connections they are fostering are not with individuals with power, which underlines the importance of transforming male-dominated spaces simultaneously to fostering spaces like EQ. The underrepresented individuals in communities like EQ need to be given meaningful and self-determining access to the main institutions of power and influence. Bolton has noticed a change within Toronto:

> Organizations that were male dominated started to realize that all men was kind of strange. Toronto Sound Festival (founded and run by [CEE member] Paul Stillwell) now features a pretty good gender ratio. I moderated a talk with an all women panel, invited by Paul, and it seemed to be incredibly successful ... Where I see a change, is that a lot of music festivals, databases, concerts, are featuring more women than before. So the optics are changing. Women are finally getting jobs in Artistic Director positions etc. It has to continue. Hopefully this phenomenon is here to stay. (personal communication, 10 August 2020)

However, Bolton still notices how she is treated as a woman within electronic music and the effects this has on her professional opportunities: "I think it is still expected that a woman artist make some kind of sacrifice to advocate for their cause. For me, the expectation was always that I continue to run EQ every year, and ultimately, my work as a composer would have suffered" (personal communication, 10 August 2020). She considers wage disparity a lingering issue: "I still notice a huge difference in the financial status of women vs. men. Even if a woman makes a lot of money, the way she spends it seems different than a man. It still feels very new, less than 4 years old that the tide is turning, so I am not ready to breathe easy yet!" (personal communication, 10 August 2020).

EQ ended up being an enormous undertaking for Bolton, but it was an initiative that she valued. She spoke to me about learning from the other participants and feeling her own community expand. The participants gained community, confidence, and, in some cases, new collaborators. Vilde even spoke of wanting to lead a similar initiative back in Norway. The role of larger institutions like the CMC is to help ensure that the gains made within these women-only spaces transform the male-dominated institutions by giving these women access to power, influence, and resources.

Conclusion

This chapter's study of the CEE's broader network connections and its own institutional power has necessitated a critique of contemporary concert music in Canada and electronic music more broadly as gendered, racialized, and classist spaces. Beyond the issues raised in this chapter, Rodgers's (2010) critique of audio technologies' implication in military technology histories and the erasure of (often female) labour in audio technology manufacturing underlines how much remains to be unpacked in the stories we tell about electronic music and the histories we preserve.

In many ways, the CEE is an "old boys' club." Brant T. Lee explains: "The idea of the old boys' club is that people with certain biological and genetic characteristics – White men – intentionally and perhaps covertly reserve economic benefits for other members of the club, particularly those who share certain social or class characteristics such as school ties, inherited wealth, or shared acquaintances" (2004, 1299). Jaeger, Lake, and Montgomery in particular shared decades' worth of school connections, mutual acquaintances, and the benefits of institutional wealth, whether from the CBC, the CCA, the OAC, or the CMC. This is not to single out the CEE or its members; rather, as Lee explains: "The operation of network standards requires no intentional, irrational discrimination, and no special, direct connections ... The network effects of Whiteness operate this way – without necessary discriminatory intent" (2004, 1299); Lee's words similarly apply to the network effects of patriarchy, given the intersectional privilege of whiteness and cis maleness in Canadian society.

We see in the CEE's history and activities (commissions, bookings, recordings, and so on) the ensemble's many social connections. The CBC Radio's music department is particularly important as a hub of power and resources to which the CEE had access through Grimes, Jaeger, and Lake. The connections within the CBC overlapped with the CMC, the CLC, the Music Gallery, and beyond. Because these social networks have been male-dominated for so long, the CEE continues the internal reinforcement of homogeneity, which in this case is white men. In alignment with Lutter's findings about project-based industry work, the main decision makers at the institutions discussed in this chapter are men, by a vast majority.[22] Lutter explains that women are further disadvantaged because so much of this kind of work relies on personal connections (2015). Bolton's EQ is one initiative that has impacted many women and non-binary electronic musicians in Toronto. However, without shifting the larger institutional networks, the impacts of initiatives like EQ will likely remain limited.

This chapter has identified many Canadian music institutions with the power and resources to provide composers and musicians with career-making and career-sustaining opportunities. These institutions maintain inequities in gender, race, and class. From composition programs to classroom dynamics, from funding opportunities to hiring in positions of power: there are many opportunities for intervention. The CEE can be part of these changes through programming, commissioning, and collaborating. The CEE used to frequently present works by composers; the CEE could return to some of this programming and consciously counter the dominance of white men in electronic music spheres. By partnering with organizations with financial means, the CEE could commission new works, exclusively by musicians from underrepresented identities within experimental electronic music. The CEE thrives on collaboration, with its own members and with guest musicians and ensembles; the CEE could seek out improvisational ensembles with diverse personnel to collaborate. The future holds exciting possibilities for the CEE to be a leader in transforming experimental electronic music into a more equitable and heterogeneous musicking sphere.

Epilogue

The CEE

Fifty Years and Counting

During the Canadian Electronic Ensemble's (CEE) residency at Carnegie Mellon University (CMU) in February 2020, the members were featured in a Steiner Lecture for Creative Inquiry hosted by the Frank-Ratchye STUDIO for Creative Inquiry. The CEE members reflected upon decades of live electronic music making, articulating the threads of their creative practice that persist through changing personnel, collaborators, and technologies while speculating on their own sonic future. This epilogue is an abridged transcription of that lecture, with additional material from their visit and follow-up communication.[1] The question-and-answer format has been edited for narrative flow.

Alexa Woloshyn: How did you become involved with the Canadian Electronic Ensemble? If you are a founding member, what do you recall about that early formation?
David Jaeger: My memories: hanging out with these guys [Jim Montgomery, David Grimes, and Larry Lake]. Just deciding where we can play this gear. It was all this rack-mounted gear. And so we did. And we thought, well, let's pull it out of the rack and take it on stage, and let's create work.

Jim Montgomery: My background was completely in classical music. In fact, I knew nothing about electronic music. When I got to the U of T, I didn't even know they had a studio. I went to the University of Toronto to study composition. All of this stuff was completely new to me. In fact, one of my more embarrassing memories was holding forth in the seminar with Gustav Ciamaga about how this wasn't really music, this was sound sculpture, and clearly, it operated under different laws and different parameters than "real" music. So that attitude was beaten out of me in about three weeks. [laugh] And once I became acquainted with the other three guys ... It's been all downhill from there. [laugh]

Paul Stillwell: I came to the ensemble at a time when I had actually quit doing music. I became so disenchanted with the way things worked at my community college music program that I dropped out and I left. I had such a bad taste in my mouth from that, it actually prevented me from touching any instruments for a period of about seven years. I had the opportunity to acquire some computer gear, and along with that, I decided that I was going to start working around electronic music. So, I put a system together; I started making some music with it. It was all done via MIDI. We had no ability to do audio recording onto a hard drive at that point. I started posting these MIDI files on a service called CompuServe. This is pre-internet. Larry Lake heard some of my compositions, reached out to me, invited me to come hear the ensemble and then commissioned me to write some music for the ensemble. And I never left. I just stayed.

Rose Bolton: I studied music at the University of Western Ontario, which is in London, Ontario. I saw that there was a course called "Electronic Music," and I was really excited about it. I took it, and that changed my life. I would spend all my time – or as much time as I could – going to the library and hunting up records and CDs of electronic music. It was so exciting, and I discovered the CEE's records. I found out there was a job at the Music Gallery. Jim was the artistic director. In the interview, I said I loved electronic music and that one of the ensembles I really liked is the Canadian Electronic Ensemble. The Ensemble commissioned me to write a piece ... for one of their concerts, and eventually I just morphed into being a member.

John Kameel Farah: My dad got me a job a summer job in a factory. On the very first day on the job, I sliced my thumb open. So, I quit the job. I went through the Yellow Pages. I was looking at music, desperately looking for music. I love experimental music. And then the Music Gallery came up. I thought: what the hell is the Music Gallery? Then I called him up, and Jim was the guy that answered the phone. The CEE invited me to jam with them, and then I became the new guy in the band. It was my turn to be the new guy in the band for a few years. Until ...

David Sutherland: I am the new guy in the band. In the '70s, I got involved in electronic music in Montreal. I was with an ensemble called MetaMusic. We did live improvised music – pretty much the same deal as the CEE. Taking the studio apart, moving into a concert hall and playing around with it. I knew about the CEE. They were the cool guys. They didn't know about me. I was a nobody. And then I moved to Toronto. There's all of this modular synthesizer stuff, so I got into that, and just hanging around, met Paul Stillwell over there. And he invited me over to his place to jam, and that was good. It was amazing. Paul actually introduced me. I got invited to play a gig, and then they said I was in the band.

Golan Levin: What is your relationship to other strains of electronic music, such as Tangerine Dream?
Stillwell: Tangerine Dream was one of the reasons I got into doing electronic music. Those instruments that they used and the sounds that they created, particularly in the early days, those were way out there and very similar to the kinds of things that we do.

Jaeger: I think one of the great attractions to the medium of electronic music and certainly live electronic music is that it is wide open, and you can go anywhere. My personal interest in electronic music, and in contemporary composition in general, is the development of musical language. I'm interested in finding ways and finding people – artists – who have the ability to transform the language of music. So, this was the thing that first got me into electronic music, and I discovered it in other forms of music. Larry Lake was a huge fan of all of these manifestations of the art form.

Stillwell: I'm one of three people who organize a festival called the Toronto Sound Festival. One of our goals is to bring interesting new electronic music that is performed live to the audience in Toronto. But at the same time, we're holding seminars during the day so that people can learn how to make music or, if they're already making music, learning how to make the music better, or produce the music better, mix and master the music better. There's a lot of electronic music happening everywhere. I think what's happening, though, is that a lot of it is very local. So, in Pittsburgh, you know, you've probably never heard of the Toronto Sound Festival. And there's a lot of stuff probably going on in Pittsburgh that we don't care about in Toronto. There seems to be a whole movement where new music is very local. I think that's kind of cool, because as you travel around and you seek out the local scene, wherever you happen to be, you're hearing different things, and it's all amazing.

Woloshyn: What have you found to be the common characteristics of a successful collaboration? Do you have any dream collaborations moving forward?

Sutherland: Buddhist monks work at a very high order of consciousness. What I've experienced with the CEE is people who are working at a very intuitive level.

Stillwell: It's not eye contact. It's ears and that other thing. Those other lines of communications. If I'm composing a piece for the band, it's very loose, and it's often just a set of instructions, because I have found that if I try and take too much control over what we're doing, it stamps the life of the band and what we do.

Jaeger: It's kind of a vibe thing. As Dave [Sutherland] describes it, it's almost like another level of communication that happens between us: a collective consciousness, if you will. And when we can work with somebody who can tap into that with us, then it's good.

Montgomery: We've had a very mixed relationship with the visual aspects of our concerts. Our concerts are not what you would call visually compelling. John is a very fine artist and has been producing some videos that we've experimented with – playing with and using his inspiration. I really think that that's an area that we could very fruitfully develop. There are a whole bunch of really interesting video artists out there that we might pursue some collaborations with.

Bolton: What would be really wonderful would be a very high ceiling, or art space, just a giant space with a big, high ceiling where the speakers surrounded the space. We'd have to figure out how not to get too much feedback. But we'd have a really good sound engineer that really was a master. And we occupied the space. It would just be this wonderful happening where people would wander around, maybe there'd be sofas, and throw themselves out on the sofa to zone out.

Woloshyn: What dreams do you have for gear?

Farah: I'm just so dependent on my one synthesizer that I use – usually my Nord Lead 3. I would just love to augment my setup, make it richer with analog gear – sounds so cliché. A couple of analog synthesizers and also more ways of treating the piano. Some more effects. Because I've got my bag that I've been using for years.

Sutherland: I just want to say that the fundamental problem for electronic music in the private sphere, and possibly in the public sphere, is real estate. Everybody that I know has run out of space.

Woloshyn: Maybe you have to get rid of something.

Stillwell: Well, that's the rule. Something new is coming in, something else has to go.

Woloshyn: I guess that's the thing moving forward as you're thinking about new developments, but also, how do you maintain the ones that you have.

Stillwell: Just because something is new, doesn't mean it's better. If that particular tool is something that you find inspiration in, you can't put a price on that. I would really, really love to have a real tape delay. I mean something like a Roland RE-301 or 501 Chorus Echo, or a Korg SE-500. Something that has the ability to also do sound on sound.

Montgomery: It was a sort of ubiquitous gadget about thirty years ago.

Stillwell: I have looked at the Echoplexes. The maintenance on them is a bit of a nightmare.

Jaeger: Apparently, they still make the cartridges.

Stillwell: The guy who originally made them is making new ones.

Bolton: I would like to see further development of small speakers that are able to make good sound. It's happening, but the price is going to have to come down.

Stillwell: I'd love to play in some place that takes full advantage of Ambisonics and has speakers in a full 360 degrees around the audience, including underneath them.

Bolton: There's interesting technology where the fabric has speakers. It's still pretty pricey at this point, but that's what I'm looking forward to.

Jaeger: It's going to be interesting when wearable technology gets into our realm. Wouldn't that be fun?

Stillwell: I don't know. There is some stuff that you can do already with that. And there are some people who are making some good use of it, particularly gloves. I'm still not ready to buy into it. No. VR, I think, holds more potential. Mike Palumbo at York University is working on doing modular synthesis in virtual reality. So, you're not dealing with cables or hardware or anything, but you still have the modules laid out in front of you. But because it's virtual reality, it's almost like you could pick up the modules and move them anywhere in space around you, have the cables stay connected the way they should. That might be cool. Because from a modular synth perspective, a big part of how you make your sounds is how the modules are placed.

Montgomery: Essentially what we've been about is inhabiting a sound world that was much larger and more expansive than the world we were coming from originally as acoustic musicians. Very important at the beginning when we first started working with this stuff. So even in terms of the quartet, in terms of the quintet, in terms of the whole sextet: it's still a matter of looking, searching for what happened. Not so much things that you've never encountered before, but for things that involve new combinations of personalities, sounds. The technology, the hardware kind of falls away at a certain point – for me, anyway. It stops mattering whether this is a DX-83 or this is a DX-42. I've always felt that you can make really good music with sticks and rocks if you want to. But it's a matter of discovery.

Woloshyn: When are you going to release another album?
Bolton: It would be a good idea to create a new album.
 Stillwell: We don't have a new album with John doing piano. We don't have one with David [Sutherland] either.
 Sutherland: It's not like booking a studio for three weeks to try to get an album out. It's like we go in, we play, we leave. It's like jazz.
 Jaeger: If you look at the entire experience of *Bluffer's Lookout* from the planning stage to the sessions, to the mixing, to the final selection and editing, that was kind of a perfect project, in my mind, in terms of just the process. The outcome was very satisfying as well. But just evaluating that as a case study of project conception and realization, I can find no fault with what we did there and how we did it. I'd be willing to do that again.
 Stillwell: From an engineering perspective and a mixing perspective, I've learned a ton since then.

Woloshyn: What do you think is coming next with the CEE?
Jaeger: We're still having fun.
 Sutherland: I'll divide the CEE into two bits. One bit is the CEE that comes out of the academic composer community. Whether we bring guest artists in, they would do regular academic composition with scores, maybe graphical scores, maybe actual common Western music notation scores. But the other piece of it is just improvisation. That's more interesting for me. And so, what does progress look like on the improvisation side? I'm going to suggest it's a little bit more like progress in a martial art. You're not doing more and more; you're going deeper and deeper into it.

Montgomery: I'm seventy-seven years old, right. Now, how much longer can I actually do this? My concern ... In fact, it's not really even a concern. I'm very confident that whatever it is – whether it's called the Canadian Electronic Ensemble or not – we're making, the way we do music, the way we involve ourselves with people, the people we come in contact with, all of that's very positive. Our collaborations and our work with other artists almost uniformly throughout our history have had that kind of openness, immediate connection. And I'm convinced that that will continue in the hands of these people.

Woloshyn: What do you hope the CEE's legacy will be?
Bolton: I would love it if the CEE made a lasting impact that continued on and on with generations to come. Our experiences as artists are shaped by the legacies of others, and so it only makes sense that we could possibly dream, or hope that we might make an impact on others in the future. For myself, coming from a classical background means that I grew up listening to music that was anywhere from ten years up to hundreds of years old. When one is raised on music of the past, do some of us musical creators ever wonder: is there a chance that people will listen to our music hundreds of years or even decades from now? This seems like a good reason to also embrace the music of the present.

I have always thought that it is already a lot to think about creating music for the present. If we have listeners in front of us, they are more important than people who may or may not listen in the future. We can create and then document our work and ensure it is available to others in the future. I think that is all we can really do. Our priority as artists is the now and the present.

Jaeger: My wish is that, as part of the legacy of the CEE, people simply continue to seek out this music in order to enjoy it.

Sutherland: It is not a hope as much as it is a wish that someone at Red Bull would identify the CEE as worth inviting to one of their events; Tokyo or Berlin would be nice. Then, we could have the marvellous experience of meeting young musicians from around the world and playing together. Doing this (meeting young musicians) on repeat until I could no longer travel isn't about legacy. It's about staying in the present moment, and making space for others, which is at the heart of the improvisation.

Montgomery: What I would hope is the legacy of the CEE is freedom. Humans are creative (they can't help it) but they're also very good at putting fences around things and deciding what's in and what's out. All the artists who have worked in and with the CEE have jumped some of those fences in order to play in a larger sound world, and equally importantly (IMHO), to hear in that world. Obviously, we didn't invent this; it was transmitted to each of us from a long line of fence-jumpers (Stockhausen and Cage in my case) each in our own way. My hope is that we will be part of that long line.

The CEE: Living Electronic Music History, Building Its Future

After fifty years of electronic music making history, the story of the CEE still focuses on relationships and the members' memories of first encounters and shared experiences. From feverish nights of experimentation as students in the 1970s to finding a mentor during summer work; from meeting a kindred spirit online to meeting one in a local interest group. The group's compatibility as both sound makers and social humans has been key to their longevity and desire to continue their work together. Their respect for each other's activities outside of the CEE has also been essential. Most members of the ensemble did not set out to create electronic music, but rather found it during the course of their studies or through independent explorations (e.g., Stillwell). The draw of electronic sound worlds has sent them in a wide-ranging search for influences and deep studies of their instruments. After decades of electronic music making, the CEE remains excited to explore and experiment through collective discovery.

The CEE also reflects on the realities of electronic music making: it takes money and space. While institutions may have budgets for new gear or for expensive maintenance of old analog gear, the CEE has not had consistent access to institutional resources across the decades, so choices must be made. Another reality after fifty years is the age of its founding members. Montgomery is plain in recognizing that his time in the CEE must come to an end, likely soon. However, all members of the group see their way of music making as something that can exist beyond this specific collection of musicians under the name "Canadian Electronic Ensemble." They hope that the way they make music will continue in the creative practices of musicians who have collaborated with or listened to the CEE.

The CEE can regale a willing listener with seemingly endless stories of performances, collaborations, travels, and technical glitches (and victories!). Many of the group's members have participated first-hand in decades of live electronic music history. And while this history lives on in the CEE's practice – not only in memory but also in their gear and repertoire – they also have an ear to the future. They are musicians who are eager to explore and experiment, both with each other and with other occasional collaborators. In Canada, there is no group like the CEE. With decades at the forefront of electronic music making, they have witnessed and helped construct the development of electronic and experimental music making across the country. In the broader world of electronic music making, the CEE distinguishes itself by its longevity; by its balance of the individual and the collective, of composed and improvised sounds; and by its Canadianness. On the global stage, the CEE's Canadianness is most apparent through its relationships with Canadian arts and media organizations, such as the University of Toronto, Canadian Broadcasting Corporation, and Canadian Music Centre. The CEE has also been deeply influenced by key Canadian creative voices, such as R. Murray Schafer, Hildegard Westerkamp, and Glenn Gould, each of whom has shaped how the ensemble and its members relate to sound, performance, listening, and recording.

The CEE, both the group and individual members, is a leader in the Canadian electronic and experimental music-making scenes. Their support has bolstered the careers of many young composers and performers whose creative approaches often resonate with their own. As the CEE heads into the next decade of music making, my vision for the group is that it will continue to use its platform and networks of privilege to generously provide opportunities for young musicians and composers through commissions, concert presentations, and/or collaborations, drawing on its half-century of experience to foster the next generation of electronic music.

Discography

CEE. 1977. *Canadian Electronic Ensemble.* Music Gallery Edition MGE 8 (LP). Artoffact Records AOF298CD (CD). Bandcamp.
CEE. 1981. *Canadian Electronic Ensemble.* Centrediscs CMC-1 (LP).
Elmer Isler Singers and "Synthescope" Digital Synthesizer Ensemble. 1982. *The Electronic Messiah.* Moss Music Group D-MMG 113 (LP).
CEE. 1990. *Catbird Seat.* Centrediscs TRAP9003 (CD).
Supertrio. 1996. *Supertrio.* Centrediscs TRAP9604 (CD).
CEE. 1998. *Canadian Electronic Ensemble: Live.* Centrediscs TRAP9805 (CD).
CEE. 2000. *MEGAJAM: 18 Musicians in Your Head at Once.* Trappist Records TRAP0006 (CD).
CEE. 2013. *Live in Cabbagetown.* Bandcamp.
CEE. 2014. *Bluffer's Lookout.* Bandcamp.
Grimes, David. n.d. *Portrait Musical/Musical Portrait: David Grimes.* CAPAC QC-1289.
Jaeger, David. n.d. *Portrait Musical/Musical Portrait: David Jaeger.* CAPAC QC-1288.
Lake, Larry. n.d. *Portrait Musical/Musical Portrait: Larry Lake.* CAPAC QC-1287.
Montgomery, James. n.d. *Portrait Musical/Musical Portrait: James Montgomery.* CAPAC QC-1290.

Appendix

Listening Guides

The Author as Listener

The first time I listened to the CEE was in the early years of my doctoral studies, when I borrowed their album *Catbird Seat* from the library. As a pianist, I was more drawn to acoustic instruments at the time, so the group's collaborations with acoustic soloists (flute, piano, oboe, accordion) brought a sense of familiarity. Listening through headphones, I was quickly drawn into the CEE's sonic world, even when acoustic sound sources were absent.

My listening encounters with the CEE have included rehearsals, concerts, and private listening experiences (mostly through headphones). Each context facilitates a different relationship of my body and ears with the CEE, their instruments/gear, and sound diffusion. Your most frequent listening encounter will likely be through individual listening on speakers or headphones. This type of encounter invites you into an intimate listening experience with the CEE's music in which you can position and move your body however you wish, play back certain sections or tracks as often as you want, and even modify your own mix (e.g., by decreasing high frequencies).

The best way to acquaint yourself with the CEE is to listen, however you want to experience that. My own listening tendencies are largely shaped by my training in teleological, "close" listening, but one may employ various strategies based on different listening priorities. Listening to electronic music can be intimidating to some because they assume they require knowledge of the electronic instruments/gear in order to listen "the right way." Or, as I discussed in chapter 4, some listeners may conclude that their confusion about sound sources (e.g., "What is that sound?" "Who made that sound?") means they cannot or should not listen to this music. But there is no single, correct way to listen to the CEE, or even a hierarchy of ways to listen. Indeed, in her book *Listening Publics*, Kate Lacey rejects the use of the word "audience" as a collective noun that is unified in its experiences and reactions (2013, 14). Dylan Robinson similarly emphasizes that "listening is guided by positionality as an intersection of perceptual habit, ability, and bias" (2020, 37), meaning we cannot speak of a single audience experience. Robinson encourages a self-reflexive listening in which a listener oscillates between layers of their positionality (2020, 60).

In what follows, I outline some potential listening approaches and then provide nine listening guides for pieces composed by and/or for members of the CEE, covering a span of four decades. My reliance on large-scale patterns or growth, a consequence of my background and musical training, has shaped these listening guides as well as my perspective on the CEE's music throughout this book. If taken as objective or prescriptive, this mode of imposing sectional structures on the music might lead one to conclude that large-scale considerations in the CEE's creative practice are more important than the momentary, or that a "correct" listening will invariably lead to the perception of large-scale patterns. The former is not the case, given the CEE's improvisation practice, and the latter would be unethical and even white supremacist, positioning European classical compositional concerns and analytical methods as objective and superior. Thus, rather than prescribing a particular way of hearing the music, I intend for these guides to serve as an example of one listener's encounter that can be in dialogue with other interpretations. Listeners will encounter the CEE in multiple ways, and this music lends itself to open and flexible interpretation, particularly because it avoids the pitch and rhythm-based features of Euro-American classical music and sometimes blurs boundaries between art and popular electronic aesthetics. As the listening guides admittedly also prioritize what Robinson (2020) calls "aesthetic listening" over more flexible kinds of listening, I encourage the reader to explore other listening positionalities alongside the one I model here, and to critique my reliance on Western ontologies of music as the unmarked norm (as discussed in chapter 5).

The chosen pieces include a solo composition by each of the four founding members of the CEE. Both *Increscents* and *Fancye* were included on Grimes's and Jaeger's respective *Portrait Musical* albums.

These four works, plus *Quivi sospiri*, were all among the most frequently performed pieces on CEE concerts during the early quartet and trio eras. This list also includes representation from five CEE albums (and three other albums have examples discussed in the preceding chapters). Thus, these works provide an overview of the CEE's compositional and performative activities across almost forty years. Beecroft's piece offers a slightly different perspective on the CEE: as performers responding to the creative vision of a commissioned composer. This work also demonstrates some important possibilities in live electronic music performance in the 1970s. All of these works reflect the CEE's affinity to combine electronic and acoustic sonic forces.

An Invitation to Listen

Listening to the CEE through headphones or speakers creates acousmatic listening contexts in which the listener cannot see any human performer. Such a listening context was required for what Pierre Schaeffer termed écoute réduite (reduced listening). Schaeffer identified four modes of listening employed in our daily lives that result in listening habits running counter to his goal of listening carefully and with intention, but rejecting sound identification and interpretation (Chion 1994):

1. écouter: when listening, we aim to identify the source of a sound
2. comprendre: processing the meaning of a sound
3. ouïr: aural sensation of hearing a sound; can be passive
4. entendre: choosing what to listen to from all of the sounds we might hear

Schaeffer theorized "écoute réduite" as an intentional listening approach specific to his "concrete music": reduced or reductive listening through which one considers only the internal perceptible properties of the sound object.[1] A sound object is a sound phenomenon that one attends to as a coherent whole while disregarding its origins (avoiding écouter) or meaning (avoiding comprendre). These sound objects are recontextualized as musical objects through creative intervention in the studio (Schaeffer 1966).

According to Schaeffer, the acousmatic listening context facilitates reduced listening by eliminating non-sonic sensory input (as opposed to Joanna Demers's [2010] desire for "aesthetic listening," discussed in chapter 5).[2] Musique concrète, though, does not hide human performers behind a curtain: there are no human performers, at least not in the conventional sense of Euro-American classical music. Listening to the CEE live is not acousmatic, therefore, as there are human performers on the stage. However, listening to the CEE's albums is an acousmatic listening experience, with the electronic sounds creating an increased sense of distance from human agency. So, you might want to try listening to the CEE through a "reduced listening" approach. This means avoiding attempts to identify sound sources or craft a narrative. Rather, reduced listening asks the listener to focus on the timbral and textural qualities of the sounds and how they transform over time, or the spectromorphology of sounds (from Denis Smalley 1986, 1996, 1997). The guide for *Attention Elk!* incorporates some reduced listening. However, it also connects the sounds and their transformations with extrinsic associations, something Smalley – unlike Schaeffer – prioritizes.

Critiquing Schaeffer's approach, Smalley characterizes reduced listening as "an abstract, relatively objective process, a microscopic, intrinsic listening" (1997, 111), and he declares it "dangerous" despite "many composers [regarding] reduced listening as an ultimate mode of perceptual contemplation" (1997, 111). Smalley emphasizes the interactivity between intrinsic features – spectromorphology – and extrinsic features contextualized by culture and experience. He worries that too much focus might be paid to "low-level" details and that once this type of focus has been established, it becomes too difficult to reintegrate it with extrinsic considerations. Smalley's indicative fields outline nine concepts that link intrinsic sound qualities and behaviours to "to the world of experience outside the composition, not only to the wider context of auditory experience but also to non-sounding experience" (Smalley 1996, 83).[3] If you attempt Schaeffer's reduced listening, consider Smalley's caution to avoid too much low-level focus and to connect the intrinsic details to associations and experiences that come to your mind.

Some listening guides here provide more technical details than others, especially *Consequences for 5*. Technical knowledge is never a requirement for the appreciation of electronic music, just as one need not be an opera singer to enjoy opera or to share one's assessment of an opera and its performers. Technical knowledge can be one path into electronic music listening – one's knowledge of gear and processes will shape how one listens – but it is not a prerequisite for deep engagement with electronic music. If you enjoy technical details, then I hope the ones provided here are interesting and insightful.

Both *Analytical Methods of Electroacoustic Music* (Simoni 2006) and *Expanding the Horizon of Electroacoustic Music Analysis* (Emmerson and Landy 2016) provide numerous models for analysis of electroacoustic and electronic works. While my listening guides are not designed as analyses, they include some of the same strategies, including visual components: score excerpts and spectrogram images.[4] Visuals can clarify or amplify aural stimuli. For example, in the listening guide for *Quivi sospiri*, I provide a spectrogram that emphasizes textural aspects, particularly a slow build in intensity and a sudden drop. Score excerpts identify pitch and rhythmic components, but they also clarify instances in which those aspects are not precisely notated. For those with training in Euro-American notated musics, score excerpts can, perhaps misleadingly, guide one into emphasizing elements that can be notated (e.g., pitch, rhythm) over those that cannot, like timbre. Furthermore, they could lead one to pay more attention to notated elements, such as focusing on the piano part in *Quivi sospiri* or the oboe part in *Psalm*. I encourage you to experiment with your focus, challenging yourself not to give the acoustic, notated components more attention than the electronic components. You might also choose to oscillate attention between them: When is your attention drawn to one kind of sound source over another? How difficult is it to shift focus between different sound sources, especially acoustic vs electronic? If you listened to the piece before reviewing the score, does anything surprise you when you listen again with the score?

I have not strictly applied any one particular approach in these listening guides. Nonetheless, teleological, structural listening is a recurring feature, owing to my training in so-called "close listening." Robinson (2020) describes the kind of fixed, close listening prioritized in Euro-American classical concerts and education as "single-sense engagement" (i.e., listening with the ears only). In this mode, repeated listening to audio-only works and score study facilitates the discovery of recurring motifs and other sectional similarities. I invite you to use my structural listening as best suits your own listening interests. Robinson encourages us to reflect on our positionality, or the "intersection of perceptual habit, ability, and bias" (2020, 37). We can listen through and between those various positionalities, to listen relationally "not merely between listener and listened to, but between the layers of our individual positionalities" (58). Perhaps you will hear different structural breakdowns than I do, or perhaps you'd prefer not to think about structure and form at all. Robinson encourages listeners to embrace flexible listening, such as embracing "the affective feel, timbre, touch, and texture of sound" (38). Have each sonic moment wash over you – mind and body.

Joanna Demers (2010) describes the kind of listening to EDM that happens at dance clubs as "aesthetic listening": in addition to taking in sonic stimuli, one also shifts attention to other attendees – what they are wearing, how they are moving, etc. – and one might focus at times on their own movement, how their body feels in that space, in relation to the other bodies. While the CEE's music is not EDM, this kind of listening can be brought to any kind of music, including the CEE's. Listen alone, and then listen with others. Don't resist when your attention shifts to the lighting in the room, or to the kind of clothing you are wearing and how it feels on your body. Listen with loudspeakers to allow the sounds to resonate more deeply through your body. Move as you listen. Embrace Gouldian ecstasy.

Listening Guides

The listening guides are presented in chronological order:
Increscents (1972) – David Grimes
Fancye (1973) – David Jaeger
Consequences for 5 (1977) – Norma Beecroft
I Have Come Through (1979) – James Montgomery
Quivi sospiri (1979) – David Jaeger
Psalm (1985) – Larry Lake
Attention Elk! (1994) – CEE
Caspin's Arrival (1998) – CEE
Improvisation #4 (2008) – CEE

INCRESCENTS (1972) – DAVID GRIMES

Increscents is a trio composed for two synthesizers and violin. Grimes explained in a CBC interview for the 2 November 1976 broadcast of the piece that his objective is to "try to strike a middle ground between

Table A.1 Formal outline of *Increscents* with descriptions of violin and synthesizer parts.

Section/timing	Violin	Synthesizers
Solo – 7:18	• With mutes • Opens with E♭. Ascending and descending M2, with ornamentations of M9 and m7 (same two pitches: E♭ and D♭)	
Trio – 8:34	• Spaced-out harmonic m7 gestures • Removes mutes, and shifts to higher range with expanded intervallic and pitch palettes; keeps returning to E♭	• Synthesizer I: A♭ and D♭; Synthesizer II: B♭ and E♭ • They retrigger their pitches at various points beneath the violin part
	• *Sul ponticello* double stops, dissonant intervals, and angular motives (10:20)	• Synthesizer extends into a lower range
	• High glissandi alternating with pizzicato • High pianissimo trill as transition	• Reverb and feedback effects
Duo – 13:12	• In two brief instances (16:40 and 17:46), the violin plays a pianississimo trill (recalling 12:59) • The second trill persists until the two synthesizers fade out	• Notated pitches without precise rhythm • Frequent use of M2 and m2
Solo – 18:11	• The violin plays brief motives (1–7 notes) • Wide range of pitches and dynamics	
Trio – 19:53	• Pizzicato-glissandi gestures • Then simple and spaced-out melodic gestures • Ends on B♭ (the fifth above the E♭ tonal centre)	• Ring modulation on the pizzicato-glissandi gestures • Pulsing on the violin's closing melodic gestures • A drone on E♭ persists until the end

traditional music and electronic music." By composing to each instrument's strengths rather than requiring one to imitate the other, Grimes creates a compellingly integrated collaboration between the three instruments.

The various combinations of the performing forces (solo, duo, and trio) divide *Increscents* into five large sections, outlined in table A.1.[5]

This piece is not tonal in any sense of containing functional harmony. However, it clearly opens and closes with a tonal centre: E♭. The muted

Figure A.1 Opening violin solo in *Increscents*.

Figure A.2 Score excerpt (p. 5) of synthesizer duo in *Increscents*.

violin then meditates on both E♭ and D♭, articulated as ascending and descending major seconds in various rhythmic iterations. Then, through major ninth and minor seventh leaps, the violin continues to play only E♭ and D♭ (see figure A.1).[6] This increased intervallic range anticipates an even bigger change: the entrance of the two synthesizers on A♭ and D♭ (synthesizer I) and B♭ and E♭ (synthesizer II). The piece is now a trio, with the violin playing E♭ and D♭ as a harmonic interval. The violin removes its mutes and expands its intervallic and pitch palettes while continuing to reinforce E♭ as tonal centre. The synthesizers punctuate unpredictably the space around the violin. The violin becomes more aggressive, with sul ponticello double stops, dissonant intervals, and angular motives. From its highest note, the violin plays brief glissandi, which soon alternate with pizzicato, all with reverb and feedback effects. With a high pianissimo trill, the violin passes the piece over almost entirely to the two synthesizers (with the exception of two brief trills).

Each synthesizer performs notated pitches, sometimes with huge contrasts in range (see figure A.2). The pitches are not notated with precise rhythm, which fosters uncertainty and anticipation. The timbres transform across the section, and vibrato effects are also varied. The pitch content also creates a sense of instability – though the frequent appearance of major second and minor second intervals offers some familiarity. The violin plays a pianissimo trill as the synthesizers fade out: a second violin solo section begins. The violin plays brief motives (one to seven notes) with rests of various lengths between each one. The violin traverses a wide range of pitches (approximately three octaves) and dynamics (from subito pianissimo to fortissimo). The piece ends as a trio, with the synthesizers modifying the violin's pizzicato-glissandi gestures through a ring modulator. The violin's simple and spaced-out melodic gestures are modified through a pulsing effect. Synthesizer II holds a B♭ and E♭ pedal until the end of the piece. The violin's final three pitches (B♭-G-B♭) reinforce not only E♭ as tonal centre but also the E♭ major triad as a kind of conventional tonal "home," despite the piece's overall avoidance of tonality through its varied pitch content.

FANCYE (1973) – DAVID JAEGER

Jaeger's organ background and electronic music studies are both reflected in *Fancye* (1973), commissioned by the University of Toronto to dedicate the Edward Johnson Building's organ in Walter Hall, an organ with two manuals (Hauptwerk and Ruckpositiv) and pedals, twenty-five stops, and thirty-four ranks.[7] For the work's premiere on 2 December 1973, Derek Healey played the organ in tandem with a four-channel electronic tape realized by the CEE in the University of Toronto Computer Centre and visuals by Carol Sutton Martin. The title, an Elizabethan spelling of "fancy," refers to English Renaissance organ music like that of John Bull (ca 1562–1628). The work's construction traces a path from Bull through Bach to the present by way of two chords from J.S. Bach's *Orgelbüchlein*. Any attempt to listen for those specific chords will leave one disappointed, because they are not present in plain sound. Rather, Jaeger analyzed the harmonics of those chords, which then form the harmonic structure of the work, to which the computer-generated sounds were tuned and the organ set.

Jaeger's score note describes the visual component:

Consists of flakes of colored light (soft colors of a Japanese fruit dessert) produced by light organs linked to the computer electronic tape and cast upon two distinct sculptural forms. The first form: hanging mirrors which move freely with the wind (as the organ is a wind instrument). The second form: high silver-surfaced columns, scattered at random on stage, catching light and reflecting it back to the audience.

Nicholas Thistlewaite and Geoffrey Weber declare that "throughout the ages the organ has been granted an elevated status in the minds of both writers and musicians" (1998, xi) because this single instrument could achieve diverse tone colours and tessituras, express intricate melodic lines, harmonize dense chords, and fill a large cathedral with its thunderous swells. For example, Irish poet Nicholas Brady referred to the organ as "Wond'rous Machine!" in a text set by Henry Purcell ("Ode for St Cecilia's Day," 1692). Thistlewaite and Weber bemoan the development of electronic organs "that electronically reproduce recorded sound," arguing that "in these the breath that gives life to the music has been extinguished altogether" (1998, xii). One might claim that the world of electronic music, both in the studio and in live performance, has also taken over as the "wond'rous machine" with vast and mysterious capabilities. However, in *Fancye*, the organ devotee is reassured of the instrument's role: the organ and the four-channel tape work as partners, weaving in and out of each other's timbres through a principally spacious and slow-moving texture. Broadly speaking, the opening and closing of *Fancye* employ the fewest stops, with a climax of tonal and harmonic colour occurring from approximately 6:20 to 7:00.[8] See table A.2 for a list of stops employed in *Fancye*.

Fancye opens and closes with relatively limited pitch material in the organ part, an approach that allows the timbre of the combined forces to take prominence. The work begins with C, which acts like a tonal centre for the opening minute through its repetition in various octaves across the two manuals and pedals. This C is soon accompanied by B♭; this minor seventh relationship becomes a stable harmony not only through repetition but also because of its familiarity from dominant seventh harmonies within Euro-American classical music common-practice functional harmony. The tape part complicates this relative tonal coherence with its own ephemeral pitch material; it is quieter than the organ, so the tape's ringing tones – though they have precise frequencies – act more as timbral colour than as pitch material.

The organ's pitch material expands slowly to embrace more dissonance and chromaticism, including augmented and diminished fourths.

Table A.2 List of organ stops used in *Fancye*.

Organ stop	Manual/pedal	Notes
Bordun 16'	Hauptwerk	Produces a massive full sound of "extreme dignity and an ecclesiastical solemnity of tone" (Locher 1914, 8)
Gedackt 8'	Ruckpositiv	Adds "body" and "a fuller and darker note to combinations" (Locher 1914, 67)
Gedacktpommer 8'	Pedal	Produces a strong harmonic at the 12th
Gemshorn 2'	Ruckpositiv	Horn-like timbre
Hohlflöte 8'	Hauptwerk	Provides a "full and pleasing intonation" (Locher 1914, 78)
Krummhorn 8'	Ruckpositiv	Resembles the horn; soft intonation
Mixtur	Pedal	
Mixtur IV	Hauptwerk	Uses four pipes per note to create various harmonics
Nasat 1 1/3'	Ruckpositiv	A quiet stop that reinforces the 2nd harmonic
Oktave 2'	Hauptwerk	Reinforces the first harmonic to add "more precision and clearness" (Locher 1914, 97)
Oktave 4'	Pedal	
Oktave 8'	Pedal	
Praestant 4'	Ruckpositiv	
Quinte 2 2/3'	Hauptwerk	Reinforces the 2nd harmonic
Rohrflöte 4'	Ruckpositiv	Brighter stop
Schalmei 4'	Pedal	Very soft reed stop
Scharf	Ruckpositiv	Similar to Mixtur with "penetrating tones" (Williams and Owen 1988, 284), including the 3rd
Sesquialtera 2 2/3'	Ruckpositiv	Adds the third in the upper voice
Spitzflöte	Hauptwerk	Bright metal stop
Subbass 16'	Pedal	
Tremulant	Ruckpositiv	
Trompete 8'	Pedal	Reed stop

Fancye contains a small number of striking gestures that unify the work across the changing timbres and pitches (see figure A.3): a descending major second (first presented as C to B♭); a short, notated trill/mordent (three to six notes), both ascending and descending (almost exclusively a major second interval); a descending perfect fifth (sometimes notated like an acciaccatura), followed by an ascending major second; and to a lesser degree, quartal chords consisting of various combinations of diminished, perfect, and augmented fourths.

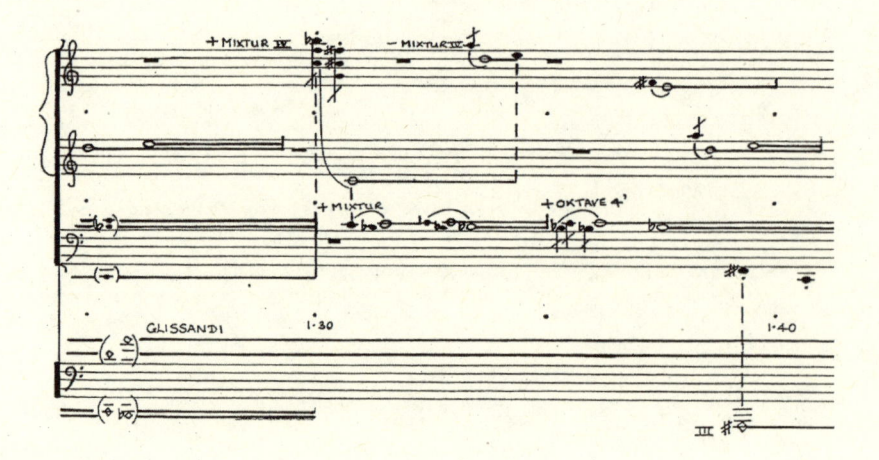

Figure A.3 Score excerpt (p. 2) showing recurring gestures in *Fancye*.

The organ and electronic tape parts are timbrally cohesive, often creating the effect of sounding like one expansive instrument. In two instances in *Fancye*, however, the electronic tape part takes a more prominent role. From approximately 3:25 to 4:05 (most noticeably until 3:47), *Fancye* suddenly increases its activity in the tape part, with rapid-moving pitch bursts resembling the ascending and descending impulse complexes of Stockhausen's *Gesang der Jünglinge* (1955–56). In that case, Stockhausen was working with an impulse generator, while the CEE used a computer. With increased amplitude, the tape part is more prominent in this section of the piece, resulting in more of an equal partnership with the organ than its more supportive previous role. This increased focus on the tape part anticipates a tape solo. From 4:08 until 5:20, the organ is silent. Perhaps surprisingly to some listeners, however, the tape part does not include any of the more active passages from the previous minute. Sustained mid-range pitches function as pedal tones, which move around and across the listening space.[9] Time slows down during this brief section of relative inaction. Additional higher-frequency pitches enter the texture in anticipation of the return of the organ.

The organ returns on C, and soon with a C to B♭ gesture, a clear harkening back to the opening section. Jaeger applies some new timbral colours to this familiar pitch material, including Tremulant (Hauptwerk), Trompete (Ruckpositiv), and Spitzflöte (Hauptwerk). The ending also resembles the opening in its spaciousness, with sustained tones and transparent layers. This recall is much more tense, however, with an

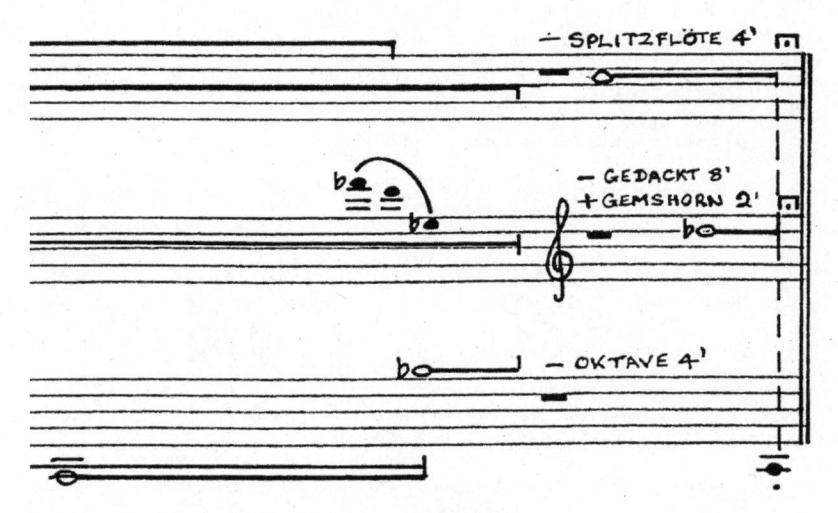

Figure A.4 Score excerpt from ending of *Fancye*.

electronic ringing above a low-range dissonant melody. Like the opening twenty-five seconds, the final seventy-five seconds are for solo organ, as it builds up its final pitch layers before arriving at C first in the pedal and then in the Hauptwerk manual. However, unlike the opening, the C is not alone: a high D♭ played on the Ruckpositiv manual resists tonal closure (see figure A.4).

CONSEQUENCES FOR 5 (1977) – NORMA BEECROFT

In her album notes, Beecroft explains two aspects of the piece connected to "consequences." First, the CEE could play both brass instruments and electronic instruments, so *consequently*, Beecroft required that versatility in the piece. Second, Beecroft points to "basic material" from which material is expanded and electronically manipulated. Building on Beecroft's own conceptualizations, I would add that because of extensive tape delay and playback, the way the performers play their parts the first time around has consequences when those delay and playback functions are implemented. The tape delay effect was achieved using an Echoplex, which includes volume, sustain, and delay time controls.

Beecroft composed a piece with clear sections, labelled in the score as Sequences I through IV and Interludes I through III (see table A.3). Each section draws on particular temporal, rhythmic, registral, textural, and pitch-based elements.

Table A.3 Formal outline of *Consequences for 5* with descriptions and technical details.

Section	Description	Technical notes
Sequence I	• All brass on C, with quarter-tone glissando; Harmon mute on trumpet • Soft piano pitches • Horn ascending slide with echo effect • Fortissimo brass crunch chord (A-B♭-B)	Echoplex (EP) on horn
Sequence II	• Piano plays only E3 and F3 • Piano expands pitch and register, with notes articulated as fast as possible • Fortissimo piano tone cluster with EP	Tape playback: brass from Sequence I Tape delay: piano + synth 1 (0:20) EP on piano at end of section
Interlude I	• Synthesizer-only section • Synthesizer I: siren-like, with slow glissando • Synthesizer II: resembles slow-changing white noise • Synthesizer III: staccato pitches with varying groupings and tempi • Section ends with a rallentando and decrescendo	
Sequence III	• Piano enters, then synthesizer, and then horn: focus on third intervals • Virtuosic piano passage: mostly ascending thirds before arriving on a fortissimo chord of fifths (C-G-D; G-D-A) with delay effect • Horn plays a series of fast staccato pitches	EP on piano EP on horn
Interlude II	• Horn lands on a loud C, followed by synthesizer-only section • Synthesizer I: low range, slow rising and falling (Patch G; see figure 6.2) • Synthesizer II: low range with similar glissandi effects (Patch G; see figure 6.2) • Synthesizer III: higher range, with quick staccato sounds that vary rhythmic pacing and frequency range • All parts fade to silence	
Sequence IV	• Piano recalls chord of fifths (C-G-D; G-D-A) • Quartal and quintal pitch relationships	Subtle piano treatment applied by synthesizer (via Patch I)
Sequence V	• Trumpet and trombone: dissonant staccato pitches, speeding up and increasing in pitch range • Synthesizer I: similar material to the brass • Piano plays fast, repeated notes and leaps to seemingly random staccato notes; rhythmic EP effect • Synthesizer II: seemingly random pitches • Trumpet and trombone land on C: trombone immediately trills to D♭; they glissando up to C and D♭, respectively • Short runs in the piano, followed by descending seven-16th-note groupings • Piano arrives on chord (LH: B♭-F; RH: C-D-G-C), with EP effect	EP on piano EP on brass Tape delay: piano + brass
Interlude III	• Piano part from Sequence IV plays back • Real-time piano part plays only fourth and fifth intervals in various directions, melodic and harmonic arrangements, and rhythmic iterations	Tape playback of Sequence IV

Section	Description	Technical notes
Sequence VI	• Staccato brass returns, then piano part (playback of Sequence V). • All brass parts, piano, and Synthesizer I play similar material to the playback: becoming higher, faster, and louder over time • Synthesizer II: quick staccato pitches • Real-time piano and brass hit Cs simultaneously (piano chord: LH: C-G-D; RH: G-D-C), while the synthesizers and tape playback continue to play higher, louder, and faster	Tape playback of Sequence V EP on piano EP on brass
Coda	• Notated in the score, but imperceptible or absent on recording	

Sequence I opens with a subdued, potentially mysterious mood. The brass – beginning with trumpet, then horn, and then trombone – articulates C. As each player crescendos and decrescendos the C, they slide a quarter tone sharp and then back down; because the three brass players articulate their Cs at different times, the quarter-tone glissandi create a beating effect. The piano's sparse and pianississimo pitches are barely audible. Sequence I's mood shifts suddenly: first, with a horn glissando and crescendo, all with an echo effect, then more dramatically with the fortissimo brass crunch chord in the brass (A-B♭-B).

As the brass crunch chord fades, the piano enters. Though Sequence II begins with a simple piano part (moving between E_3 and F_3 in different rhythms), the pianist soon reveals their virtuosity. In this section, the brass part from the opening section plays back. And soon enough, the piano also has a second layer via a twenty-second tape delay from the start of Sequence II, an intriguing and possibly confusing effect for a listener. Sequence II ends with the fortissimo cluster chord, to which the Echoplex immediately applies a delay effect (see figure A.5).

Interlude I begins as the piano's Echoplex effect is still fading. The remainder of the interlude contains only synthesizers. Beecroft has indicated specific roles for each synthesizer based on frequency and durational components. The first synthesizer plays slow glissandi, like sirens. The next synthesizer is instructed to sit in the high to medium-high range and to vary the filter/oscillator frequency and response; the result is like a gentle white noise with subtle frequency changes. The third synthesizer provides contrast by improvising random pitches with short attacks and decay, beginning with slower articulations and then alternating between fast and slow sequences. Despite constant change

Figure A.5 Score excerpt (p. 2) from Sequence II of *Consequences for 5*.

on the micro level, the overarching electronic sound world here is stable, allowing a listener to shift attention between the three synthesizers or to focus on the subtle changes produced by a single performer. This section ends calmly with a decrease in both tempo and dynamics.

The piano returns in Sequence III. At first, the piano offers only sparse thirds (E to C; C to A; G♯ to E; E♭ to C); the Echoplex's delay effect adds a rhythmic echo. A synthesizer and the horn join the piano and its meditation on thirds, both with pianissimo indications. The piano part expands from single pitches to third, fifth, and sixth harmonic intervals. Due to the delay effect, we hear more articulations than are actually being played. The piano has another virtuosic flourish, consisting principally of ascending thirds played as fast as possible over a crescendo. The piano strikes a fortissimo chord built on fifths (LH: C-G-D; RH: G-D-A), to which a dramatic delay effect is applied. The horn follows suit with a series of staccato pitches played as fast as possible until it arrives on the loud C with a delay effect.

Interlude II is similar to the first: it consists of three synthesizers, two of which play slow-moving glissandi (both instructed to use Patch G on the Synthi As; see figure A.6), with the third playing rapid staccato pitches. In contrast to the previous interlude, it is the slow-moving synthesizers that are in a lower frequency range. All three synthesizer parts subtly transform dynamic levels and frequency ranges until they fade into silence.

Sequence IV begins where Sequence III ended: a stacked fifths chord. The piano remains almost obsessed with the perfect fifth interval (other than a single tritone near the start of the section) until it begins to switch

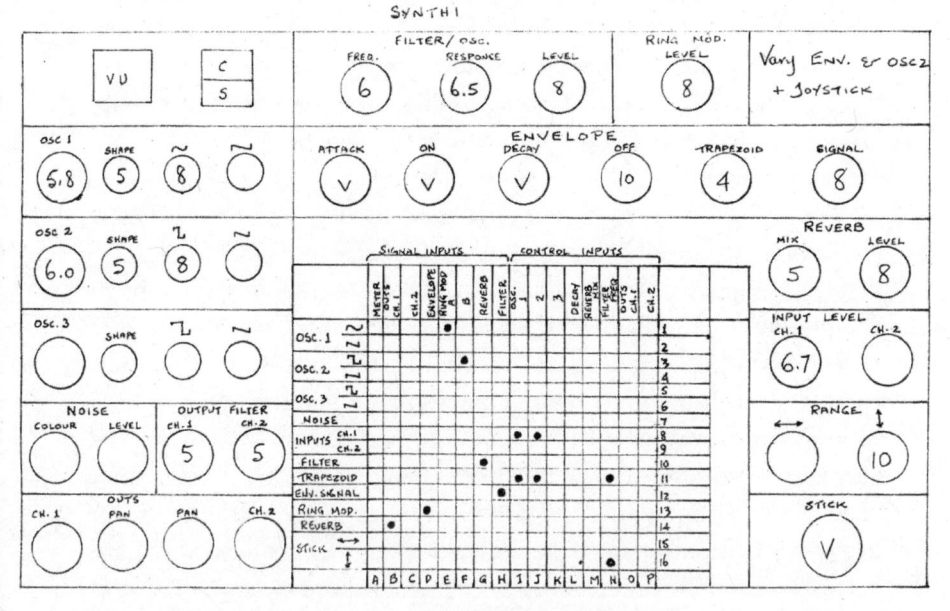

Figure A.6 Patch G instructions for *Consequences for 5*.

between quartal pitch relationships when descending and quintal pitch relationships when ascending. A tremolo quintal (LH) and quartal (RH) gesture heralds the next sequence.

In Sequence V, the trumpet and trombone are instructed to improvise: the score includes some notated suggestions of staccato pitches, mostly in minor second and diminished octave melodic intervals, at a quiet dynamic level and relatively slowly; they gradually play faster and louder. The piano joins the increasing cacophony with fast repeated notes plus an abundance of leaps to seemingly random staccato notes across a large range. One synthesizer and then another joins in the rhythmic and pitched cacophony. The live pianist takes a brief pause before returning with quick ascending runs and leaps. Following a long series of improvised staccato pitches, the trombone and trumpet settle on a sustained C. The trombone, though, trills between C and D♭, creating dissonance following that brief moment of consonance. The trumpet and trombone both slide up and land on a loud C and D♭, respectively. Through this, the piano has continued its virtuosic playing, now with a series of descending seven-16th-note patterns. During almost this entire section, we have heard the brass and piano parts on tape delay. This tape delay part reinforces the impression of cacophony and also allows the listener to hear the impressive piano passagework twice. When the tape delay version arrives at the piano's final chord – mostly fourths and fifths (LH: B♭-F; RH: C-D-G-C), unsurprisingly – the Echoplex adds a dramatic delay effect.

While the previous two interludes had been synthesizer-only sections, Interlude III is piano-centric. We hear playback of the piano part from Sequence IV as the piano improvises fourths and fifths above. Sample patterns have been provided in the score to communicate expectations to the performer: ascending and descending; melodic and harmonic; different rhythmic iterations. When the tape playback continues into Sequence VI (Conclusion), we are hearing Sequence V. Someone listening to this piece without access to the live performance likely wouldn't know that this is a playback. I suspect, though, some perceptual dissonance for a live audience when they are hearing sounds but seeing no physical movement. Following about twenty seconds of this playback alone, the piano, three brass, and a synthesizer join in the staccato leaps heard on the playback. They are instructed to begin slowly and in a lower range, increasing dynamics and speed and raising the overall frequency of their random pitch leaps. Another synthesizer joins in the fun; by this point, the dense texture makes it difficult to discern the discrete number of performers, but that doesn't really seem to be the point anyway. The piano and brass arrive simultaneously on forte or fortissimo Cs (the piano plays a chord; LH: C-G-D; RH: G-D-C) while the synthesizers and playback continue. One synthesizer's pitches become unhumanly fast and continue ascending while the other synthesizer's long ascending glissandi sound like a rocket taking off. The piece ends suddenly, perhaps as the synthesizers blast into space.

I suspect that *Consequences for 5* creates strikingly different impressions when experienced in live performance as opposed to through audio recording only. Beecroft's use of tape playback and delay throughout the piece results in often dense textures that are only in part the result of the performers' physical actions. Because of the clear overlap of piano parts and brass parts, a listener might conclude that some kind of playback or delay must be present. However, without access to the score, it is nearly impossible to precisely delineate between the recording and real-time playing when they are presented simultaneously. Listening to the piece without referencing the score, someone might interpret the piece as having two pianists, or at the very least more piano action than the performer physically provides. The listener might also assume that the piece involves more than three brass players, particularly at the end when both the tape playback and the real-time brass parts articulate rapid staccato pitches.

When I listen to *Consequences for 5* without referencing the score, I am more caught up in colours, contrasts, and recollections. When I listen along with the score, my perception is pulled in two directions: the sound world of the piece and the technical details required to pull it off, such as the many patch changes, turning playback on and off, changing Echoplex settings, and so on. I have not seen a live performance of this piece, but I suspect that in live performance, a listener would be impressed both by the physicality of the acoustic playing and by the technical prowess to engage playback, delay, and the Echoplex in real time: a listener may deem such a live performance "virtuosic." My discussion here draws on the score, additional technical notes supplied by Beecroft, and the recording from Beecroft's *Anthology for Canadian Musicians*. This recording, featuring guest brass players alongside Kieser on piano and the CEE on synthesizers, captures a very different kind of live performance in terms of effort and physicality than the premiere, in which CEE members doubled on brass and synthesizers. (In her liner notes, Beecroft explains that the premiere "posed considerable logistical problems," and as a result, she simplified the piece and the brass parts were passed along to other performers.) My reflection above at times considers the non-recorded premiere and imagines what this piece would be like when performed spatially and temporally live as originally composed – for five. William Littler's *Toronto Star* review (22 April 1977) of the 21 April premiere aids my imagination of the work's impressive complexity:

> [This piece requires] having them perform live on brass instruments, act as composers of improvised sequences and operate a vast array of electronic hardware, including four synthesizers, two of them to treat the brass and piano, tape delay, tape play back, echo units, microphones, mixers – the works.
>
> The result resembled a kind of sound sensorium, multi-layered and textured, with a regular interplay of present and past, live and electronic instruments, and a keyboard part solidly in the virtuoso piano tradition.

What makes the complexity and labour of this premiere all the more striking is the story that a power outage meant that the piece was interrupted and had be started a second time.

I have provided a number of technical details above, yet I do not assert that such a precise knowledge of the mechanisms of production is what makes *Consequences for 5* interesting for me as a listener or that such knowledge will lead anyone to a more "valid" or "true" assessment of this piece. If appreciation of electronic music necessitated intimate technical knowledge, then the reach and impact of the genre would be limited indeed. Nonetheless, the technical details are revealing – what technologies were available at the time, what labour those technologies necessitated, what timbres those technologies created – and they enable us to imagine what a live performance would look like in addition to its sound based on acoustic, electronic, and performative elements.

I HAVE COME THROUGH (1979) – JAMES MONTGOMERY

Montgomery's *I Have Come Through* (1979) for piano and electronics was commissioned by the CBC and is dedicated to pianist Monica Gaylord, with whom the CEE performed on a few occasions in the 1970s and '80s. The piece was featured during the 1979 European tour with Karen Kieser on piano. *I Have Come Through* highlights the wide-ranging textural and timbral capabilities of the piano, including extended technique. The title comes from the D.H. Lawrence poem "Song of a Man Who Has Come Through," and Montgomery included an excerpt of this poem on the title page of his work: "If only I am keen and hard like the sheer tip of a wedge / Driven by invisible blows, / The rock will split, we shall come at the wonder, we shall find the Hesperides." The work could be experienced as a kind of sonic dramatization or evocation of the original poem, especially the lines quoted above. A listener might also think about all that the piano/keyboard as an instrument "has come through" historically in terms of repertoire, from Bachian counterpoint to Mozartian galant to Cageian prepared piano. Indeed, this work features many different approaches to both the piano keyboard (e.g., fast passagework and extreme registers; see figure A.7) and the piano as a physical instrument (specifically as a kind of string instrument with a keyboard interface).

Figure A.7 Fast, descending passagework in *I Have Come Through* (mm. 15–16).

Figure A.8 Performance indications for techniques 2 and 4 in *I Have Come Through* (mm. 63–72).

Montgomery provides detailed notes on how to perform both the piano and the electronics. Of particular note for the pianist are four extended techniques: 1) strike a bell or bowl-gong that has been placed on the low strings of the piano (up to the lowest F♯); 2) blow air on strings in the indicated register by using a thin tube; 3) slide resin on the designated string; 4) slide the bell/bowl-gong along the low F♯ string (see figure A.8).

The electronics part can be achieved with a pre-recorded tape, but Montgomery's design is for live amplification, signal processing of the piano (using a voltage-controlled oscillator and ring modulator), synthesized sound production (using a stick controller, voltage-controlled oscillator, and envelope shaper), and a tape delay. *I Have Come Through* is a showcase for the pianist, rather than a duet for piano and electronics. The electronics serve to expand the timbral range and spatialization of the piano's acoustic capabilities in a limited portion of the piece.

The work has an ABA' structure, with the A sections focused on pianistic writing and the B section exploring extended technique and expansions through electronics. Table A.4 outlines the main features of each section.

The piece opens with virtuosic descending sixteenth-note passagework that consists primarily of parallel fifths and fourths. The rhythmic pace slows as the sixteenth-note groupings change to triplets before

Table A.4 Formal outline of *I Have Come Through* with descriptions of piano and synthesizer parts.

Section	Piano	Electronics
A (mm. 1–40)	• Virtuosic descending passage (mm. 1–24) • Hectic pace slows until it arrives at an andante eighth-note pulse in the right hand (mm. 25ff) • Left hand punctuates the relatively static texture with an augmented fifth interval (and then alternating P5 and A5) in quarter-note and eighth-note triplets	
B (mm. 40–82)	• Sliding resin along string in crescendo/decrescendo creates a distinctive squawking timbre	• Synthesized A eighth-note pulse (begins at m. 37, before the piano material of Section A has completely finished)
	• The piano plays limited pitch material: major seventh and major ninth intervals (mm. 42–7); angular descending gestures, followed by repeated notes (mm. 53–7) • Striking the bell/bowl-gong creates a buzzing sound from the low strings as well as a high bell sound (mm. 49–57) • Sliding the bell/bowl-gong along the strings creates a complex scraping timbre (mm. 63–8) • Blowing air through a tube onto the strings creates a contrasting gentler sound (mm. 69–75)	• Starting in m. 42, the ring modulation processes the live piano sound, creating a prepared piano effect • Pulse stops in m. 48 • Delay (mm. 49–82) increases the presence of the piano's gestures
A' (mm. 83–225)	• Loud, low-range crunch chords keep the piano "noisy" but mark a return to idiomatic keyboard playing • Two-voice counterpoint (mm. 92–9) • Aggressive P5 alternations between crossed hands (mm. 100–115; left hand = B and F♯; right hand = A and E) • Pattern shifts between slower/quieter and faster/louder • Return to a two-voice counterpoint, but with "espressivo" indication (mm. 116–34) • Left-hand motion stops beneath right-hand oscillating pattern • Single pitches spaced by time and interval create a contrasting moment (mm. 143–73) before shifting to faster passagework (mm. 174–86) • Return to a two-voice contrapuntal texture with increased dissonant pitch material (mm. 187–94) • Recall of mm. 177–8 (mm. 195–201), then recall of mm. 179–80 (mm. 204–10) • Arrival at C as tonal centre • Right-hand pattern continues, with dissonant left-hand octaves (mm. 211–20) • Final closure on C, with added 9th (D) in final rhythmic flourish	• Ring modulation (mm. 90–115). Adds a kind of siren effect (mm. 100–15)

arriving an andante eighth-note pulse. In contrast to this right-hand pulse, the left hand plays in quarter-note and eighth-note triplets. The piano pulse is picked up by the synthesizer, which transitions us into the B section. Compared to the A section, the piano part is sparse in this section, with timbral modifications achieved by the extended techniques outlined above. Some of the new timbres include a distinctive squawking timbre, buzzing, a high bell sound, and a scraping timbre. The live electronics extend these timbral modifications through ring modulation and delay.

The emphasis on noise and sound rather than pitch in this B section persists with the return to the A section. However, the piano presents idiomatic keyboard playing rather than extended techniques. The piano explores several different textures, beginning with low-range crunch chords, shifting to two-voice counterpoint, followed by aggressive alternations between crossed hands. Montgomery continues to juxtapose various textures and rhythmic pacing, each time recalling earlier material. Though the piece has resisted any sense of tonality, its arrival on octave Cs achieves a sense of closure.

QUIVI SOSPIRI (1979) – DAVID JAEGER

Jaeger composed *Quivi sospiri* in 1979 for the CEE quartet and William Aide. The CEE performed the piece during their 1979 European tour with Karen Kieser, and it became a staple in the CEE's repertoire for over a decade (hence its inclusion on *Catbird Seat*). The title refers to a line from Dante's *Inferno*:

> Quivi sospiri, pianti, ed alti guai
> risonavan per l'aere senza stelle,
> per ch'io al cominciar ne lagrimai.
>
> Here sighs, with lamentations and loud moans,
> Resounded through the air pierced by no star,
> That e'en I wept at entering.[10]

While the piece was originally written for four monophonic synthesizers (two EMS Synthi As, a Roland SH 5, and an ARP Odyssey), this 1990 recording on *Catbird Seat* was performed on piano (Christina Petrowska Quilico), a sequencer that realized most of the synthesizer parts, an analog synthesizer (Yamaha CS-60) for some parts, and a Roland DC-10 Analog Echo for the live processing. The work's star is the piano, with the synthesizer parts acting either in accompaniment or in dialogue.

The ten-minute piece can be divided into four main sections, each of which presents a main musical idea, whether textural, melodic, and/or rhythmic; the first, second, and fourth sections can be further subdivided into two sections each (see table A.5).

The first section (0:00–2:16) is characterized by its counterpoint between the piano and synthesizers. Two-voice counterpoint in a low register opens the piece, including a three-note pattern in the piano octaves and a four-note pattern in the synthesizer. The counterpoint expands to three and then four voices with additional piano parts. Intensity builds through increased rhythmic activity, with smaller note values in the piano voices, while the melodic range of the piano finally rises above middle C. A chromatic figuration leads into section 1b, which arrives with a fortissimo chord (1:40). Immediately, we are introduced to a new piano pattern: a right-hand crunch chord oscillates with left-hand quartal harmony. The synthesizers' pitches glisten in the left and right channels as the piano extends up into its highest range with accented dissonances moving from major to minor sevenths. Above sustained synthesizer tones, the piano plays a flurry of chromatic passages in octave unison (see figure A.9).

This spectrogram (figure A.10) reflects the increased intensity (rhythm, energy) that leads to the arrival of section two (2:16–4:22), shown here in the striking vertical line: piano and synthesizers have united rhythmically across a wide frequency spectrum. This second section highlights both the agility and lyrical capacity of the piano; ornamentation focuses on trills and chromatic turns. This section establishes E as the new tonal centre in all parts with a $ffff$ articulation. The piano shifts to E♭ a couple of times, each time returning to the E centre. Below these tonal shifts, the synthesizers play in two-voice counterpoint, recalling the first section. The piano arrives firmly back at E, emphasized first with a trill and then with an octave oscillating pattern in the piano; this is the start of section 2b (2:48). As seen in figure A.10 this subsection has three aggressive articulations before the pitched material of the synthesizers disintegrates into a soft white noise below the piano. The piano continues with an E pedal, slowly pulsing, while it sounds out a chromatic melody that alternates descending and

Table A.5 Formal outline of *Quivi sospiri* with descriptions. Timings based on the recording from the 1990 album *Catbird Seat*.

Time	Section	Description
0:00–1:40	1a	• Counterpoint between the piano and synthesizers (expanding from two to four voices) • Increased rhythmic activity • Transition to 1b with chromatic figuration
1:40–2:16	1b	• Fortissimo chord and new piano pattern: right-hand crunch chord oscillates with left-hand quartal harmony • Glistening synthesizer pitches • Extended piano range with accented dissonances moving from major to minor sevenths • Piano chromatic flurries in octave unison
2:16–2:48	2a	• E is the new tonal centre • Piano ornamentation: trills and chromatic turns • Shifts from E to E♭, back to E, then E♭ again • Synthesizer two-voice counterpoint
2:48–4:22	2b	• Assertion of E as tonal centre with piano trill and octave oscillating pattern • Synthesizers decrescendo into white noise • Slow, pulsing E pedal in the piano below a chromatic melody • Destabilized tonal centre, with F as new tonal centre
4:22–6:20	3	• Notated in 4/2; F pedal played as pulse by synthesizer • Muted strings on piano • Jarring low mezzo-piano F in the synthesizer • Quick chromatic passages in the piano
6:20–7:24	4a	• New tonal centre: D • Delay on piano • Roland synthesizer pulses the basic beat (as in Section 3) • Recall of earlier piano patterns: quick chromatic inflections (cf. 2:20) the ascending chromatic melody (cf. 3:10) • Piano chromatic melody in octave unisons and increased rhythmic pace • Sixteenth-note passages in octave unison • New motive E♭-F-E is played *fff* by two synthesizers and the piano left hand
7:24–10:08	4b	• Return to E pedal • Piano delay with rhythmic echo • Synthesizers drop out • Return of previous musical ideas: chromatic ornaments (cf. 2:20), chromatic melody over an E pedal (cf. 3:02), and the opening multi-voice counterpoint (cf. 0:00) • Piano creates a four-voice counterpoint • Piano ritardando and diminuendo

ascending motion while expanding the length of its phrases. A gentle plucked timbre from the synthesizer traces the same melodic path. The E is destabilized by D♯ and F, and soon F prevails. The piano on F sustains, and all synthesizer sounds drop out in anticipation of section 3.

Figure A.9 Score excerpt (p. 3) of piano part in *Quivi sospiri*.

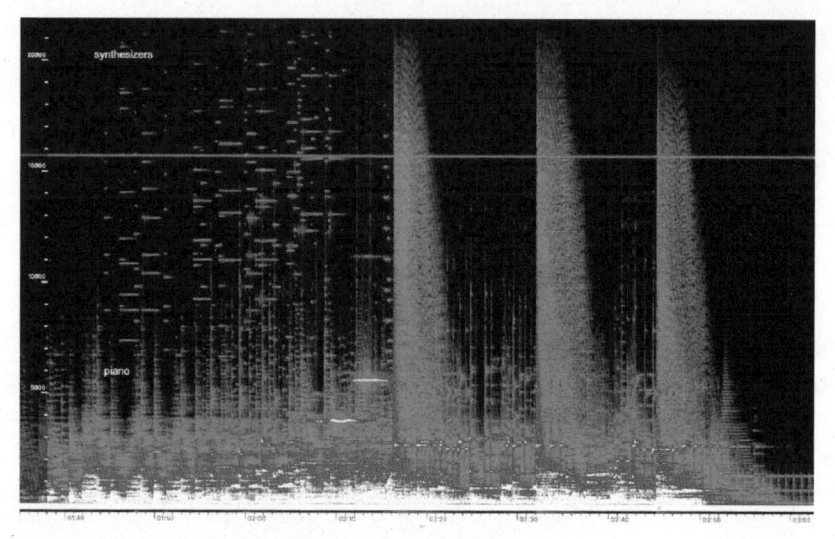

Figure A.10 Spectrogram of *Quivi sospiri* (ca 1:40–3:00).

The third section (4:22–6:20), now notated in 4/2 metre, begins with a dramatic shift to an F tonal centre (emphasized harmonically in the synthesizers) and a pedal pulse from the Roland synthesizer. A second synthesizer reinforces the new tonal centre through a V–I gesture (C to F). The piano presents a new and unusual timbre achieved by muting the strings of notated pitches. The muted piano figurations are also pulsed by the Analog Echo (see figure A.11).

Figure A.12 clearly visualizes the steady pulse and the sparseness of this section. Because of this quiet sparseness, it builds anticipation for an increase in action that must be ahead. Jaeger startles the listener with a low mezzo-piano F in the synthesizer – a jarring effect in this pianissimo section. The piano's quick chromatic passages contrast with the steady synthesizer pulse below.

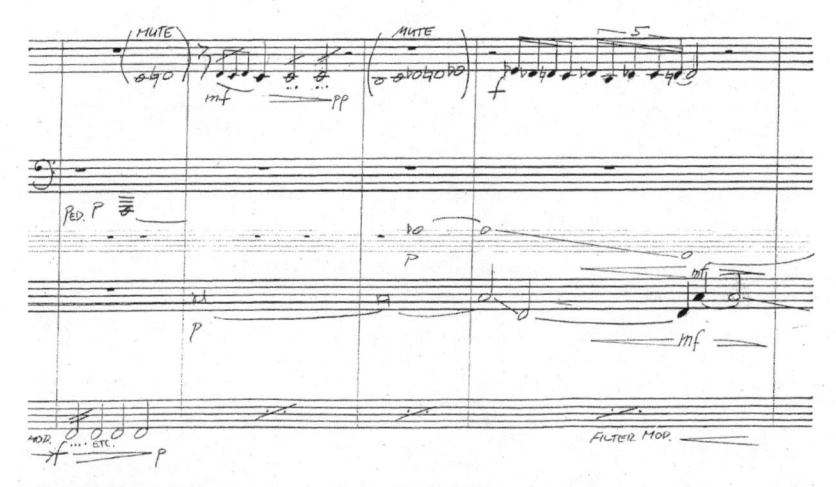

Figure A.11 Pulse-oriented piano and synthesizer parts on p. 5 of the score for *Quivi sospiri*.

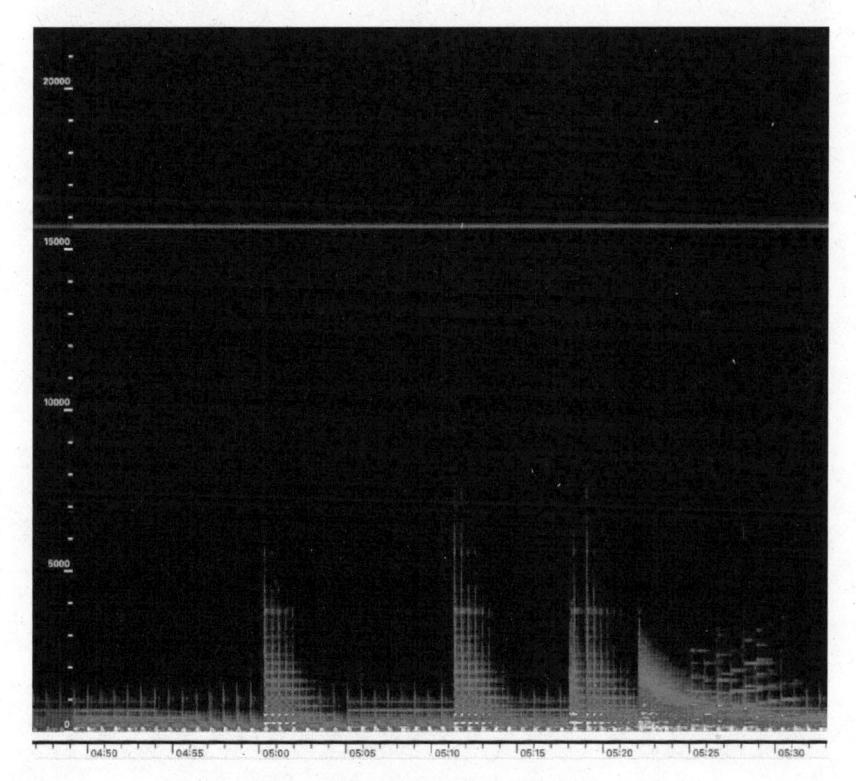

Figure A.12 Spectrogram of *Quivi sospiri* (ca 4:47–5:31).

Figure A.13   Four-voice counterpoint in piano in final measures of *Quivi sospiri*.

The final section (6:20–10:08) acts in many ways like a recapitulation, with the return of many previous motifs, textures, and gestures. However, it begins with a new tonal centre: a low D in the synthesizer, harmonized with an F♯ in the piano. The rhythmic pulsing and echo of the previous section returns: delay on the piano, which creates a rhythmic echo, while the Roland synthesizer pulses the basic beat. The piano's quick chromatic inflections recall section 2a (cf. 2:20), while the ascending chromatic melody recalls section 2b (cf. 3:10). The piano intensifies its chromatic melody through octave unisons and increased rhythmic pace. Sixteenth-note passages in octave unison recall the end of section 1b, in which a similar gesture was used to build tension into the arrival of a new section. The synthesizer's pulsing pedal stops, and instead, the synthesizers have a new role: the motive E♭-F-E is played *fff* by two synthesizers and the piano in the left hand.

Section 4b also makes a return: in this case, to the E tonal centre, here articulated by oscillating octaves in the right hand. The delay on the piano creates an echo quality that reinforces the overall sense of echo in many other sections in the work. The synthesizers are now absent from the texture, but the piano maintains the polyphony. Several musical ideas return: chromatic ornaments (cf. 2:20), chromatic melody over an E pedal (cf. 3:02), and the opening multi-voice counterpoint (cf. 0:00). The piano creates a four-voice counterpoint based on three three-note patterns and one four-note pattern (see figure A.13). With a mild tape delay still in effect, the piano gradually slows down and fades into pianissimo.

PSALM (1985) – LARRY LAKE

Lawrence Cherney premiered Lake's *Psalm* on 27 January 1985, in St Catharines, Ontario. This piece for oboe and tape is not a liturgical work and it makes no reference to specific psalm texts. Rather, according to Lake, his aim was to capture the overall goal of the various psalms: praise and contemplation. While Lake uses some more animated rhythmic features to capture a sense of praise, *Psalm* seems to focus mostly on the sense of contemplation, particularly through the long, sustained pitches and minimal rhythmic action. This work is spacious in terms of rhythm, texture, dynamics, structure, and spatialization.

Psalm contains no obvious structural divides, but rather transitions through sections of relative activity versus stasis. Some basic materials serve as recurring elements: the interval of a perfect fifth and, to a lesser extent, the minor third (both melodic and harmonic) and descending major second; quick rhythmic figurations of either eighth or sixteenth notes; and C as tonal centre and C major as tonic harmony, though the piece does not follow functional harmony (see figure A.14). The oboe is the star, and it is from the oboe's part that I perceive the strongest sense of structural contrast.

From the distinctive melodic, harmonic, and rhythmic characters within the piece, a broad formal structure can emerge: A B C B' C' A' (see table A.6).

Psalm establishes a contemplative mood in its brief introduction with a low, rumbling drone and layers of indeterminate pitches in the tape part. The oboe enters on the same A as the tape part, making them almost indistinguishable for the first few seconds. This A section consists mainly of long tones as the oboe plays "freely and lyrically." Across the section, the rhythmic pace quickens slightly, a shift that pairs effectively with the tape part's light dissonance. The A section ends with a two-voice counterpoint using only formally "acceptable" intervals: minor and major thirds, perfect fifth, and major sixth (see figure A.15). The closing A' section will recall this contrapuntal texture. Lake anticipates a new section with a change to a flute-like timbre in the tape part. The B section is characterized by a chordal accompaniment in the tape part (alternating C-G-C and D-G-D) below an oboe melody with strong intervallic and rhythmic profiles: the melody features an ascending perfect fifth and has a clear pulse. The C section begins when the oboe

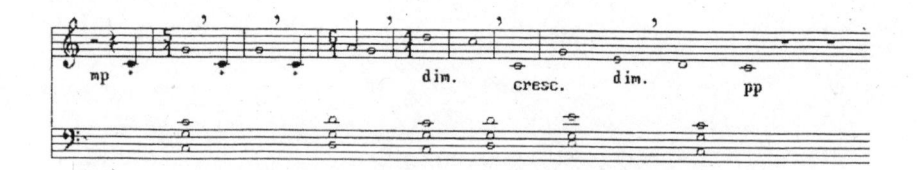

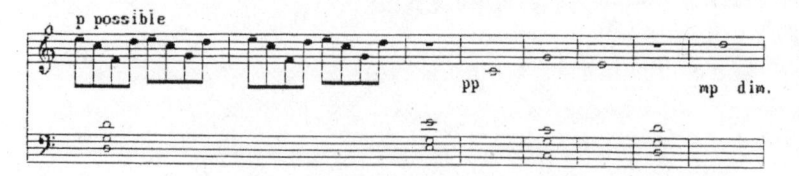

Figure A.14 Score excerpt demonstrating recurring intervallic, melodic, harmonic, and rhythmic characteristics of *Psalm* (ca 4:45–5:58).

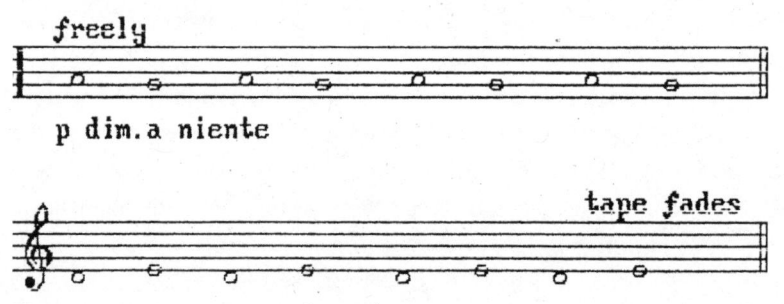

Figure A.15 Score excerpt of two-voice counterpoint (9:26–10:15).

presents a new eighth-note pattern and soon enough sixteenth-note pattern, which alternate with brief sections of longer tones.

Lake begins to recall earlier material, starting with the ascending perfect fifth motive of the B section. Both the melody and the tape chordal accompaniment, however, contain different pitches. In contrast to the first B section, here the tape part switches to a "string" timbre and adds more pitch variety, all while a slowly ascending and descending glissando gradually crescendos into the mix. Lake hearkens back to the C section with oboe patterns in quarter notes, followed by eighth notes, and then finally in sixteenth notes. In contrast to this increased activity in the oboe, the tape part rests on a low C pedal, which functions as a kind of tonal closure for the remainder of the piece. *Psalm* closes with a two-voice counterpoint, played "freely" by the oboe, as both the tape and oboe slowly fade to silence.

Table A.6 Formal outline of *Psalm* with descriptions. Timings based on recording from the 1988 album *Shadow Box*.

Time	Section	Notes
0:00	Introduction	• Tape part only: low rumbling drone, with layers of indeterminate pitches • Ends with a clear A (notated in the score)
0:50	A	• The oboe enters on the same A as the tape part, making them almost indistinguishable for the first few seconds • The oboe plays long tones ("freely and lyrically") • Intervallic emphasis on P4, m2, and M6
1:34		• The oboe's rhythmic pace quickens slightly • C emerges as a kind of tonal centre • The tape part adds some light dissonance to the oboe's pitch material, particularly when a D♭ sounds at 2:18
2:50		• The oboe's rhythmic pace remains the same, but it performs with alternating crescendos and diminuendos • The oboe and tape perform a kind of two-voice counterpoint with "acceptable" intervals, such as m3 and M3, P5, and M6
4:05		• The tape part changes to a flute-like timbre
4:28	B	• The tape part changes to a chordal accompaniment, alternating C-G-C and D-G-D
4:45		• The oboe plays a melody with a clear pulse • The melody is based principally on an ascending P5, and to a lesser extent, a descending M2 • The tape part adds high, bell-like passagework
5:32	C	• The oboe has a new eighth-note pattern
5:43		• The oboe returns to long notes while the tape part continues with its chordal accompaniment • The oboe outlines a C major triad that aligns with the tape part's C-G-C
5:59		• The oboe plays a sixteenth-note pattern followed by a high D-C (descending M2)
6:17		• The oboe plays a different sixteenth-note pattern whose pitch material is more varied but still belongs within C major • The oboe then plays a different sixteenth-note pattern, then an eighth-note pattern, followed by descending M2s
6:58	B'	• The oboe returns to the ascending P5 motive, this time with A and E
7:25		• The tape part switches to a "string" timbre and adds more pitch variety • A slowly ascending and descending glissando gradually crescendos into the mix
7:48		• The oboe's melody slows down • The tape part's glissando effect is in the higher register
8:26		• The tape part slowly crescendos in a high pizzicato effect
9:02	C'	• The oboe plays patterns in quarter notes, eighth notes, and then sixteenth notes • The tape part arrives at a low C pedal that will remain until the end of the piece • The pizzicato effect remains but decrescendos
9:26	A'	• The two-voice counterpoint returns • The two parts are slightly misaligned, but they still clearly alternate between a P5 (D and A) and m3 (E and G), all over the tape's C pedal

ATTENTION ELK! (1994) – CEE

Jaeger describes *Attention Elk!* as "more 'in the pocket' of a recognizable CEE approach" (personal communication, 20 May 2020) compared with the other collaborative Supertrio tracks. If the listener was unaware of the performing forces for this piece, they would likely conclude it consisted of a vast array of percussion instruments (perhaps chimes, marimba, and xylophone) and a collection of synthesizers. About the latter, they would be correct. However, there are no acoustic instruments in this piece, and all sounds resembling acoustic percussion instruments are created by the synthesizers. The piece plays on several contrasts: register (especially between low- and high-range sounds), pitched and unpitched, rhythm (sustained versus intermittent articulations), and timbre (impressions of the acoustic world versus synthesized sounds). *Attention Elk!* is constantly in flux, but its ametrical, drone-saturated sound world creates an overall sense of stability. Nonetheless, this relatively brief work has clear sections, even as the boundary between one and the next is often amorphous. I perceive four larger sections with three additional subsection divides (see table A.7).

Section 1 (0:00–2:22) is characterized by layers of drones (both pitched and unpitched), bell rings, high synthesized pitches, and seemingly real-world sounds. The piece opens with a low, growling, unpitched drone that might escape the listener's ears if the volume is low or there is ambient noise in the listener's environment. However, the new pitched drone (D) at 0:09 is much more assertive in the mix. Ambient sounds like breath or wind begin to fill the sonic space. Additional drone layers are added, some clearly pitched on F♯ and G, others with less emphasis on their pitch content as they glissando up and down. The piece fills out more of the upper register with occasional bell rings. If one is looking to interpret the title in the piece's soundworld, the sounds beginning at 1:13 could evoke two elk chirps, which are discrete, high-pitched vocalizations.[11] Section 1b maintains some similar sounds to 1a, such as drone, high synthesized ringing, and the imagined elk calls, but the low drone fades away (beginning at 1:26) and the overall texture thins out. In this thinner texture, the "elk calls" (1:40) are more pronounced in the mix (see figure A.16); this time, the "elk calls" resemble the high-pitched portion of an elk bugle and chuckle, with a crescendo on each wobbling note. The calls seem to trigger a series of synthesized ringing

Table A.7 Formal outline of *Attention Elk!* with descriptions. Timings based on the recording from the 1996 album *Supertrio*.

Time	Section	Description
0:00–1:30	1a	• Low, growling drone (0:00) and then pitched D drone (0:09) • Ambient sounds • Pitch layers • "Elk calls" (1:13)
1:30–2:22	1b	• Thinner texture • "Elk calls" (1:40) • New drones in low and high registers (F♯ and G)
2:22–3:40	2a	• Low C drone • Percussive tapping in chromatic descents and unpitched gestures • High-range ringing metallic pitches (3:16)
3:40–4:44	2b	• Synth chords: consonant and then increasingly dissonant • More second-interval motives • Low rumble as transition material
4:44–5:27	3	• Low rumble continues until fade-out at end of section • Percussion-like and woodwind-like timbres in increased rhythmic material
5:28–6:48	4a	• Chime timbres return • M2 and m2 motives • Increased noise and aggressive gestures
6:48–7:53	4b	• Dissonant tone clusters • Recall of chime and drone material • Cacophony drops to reveal the final A drone

tones that slide up and down in the higher range. New drones emerge, including a low F♯ and a high G; the interval of a second, both major and minor, is a recurring motive in this piece. As the movement of pitched material quickens, pitch class G is emphasized in both the high and mid ranges.

Section two (2:22–4:44) is characterized by a decrease in density. It begins with a low C drone, above which we hear lightly percussive taps like fingers on pitched glasses, producing a chromatic descending pattern. Layers of percussive tapping continue alongside ringing synthesized pitches. Additional percussive taps are added with a pronounced echo effect. Shimmering high-range pitches with a bright, metallic timbre appear rather startlingly in this relatively subdued atmosphere (3:16). Layers of percussive glass taps continue alongside new light clicking sounds. These new sounds fade into silence as we transition to section 2b (3:40–4:44). In the overall structure of the work, I hear this as still part of section two because of its overall thin texture, decreased emphasis

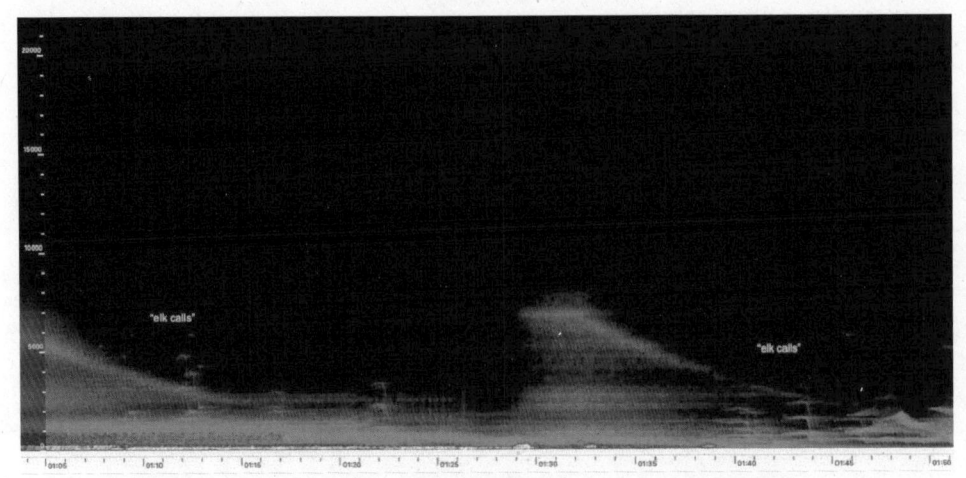

Figure A.16 Spectrogram of *Attention Elk!* (1:05–1:50) with label above "elk calls."

on drones, and increased rhythmic activity. There is an atmosphere of anticipation, with occasional surprise strikes and clicking interjections with an echo effect. Synth chords first outline some conventional harmonies (C♯, E, G♯, or C♯ minor; then G♯ and B♯, with E still ringing above). However, the chords become crunchier as pitches like F𝄪 and D♯ are added. Again, we hear a major second motive with a mid-range A to B motion (quietly coloured with a G♯ above) (4:23). A high F♯ rings out as a low rumble transitions us into section three.

Section three (4:44–5:27) maintains the low rumble, with contrasting light and quick articulations above it in a timbre at times resembling xylophones and wind chimes. The mid-range inserts sustained pitches with a woodwind quality, which later bears closer resemblance to a vocal timbre. This section ends as the low rumble fades out and the vocal timbre fades into near-complete silence.

The final section (5:28–7:53) can also be divided into two subsections. Section 4a is somewhat reminiscent of section 2b with its chime-like timbres. The emphasis on major and minor seconds persists here, with a high C to B♭ (5:40) and mid-range D to C♯ (5:46). The D to C♯ repeats (5:56), but this time the C♯ is sustained (until 6:08). I hear what sounds like a cluster of sawtooth pitches with heavy reverb. The wind sounds of section 1a seem to have returned, but much stronger. The piece continues to surprise the ears. First, an aggressive bass note (6:26) shakes the atmosphere, but its strength fades as it slowly ascends. Second, a low,

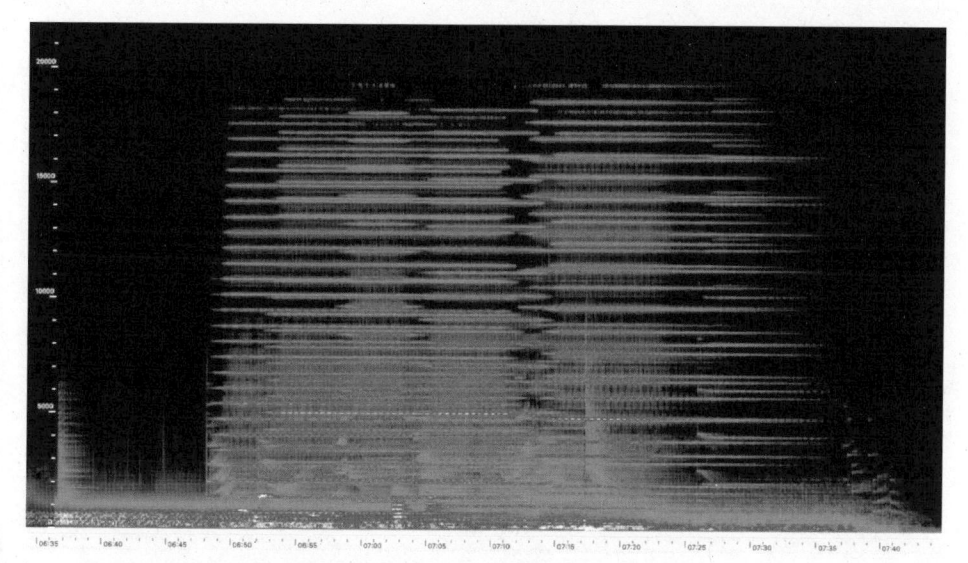

Figure A.17   Spectrogram of *Attention Elk!* (6:36–7:44).

noisy growl reminiscent of section 1a emerges and continues into the final subsection. Third, an assertive strummed echo effect (6:36) is split between the left (L) and right (R) channels. The final part of *Attention Elk!* (6:48–7:53) begins with the low, noisy growl from the previous subsection. Above it, we hear a clear chime followed by a dissonant harmonic minor second (E and F), which is then further harmonized with a D above and a B below the D. The chimes and drones of previous sections return, creating a cacophony (see figure A.17). Because of this density, it is difficult to pinpoint exactly when the final drone A (with E more quietly above) begins, but by 7:26, it is dominant in the mix. The drone is essentially alone for the remainder of the piece, but we hear one final statement from the chimes (7:43) as the entire piece fades into nothing.

CASPIN'S ARRIVAL (1998) – CEE

The track *Caspin's Arrival* was written as a CEE collaboration to honour Paul and his wife upon the birth of their son on 22 January 1998. Stillwell recalls asking Wilcox to imitate seagulls and wanting the overall effect of the piece to be "gentle" (personal communication, 25 February 2020). The result is one of the CEE's shortest pieces (3:43). In addition to its sonic appeal, this length is likely a reason why this piece has been on rotation on CBC Radio since its release.

Table A.8 Formal outline of *Caspin's Arrival*.

Section	Description
Intro (0:00–0:17)	• Opens softly with gentle cymbal strikes (left channel) • Fog horn sounds (D♭), quiet at first and then a bit louder • Viola imitates the sound of seagulls
A (0:17–1:12)	• Viola plays a melody (D-G-A-D) that moves across the mix • Assertive low bass note (0:21) contrasts atmosphere • Viola part becomes more percussive, with bouncing effect • Thickening texture (beginning 0:32): rushing air; low drone moving back and forth in the mix; bass notes (0:40); seagull sound; cymbal crash (0:56); descending chromatic motive (0:57); trills
B (1:12–2:03)	• Rhythmic gestures in synthesizer and viola • Viola shifts between short, rhythmic gestures (on repeated notes) and longer, bowed pitches (A-D-G) • Two-pitch drone: C and G (1:32) • Recall of introduction material: seagulls (1:35) and cymbal parts (played with a faster rhythm; 1:39) • Crescendo to vocal synth drone (pitches: A and C) • Bass notes on a steady pulse on D (1:51) that resolves to C (1:56)
C (2:03–3:24)	• No discernible viola part • Increase in volume, echo and reverb, and electronic layers • Increased rhythmic activity with fast-moving bass pitches (2:11) • Low bass notes (2:21): E, then D • Expansion of high-range sounds: high bell-ringing timbres; vocal synths sustained and in melody (at 2:41, A-G-D-D-E-A-G; melody returns with similar pitches) • Chromatic motive heard briefly in A returns at 2:55, in both ascent and descent (xylophone-like timbre) • Seagull-like sounds return (3:20)
Coda (3:24–3:43)	• Dynamics and density reduce quickly • Return of bouncing viola effect (3:33) • Fade into silence

Because of its relatively brief length, it's easy enough to perceive *Caspin's Arrival* as a single section, with a slight build up (introduction) and build out (conclusion or coda). With the various sounds present in this piece, I find it helpful to break it down into three main sections bookended by an introduction and coda (see table A.8). These sections have little relationship to each other apart from some shared sound sources; there isn't a sense of arch form or restatement of previous sections.

Caspin's Arrival opens gently (as per Stillwell's request), with delicate cymbal strikes and soft seagull-like sounds (which we know are coming from Wilcox's viola). The piece settles into the first main section (A, 0:17–1:12) with a viola melody that moves across the mix. The piece is still fairly spacious and gentle at this point, but with an assertive low bass note and bouncing viola bowing, the mood begins to shift. The texture thickens even more with sounds of rushing air and a low drone (moving between left and right channels). The piece continues to contrast between high and low timbres, with bass sounds, the seagull sounds, and a cymbal crash. We hear a soft, descending chromatic motive (0:57) that will be recalled in section C. Increased viola activity with trills leads to the second main section, B (1:12–2:03).

The B section is characterized by a contrast between sustained sounds like the drones and viola melody and more rhythmic, discrete sounds from the synthesizer and viola. While *Caspin's Arrival* makes little sense to hear within any tonal hierarchy, this section has clearly pitched material, most of which comes from a C pentatonic scale (C, D, G, A), with no pitches declaring major/minor mode or leading tone–tonic relationships.

The C section (2:03–3:24) begins with a marked increase in timbral and textural density as well as volume. With new electronic layers and expansion of both the high- and low-range elements, the viola is either masked in this section or is completely absent. Pitch content in the bass notes and in a voice synth melody are similar to the B section, though we now hear the pitch E. The chromatic motive heard briefly at 0:57 returns: it is more prominent in the mix and can be heard in both ascending and descending motion. Seagull-like sounds from the introduction and section A also return, but they sound more electronic and less like they come from the viola.

Shortly after the recall of the seagull-like sounds, the piece makes a quick reduction in dynamics and density: this is the coda of *Caspin's Arrival*. The bouncing viola effect returns (3:33), and soon all remaining sounds fade into silence.

IMPROVISATION #4 (2008) – CEE

Improvisation #4 stands out to my ears within the CEE's practice for two reasons. First, as on the album as a whole, Lake contributes a lot of trumpet material, giving the instrument a prominence not heard on their other albums. Second, there is a relatively long unit with a steady drumbeat. As I discussed in chapter 3, steady pulses are rare in the CEE's sound, so when they appear, they are striking. This piece's use of a steady pulse is all the more noteworthy because it's presented through the timbres of a drum kit. The CEE's 2012 performance of John S. Gray's *No Dim Pearls* also includes a synthesized drum kit pattern.

Based on Iyer's concept of smaller units, I perceive this improvisation in six smaller units; a different listener may hear more or fewer. The

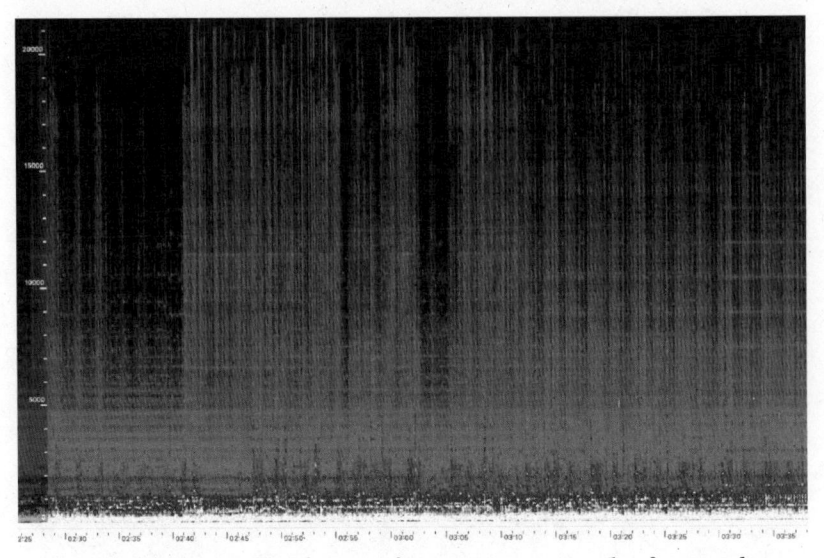

Figure A.18 Spectrogram of unit 2 of *Improvisation #4*, with a fast-paced steady groove in both keyboard and drum kit, represented here by thin vertical lines (ca 2:38–3:36).

first unit is keyboard-centric, with Farah's atonal pianistic synth notes above some noisy synth layers. Farah settles into a steady groove, and a drum pattern joins in around 2:41 (see figure A.18); I would consider this a new smaller unit, despite some continuity with the keyboard material of the first unit. Farah switches to chords (3:53) as the drum beat continues, with slight changes to the pattern. Stillwell brings in a sample of Tibetan monks' multiphonic vocalizations, and this striking new timbre signals a new unit within the improvisation. Farah returns to his "busy" pianistic playing, or what he describes as "freaking out" (personal communication, 9 July 2020). With a shift at 4:50 in Farah's part to the Nord Lead 3's Patch 6:24, I hear a new small unit, though the multiphonic vocalizations continue for a bit. The overt action of the synth layers halts to sustain beneath Lake's trumpet part. While the previous small unit was very brief, I nonetheless hear the entry of the trumpet as a new small unit. Chimes ring out, the multiphonic vocalizations return (with more of a didgeridoo timbre), and occasional drum strikes punctuate the scene. We are left with the trumpet and resonant chimes: a new small unit. The chimes ring out, and the trumpet performs a brief duet (higher part: D B F♯ G♯ F♯ D; lower part: B G♯ D E D B),[12] bringing the improvisation to an end.

Notes

Prologue

1. I explain my departure from the typical CEE origin date of 1971 in chapter 2.
2. Unfortunately, the only correct piece of information on the CEE in the latter source is the name of the group. Keillor writes that the group formed in 1973, when in fact Jaeger and Montgomery first performed in 1971 and the CEE officially debuted in 1972. She also credits the CEE as "the first group in the world to create live electronic music in concert" (265); this is not the case, as such groups in Europe and the United States had formed in the 1960s.
3. The Vietnam War did not factor into David Jaeger's decision; he explained that he had a relatively high number in the US Army draft lottery.
4. George Proctor remarked: "For the first time Canadian composers had a relatively high profile, and a few even earned a significant proportion of their income through the various commissions they received" (1980, 150).

Chapter One

1. Due to his increasing dissatisfaction with GRCM's direction, Schaeffer resigned in 1958 and created the Groupe de Recherches Musicales (GRM). The GRM continued Schaeffer's emphasis on research and experimentation. One major outcome of his research was the 1966 publication *Traité des objets musicaux*.
2. For an accessible summary of basic studio techniques, see Collins, Schedel, and Wilson 2013, 56–8.
3. Gayle Young's book *Sackbut Blues* (1989) offers a detailed study of Le Caine's personal life, scientific research, and electronic instrument innovations.
4. Keane (1984) provides a table outlining the location, year of founding, relative size, and directors known to date of publication.

5 The status of electronic/electroacoustic music making has shifted in more recent decades, as some institutions' studios have lapsed into disuse and disrepair (e.g., the studio at the University of Saskatchewan), while others have raised their status or opened new facilities. For example, while the Université de Montréal didn't open its studio until 1983, the institution has since secured a world-renowned reputation in musique acousmatique. Memorial University opened its Electroacoustic Music Research Laboratory in 2012 under the direction of Andrew Staniland.
6 Otto Joachim had already set up his own private studio in 1955 (Strachan 2016), but this was rare at the time.
7 Kevin Austin, trained at McGill University, was also a member of Montreal-based electronic improvisation ensemble MetaMusic (1971–78), of which David Sutherland was also a member.

Chapter Two

1 Helmut Kallmann wrote particularly harsh criticism of professors Willan and Leo Smith in his essay "Studying Music at a Canadian University 1946–1949," which was republished in *Mapping Canada's Music: Selected Writings of Helmut Kallmann*, ed. John Beckwith and Robin Elliott (Waterloo, ON: Wilfrid Laurier University Press, 2013).
2 The Faculty of Music website boasts: "We are the largest music research collection in Canada and among the top 3 academic library systems in North America."
3 Some sources (including Keane 1984) state that the University of Toronto EMS was the second studio.
4 For more explanation about Le Caine's Multi-Track Tape Recorder, see Collins, Schedel, and Wilson 2013, 52–4.
5 He laughed and told me that he burned this music. He was also sure to clarify that he meant no disrespect to Shostakovich's music.
6 Composition credits for collaborative works appear in the following combinations: Grimes and Lake; Grimes and Montgomery; Jaeger and Lake; Jaeger, Lake, and Montgomery; and Jaeger and Montgomery.
7 Performance numbers in all tables are tabulated from extant records maintained by James Montgomery. The relatively few concerts with unknown programs could not be included in these numbers.

Chapter Three

1. Wraggett taught at the Royal Conservatory of Music Electronic Music Studio.
2. Upstream's founding members were Bob Bauer, Jeff Reilly, Paul Cram, Don Palmer, Steven Naylor, Steve Tittle, Sandy Moore, and Tom Roach.
3. Standing Wave was Francois Houle, Peggy Lee, Lauri Lyster, and Leslie Wyber.
4. *Wildfire* had been featured on the 1985 Holland Festival tour, which included Richard Armin's ensemble Armin Strings.
5. Lake appears on one track, "Star Song," which is from 1975 and includes the entire original CEE quartet.
6. https://thecee.bandcamp.com/.
7. Sutherland bought his own in 1975 with the money he earned scoring films for Radio Canada.
8. One area of electronic music performance that deserves more study in terms of the analog/digital debate and physicality is accessibility and disability. I would caution against demonizing "buttons" over "knobs," as decreased physical demands can also make electronic music more accessible for musicians with joint pain (e.g., arthritis) or decreased fine motor skill, to name only two examples.

Chapter Four

1. One memorable exception is the performance of *Something Celtic* at the 2004 Sound Symposium: Bolton described the piece to me: "[It] would start with me playing a jig on the fiddle, and then all the synths coming in in a massive tonal swell" (personal communication, 23 June 2020).
2. The final piece was what they called "a short ditty," and they laughed as they called it "Everyone Goes First."
3. As I discuss in chapter 5, *This Is This* is also quite different between the 2004 performance and the 2014 album version: the album version was not designed to be replicated in live performance.
4. It is sometimes also referred to as the Cabbagetown Arts & Crafts Festival, or simply the Cabbagetown Festival.

Chapter Five

1. There was some laughter when the CEE prepared to perform this improvisation because while Farah, the pianist, would not need to adjust anything for a pitch-centric improvisation, the modular synthesizers needed to be tuned, and that isn't always an easy task. This was a rare moment when

the technical and aural skills of actually getting the machines to do what you need them to do was plain to the audience.
2 *Camden*, a collaboratively composed piece performed in 1978, does not appear on any album.
3 Jaeger recently collaborated with Petric, who, on 3 April 2021, premiered the work entitled *Spirit Cloud* for accordion and fixed electronic tracks.
4 A video of the performance is available on YouTube: https://youtu.be/RO1ioTzwdgs. Any timings mentioned here are based on that video.
5 I discuss a similar performance at the Arts & Letters Club in chapter 1.
6 This phrase is found in Wallace Stevens's poem "Peter Quince at the Clavier," published in 1915.
7 Bolton explained to me the difference between the two versions as follows: vocalist Janice Jackson was collaborating with the CEE during their residency at the 2004 Sound Symposium in St John's, Newfoundland. For *This Is This*, Bolton read statements from current news and Jackson improvised a response. Beneath these live vocal layers were recordings of Bolton reading from a science textbook and texts by John Donne. When the CEE was recording the piece to include on *Bluffer's Lookout*, the members did not have the same skills of vocal improvisation, so Bolton decided to use fixed texts. She also needed to use texts that were not copyrighted (personal communication, 29 November 2020).

Chapter Six

1 Kurt Stone's 1967 review of the series does not remark on the gender disparity but rather focuses on stylistic issues, the lack of electronic music content (though there is one piece by Beecroft), the dominance of "a decidedly French flavor" (441), and limited material composed after 1960. Stone notes early on that of the thirty-two Canadian composers in the series, twenty-five were born in Canada (440).
2 This calculation is based on the total number of individually named performers in the series; some individuals performed more than once across the series. It could be illuminating to calculate percentages based on total performances, or even minutes performed. These percentages do not account for ensembles, whose memberships were not identified on the albums.
3 Aitken still runs NMC as of this writing, while Beecroft left in 1989.
4 Recent seasons reflect the organization's intentions to program more diversely.
5 The Winnipeg Symphony Orchestra was the first to host a New Music Festival, but many major orchestras followed suit, including Vancouver, Toronto, and Montreal. 2NH travelled across the country to record and broadcast these orchestral performances.

6 Not everyone approved of 2NH's programming – its detractors even included featured composer Weinzweig. Alan Gillmor quotes the often-acerbic composer in his chapter "In His Own Words" from *Weinzweig: Essays on His Life and Music*. He declared to Otto Joachim in 1986: "I've heard some pretty bad compositions lately, especially on [CBC's] Two New Hours. So bad, that the composer should have his license revoked. They should be fined for malpractice!" (2011, 276). In a January 2001 letter to Elaine Keillor, his sentiments remained unchanged: "But my main opus is battling the CBC's Radio Music policy ... they continue to resist – we continue to persist. That Two New Hours programme has become a dumping ground for Canadian music. Into darkness – out of mind" (quoted in Cherney 2011, 65).
7 As of this writing, there has not been another non-European president.
8 By "programmed," I mean that the CEE performed the pieces; by "presented," I mean that the CEE hosted and produced the concert but did not perform the pieces themselves.
9 In this role, Roberts's original job title was general member, then director general, before settling on executive director.
10 Elmer Iseler (1927–1998) founded the Elmer Iseler Singers in 1979, following two and a half decades with the Festival Singers of Toronto (1954–1978; in 1968, the name was changed to Festival Singers of Canada).
11 Capitalizations within these titles is based on those published on *The Electronic Messiah* album.
12 Sir Thomas Beecham's 1927 Columbia recording has a tempo of about 114–116 bpm. Sir Adrian Boult's 1954 Decca recording with the London Symphony Orchestra is a fair amount slower, at 100 bpm. Colin Davis's 1966 Philips recording with the London Symphony Orchestra picks the tempo back up to 110 bpm, a tempo that Tafelmusik, a historically informed Baroque orchestra and choir, performed in its 2012 recording. Christopher Hogwood's 1980 Decca recording slows the tempo back down to about 100–102 bpm.
13 Jaeger maintained a good relationship with Southam, as evidenced by his commissioning her to compose for 2NH in 1998. The resulting work, *Qualities of Consonance*, is dedicated to Jaeger and Eve Egoyan, the pianist for whom the piece was written and whom Jaeger had suggested to Southam.
14 Southam later explains in the score that objects like cardboard, metal jars, bottle tops, and tin cans can be included, though these objects were not in the original set she provided to the CEE.
15 Southam concludes her instructions by saying that "the rules can be varied" (1981, 16), so even her elaborate plan can be revised.
16 These two guest musicians also performed pieces by Jaeger (*Fool's Paradise*) and Lake (*Slowly I Turn*) during the concert on 7 June 1985.

17 Of the thirty composers commissioned by the CEE, 80 per cent of them are men.
18 While "multiculturalism" may be invoked as a general ideal in a country like Canada with its diverse population, it is also official policy. Following the Royal Commission on Bilingualism and Biculturalism (1963–69), Pierre Trudeau's Liberal government instituted the Official Languages Act (1969) to address inequality between English-speaking and French-speaking populations in Canada. Trudeau expanded the focus on biculturalism to multiculturalism, which was adopted as a federal policy in 1971; the policy positioned Canada as a "cultural mosaic." When the Canadian Constitution was repatriated in 1982, it added the Canadian Charter of Rights and Freedoms; Section 27 specifies that the Charter "shall be interpreted in a manner consistent with the preservation and enhancement of the multicultural heritage of Canadians." Brian Mulroney's Progressive Conservative government passed the Canadian Multiculturalism Act in 1988.
19 Fava stayed out of the room during EQ sessions other than occasionally bringing in the much-appreciated snacks and taking orders for water or tea, a reversal of typical gendered domestic labour.
20 Since its first iteration, EQ has been clear about embracing women defined broadly as "trans/cis/non-binary." The first call for applicants identified a desired age range of eighteen to twenty-four, while the latest program increased it to thirty, but without imposing a strict cutoff.
21 The first year was open to four participants. Because of its initial success and the increasing pool of applicants, Bolton expanded EQ to eight slots for the 2017 and 2018 iterations.
22 Lutter's study (2015) centres on the film industry, but he encouraged application to other project-based contexts.

Epilogue

1 Class visit on 24 February 2020; in-person group interview on 27 February 2020; email correspondence 11–18 March 2020.

Appendix

1 Schaeffer outlined a typo-morphology that described and classified sound objects according to their type (e.g., pitched) and behaviour (e.g., steep attack).
2 As opposed to "acousmatic" as a listening context that can apply across genres and even non-musical contexts (e.g., talk radio), musique acousmatique refers to a specific genre within electroacoustic music associated with France and Quebec (see Bayle 1993).

3 The nine indicative fields are gesture, utterance, behaviour, energy, motion, object/substance, environment, vision, and space.
4 All spectrograms in this book were created using the sound analysis template in Pierre Couprie's software *iAnalyse* with the following parameters: Window type: Hanning; window size: 2,048; window step: 75%; dynamics: −80 dB.
5 Timings are according to the 2 November 1976 broadcast streaming on the Canadian Music Centre website. Grimes and Montgomery are on synthesizers and Morry Kernerman is on violin.
6 Score excerpts have been taken from the official scores held by the Canadian Music Centre library. Most of these scores are in the composers' handwriting. Larry Lake engraved his score for *Psalm* in computer music notation software; its appearance reflects the materiality of computers, notation software, and printers at the time (he submitted the score to the CMC in 1990).
7 The score is available as a non-printable PDF: https://www.musiccentre.ca/node/2552.
8 The score indicates when the organist should engage or disengage a given stop, as opposed to when a pitch will be sounded using that stop. To coordinate with the tape part, the organ score is organized by lengths of time.
9 The original four-channel tape part is reduced to two-channel when listening through headphones.
10 English translation is from Henry F. Clay's 1805 publication.
11 Elk calls vary, depending on the season, age, sex, and situation. *Attention Elk!* does not include any recordings of actual elk calls. The title, though, might inspire some listeners to interpret certain sounds as elk calls.
12 These notes are at concert pitch. Farah recalls Lake adding a slight pitch shift effect.

References

Andean, James. 2020. "Rhythm in Acousmatic Music." *Organised Sound* 25 (2): 214–20. doi:10.1017/S1355771820000126.

Applebaum, Barbara. 2016. "Critical Whiteness Studies." *Oxford Research Encyclopedia of Education*. 9 June 2016. https://oxfordre.com/education/view/10.1093/acrefore/9780190264093.001.0001/acrefore-9780190264093-e-5.

Auner, Joseph. 2013. "Wanted Dead or Alive: Historical Performance Practice and Electro-Acoustic Music from IRCAM to Abbey Road." In *Music in Print and Beyond: Hildegard von Bingen to the Beatles*, edited by Craig A. Monson and Roberta Montemorra Marvin, 213–31. Rochester, NY: University of Rochester Press.

Auslander, Philip. 2002. "Live from Cyberspace: Or, I Was Sitting at My Computer This Guy Appeared He Thought I Was a Bot." *PAJ: A Journal of Performance and Art* 24 (1): 16–21.

– 2008. *Liveness: Performance in a Mediatized Culture*, 2nd ed. London: Routledge.

Babbitt, Milton. 1964. "An Introduction to the R.C.A. Synthesizer." *Journal of Music Theory* 8 (2): 251–65.

Barcelos, Lendl. 2013. "Interfacing against the Grain." *Notations* (Fall): 9–13.

Bayle, François. 1993. *Musique acousmatique: propositions – positions*. Paris: Buchet-Chastel.

Beecroft, Norma. 2018. *Conversations with Post World War II Pioneers of Electronic Music*. Toronto: Canadian Music Centre.

Berland, Jody. 1990. "Radio Space and Industrial Time: Music Formats, Local Narratives and Technological Mediation." *Popular Music* 9 (2): 179–92.

– 2009. *North of Empire: Essays on the Cultural Technologies of Space*. Durham, NC: Duke University Press.

Blatterer, Harry, Pauline Johnson, and Maria R. Markus, eds. 2010. *Modern Privacy: Shifting Boundaries, New Forms*. Basingstoke, Hampshire; New York: Palgrave Macmillan.

Born, Georgina. 2011. "Music and the Materialization of Identities." *Journal of Material Culture* 16 (4): 376–88.

Bosma, Hannah. 2006. "Musical Washing Machines, Composer-Performers, and Other Blurring Boundaries: How Women Make a Difference in Electroacoustic Music." *Intersections: Canadian Journal of Music* 26 (2): 97–117.

Brackett, David. 2016. *Categorizing Sound: Genre and Twentieth-Century Popular Music*. Oakland: University of California Press.

Braxton, Anthony. 1985. *Tri-Axium Writings* 1. [San Francisco?]: Synthesis Music.

Britton, Eliot. 2016. "Genre and Capital in Avant-Garde Electronica." *Organised Sound* 21 (1): 61–71. doi:http://dx.doi.org/10.1017/S1355771815000382.

Cage, John. 1973. *Silence: Lectures and Writings by John Cage*. Middleton, CT: Wesleyan University Press.

Canadian Music Centre. n.d. "About Centrediscs." *CMC: Canadian Music Centre/Centre de Musique Canadienne*. https://cmccanada.org/recording-on-centrediscs/.

Carlson, Marvin. 2004. *Performance: A Critical Introduction*. 2nd ed. New York: Routledge.

Cascone, Kim. 2003. "Grain, Sequence, System: Three Levels of Reception in the Performance of Laptop Music." *Contemporary Music Review* 22 (4): 101–4.

"CCMC." 2013. In *The Canadian Encyclopedia*. Historica Canada. Article published 16 March 2008; last edited 15 December 2013. https://www.thecanadianencyclopedia.ca/en/article/ccmc-emc.

Cecchetto, David, and Jeremy Strachan. 2015. "Modernism and Music in Canada and the United States." In *The Modernist World*, edited by Stephen Ross and Allana Lindgren, 546–54. London/New York: Routledge.

Chadabe, Joel. 1967. "New Approaches to Analog-Studio Design." *Perspectives of New Music* 6 (1): 107–13.

– 1997. *Electric Sound: The Past and Promise of Electronic Music*. London: PrenticeHall International.

Cherney, Brian. 2011. "The Activist." In *Weinzweig: Essays on His Life and Music*, edited by John Beckwith and Brian Cherney, 47–73. Waterloo, ON: Wilfrid Laurier University Press.

Chion, Michel. 1983. *Guide des objets sonores: Pierre Schaeffer et la recherche musicale*. Paris: Buchet-Chastel.

Ciamaga, Gustav. 1967. "Some Thoughts on the Teaching of Electronic Music." *Anuario* 3: 69–74.

Clarke, Eric F. 2007. "The Impact of Recording on Listening." *Twentieth-Century Music* 4 (1): 47–70.

Clokie, Hugh McDowell. 1942. "Canadian Contributions to Political Science." *Culture* 3 (4): 467–74.

Collins, Nick, Margaret Schedel, and Scott Wilson, eds. 2013. *Electronic Music*. Cambridge/New York: Cambridge University Press.

Collins, Nicolas. 2017. "Live Electronic Music." In *The Cambridge Companion to Electronic Music*, 2nd ed., edited by Nicolas Collins and Julio d'Escriván, 40–57. Cambridge: Cambridge University Press.

Collins, Nicolas, and Julio d'Escriván. 2017. *The Cambridge Companion to Electronic Music*, 2nd ed. Cambridge: Cambridge University Press.

Cook, Nicholas. 2018. *Music as Creative Practice*. Oxford: Oxford University Press.

Cope, David. 1993. *New Directions in Music*. Madison, WI: Brown and Benchmark.

Cormack, Patricia, and James F. Cosgrave. 2013. *Desiring Canada: CBC Contests, Hockey Violence, and other Stately Pleasures*. Toronto: University of Toronto Press.

Croft, John. 2007. "Theses on Liveness." *Organised Sound* 12 (1): 59–66.

Cvejić, Žarko. 2016. "From Men to Machines and Back: Automata and the Reception of Virtuosity in European Instrumental Art Music, c. 1815–c. 1850." *New Sound: International Magazine for Music* 48: 65–80.

Dalgleish, Mat. 2016. "The Modular Synthesizer Divided: The Keyboard and Its Discontents." *eContact!* 17 (4). https://econtact.ca/17_4/dalgleish_keyboard.html.

Daniels, Arlene Kaplan. 1987. "Invisible Work." *Social Problems* 34 (5): 403–15.

Demers, Joanna. 2010. "Genre, Experimentalism, and the Musical Frame." In *Listening through the Noise: The Aesthetics of Experimental Electronic Music*, 135–54. Oxford/New York: Oxford University Press.

d'Escriván, Julio. 2006. "To Sing the Body Electric: Instruments and Effort in the Performance of Electronic Music." *Contemporary Music Review* 25 (1–2): 183–91. doi: 10.1080/07494460600647667.

Diamond, Beverley. 2019. "Purposefully Reflecting on Tradition and Modernity." In *Music and Modernity among First Peoples of North America*, edited by Victoria Lindsay Levine and Dylan Robinson, 240–57. Middletown, CT: Wesleyan University Press.

Dibben, Nicola. 2009. "Vocal Performance and the Projection of Emotional Authenticity." In *The Ashgate Research Companion to Popular Musicology*, edited by Derek B. Scott, 317–34. Surrey, England: Ashgate.

Dovercourt, Jonny. 2020. *Any Night of the Week: A D.I.Y. History of Toronto Music, 1957–2001*. Toronto: Coach House Books.

Eatock, Colin. 2008. "Culture Wars at the CBC." *Queen's Quarterly* (Summer): 261–73.

Eaton, John. 1968. "The Humanization of Electronic Music." *Music Educators Journal* 55 (3): 101–2.

Egerman, Gina, and Hauke Egermann. 2017. "Mapping, Causality and the Perception of Instrumentality: Theoretical and Empirical Approaches to the Audience's Experience of Digital Musical Instruments." In *Musical Instruments in the 21st Century*, edited by Till Boverman et al., 363–70. Singapore: Springer.

Eimert, Hebert. 1958. "What Is Electronic Music?" *Die Reihe* 1 (English edition), edited by Herbert Eimert and Karlheinz Stockhausen, 1–10. Bryn Mawr, PA: Theodore Presser.

Emmerson, Simon. 2007. *Living Electronic Music*. Aldershot, England: Ashgate.

Emmerson, Simon, and Leigh Landy, eds. 2016. *Expanding the Horizon of Electroacoustic Music Analysis*. Cambridge: Cambridge University Press.

Emmerson, Simon, and Denis Smalley. 2009. "Electro-acoustic Music." In *Grove Music Online*. *Oxford Music Online*. https://doi.org/10.1093/gmo/9781561592630.article.08695.

Erickson, Rebecca J. 2005. "Why Emotion Work Matters: Sex, Gender, and the Division of Household Labor." *Journal of Marriage and Family* 67 (May): 337–51.

Finch, Mark. 2015. "'Toronto Is the Best!': Cultural Scenes, Independent Music, and Competing Urban Visions." *Popular Music and Society* 38 (3): 299–317.

Garner, Steve. 2007. *Whiteness: An Introduction*. London: Routledge.

Gherardi, Silvia, and Barbara Poggio. 2007. *Gendertelling in Organizations: Narratives from Male-Dominated Environments*. Liber, Sweden: Copenhagen Business School Press.

Gillis, Carla. "Toronto Wants to Talk about Racism in Music Badly." *NOW Magazine*. 25 November 2015. https://nowtoronto.com/toronto-wants-to-talk-about-racism-in-music.

Gillmor, Alan. 2011. "In His Own Words." In *Weinzweig: Essays on His Life and Music*, edited by John Beckwith and Brian Cherney, 267–85. Waterloo, ON: Wilfrid Laurier University Press.

Gould, Glenn. 1966. "The Prospects of Recording." *High Fidelity* 16 (4): 46–63.

– 1990. "Glenn Gould Interviews Glenn Gould about Glenn Gould." In *The Glenn Gould Reader*, edited by Tim Page, 313–28. New York: Vintage Books, 1990; reprint of 1984.

Green, J. Paul, and Nancy F. Vogan. 1991. *Music Education in Canada: A Historical Account*. Toronto: University of Toronto Press.

Green, Owen. 2008. "Pondering Value in the Performance Ecosystem." *eContact!* 10 (4). https://econtact.ca/10_4/green_ecosystem.html.

Griffiths, Paul. 1979. *A Guide to Electronic Music*. [New York]: Thames and Hudson.

Harris, Cheryl I. 1993. "Whiteness as Property." *Harvard Law Review* 106 (8): 1707–91.

Hennion, Antoine. 2012. "'As fast as one possibly can …': Virtuosity, a Truth of Musical Performance?" In *Critical Musicological Reflections: Essays in Honour of Derek B. Scott*, edited by Stan Hawkins, 125–38. Farnham, Surrey/Burlington, VT: Ashgate.

Honisch, Stefan Sunandan. 2018. "Virtuosities of Deafness and Blindness." In *The Oxford Handbook of Music and the Body*, edited by Youn Kim and Sander L. Gilman. Oxford University Press. doi: 10.1093/oxfordhb/9780190636234.013.9.

Iyer, Vijay. 2008. "On Improvisation, Temporality, and Embodied Experience." In *Sound Unbound: Sampling Digital Music and Culture*, edited by Paul D. Miller, 263–82. Cambridge, MA: MIT Press.

Jaeger, David. 2013. "Larry Lake [2 July 1943 to 17 September 2013]." *The WholeNote*. 30 September 2013. https://www.thewholenote.com/index.php/newsroom/musical-life/remembering/24400-larry-lake-2-july-1943-to-17-september-2013.

– 2015a. "Ann Southam – By Hands for Hands." *The WholeNote*. 27 November 2015. https://www.thewholenote.com/index.php/newsroom/feature-stories/25761-ann-southam-by-hand-for-hands.

– 2015b. "CBC Collaborations with the New Music Community." *The WholeNote*. 30 September 2015. https://www.thewholenote.com/index.php/newsroom/feature-stories/25637-cbc-collaborations-with-the-new-music-community.

– 2015c. "Remembering Glenn Gould." *The WholeNote*. 29 April 2015. https://www.thewholenote.com/index.php/newsroom/feature-stories/25421-remembering-glenn-gould.

– 2016a. "A Point To Prove: Pierre Boulez – March 26, 1925 – January 5, 2016." *The WholeNote*. 27 January 2016. https://www.thewholenote.com/index.php/newsroom/feature-stories/25840-a-point-to-prove-pierre-boulez-march-26-1925-january-5-2016.

– 2016b. "This Isn't Silence." *The WholeNote*. 1 June 2016. https://www.thewholenote.com/index.php/newsroom/feature-stories/26101-this-isnt-silence.

- 2018. "A Singular Recognition Seen in Context." *The WholeNote*. 30 August 2018. https://www.thewholenote.com/index.php/newsroom/feature-stories/28247-a-singular-recognition-seen-in-context.
- 2019a. "Marjan Mozetich in a Film by Jamie Day Fleck." *The WholeNote*. 29 March 2019. https://www.thewholenote.com/index.php/newsroom/blog/music-and-the-movies/28908-marjan-mozetich-in-a-film-by-jamie-day-fleck.
- 2019b. "Voices in the Wilderness: Thinking about Murray Schafer in 2019." *The WholeNote*. 31 May 2019. https://www.thewholenote.com/index.php/newsroom/feature-stories/29212-voices-in-the-wilderness-thinking-about-murray-schafer-in-2019.
- 2020. "Lessons Learned from the CEE's COVID-Era Experiences." *The WholeNote*. 1 September 2020. https://www.thewholenote.com/index.php/newsroom/feature-stories/30319-lessons-learned-from-the-cee-s-covid-era-experiences.
James, Al. 2013. "The Secret World of Modular Synthesizers." *SOS: Sound on Sound* (April 2013). https://www.soundonsound.com/reviews/secret-world-modular-synthesizers.
Jones, Pamela. 2007. *alcides lanza: Portrait of a Composer*. Montreal and Kingston: McGill-Queen's University Press.
Jordà, Sergi. 2017. "Interactivity and Live Computer Music." In *The Cambridge Companion to Electronic Music*, 2nd ed., edited by Nicolas Collins and Julio d'Escriván, 86–103. Cambridge: Cambridge University Press.
Kasemets, Udo, "James Montgomery." In *The Canadian Encyclopedia*. Historica Canada. Article published 7 February 2006; last edited 14 December 2013. https://thecanadianencyclopedia.ca/en/article/james-montgomery-emc.
Keane, David. 1979. "Some Practical Aesthetic Problems of Electronic Music Composition." *Interface: Journal of New Music Research* 8 (4): 193–205.
- 1984. "Electroacoustic Music in Canada: 1950–1984." In *Célébration*, 57–72. Toronto: Canadian Music Centre/Centre de Musique Canadienne.
Keep, Andy. 2009. "Instrumentalizing: Approaches to Improvising with Sounding Objects in Experimental Music." In *Ashgate Research Companion to Experimental Music*, edited by James Saunders, 113–29. Farnham, Surrey/Burlington, VT: Ashgate.
Keller, Hans. 1990. "The Gramophone Record." In *The Keller Column*, edited by Robert Matthew-Walker, 22–5. London: Alfred Lengnick.
Kramer, Lawrence. 2012. "The Virtuoso Body; Or, the Two Births of Musical Performance." In *Critical Musicological Reflections: Essays in Honour of Derek B. Scott*, edited by Stan Hawkins and Derek B. Scott, 231–44. Farnham, Surrey/Burlington, VT: Ashgate.

Kroetsch, Robert. 1989. "Disunity as Unity: A Canadian Strategy." In *The Lovely Treachery of Words: Essays Selected and New*, 21–33. Toronto: Oxford University Press.

Kuffert, Len. 2016. "'WHAT DO YOU EXPECT OF THIS FRIEND?' Canadian Radio and the Intimacy of Broadcasting." *Media History* 15 (3): 303–19.

Kuivila, Ronald. 2009. "Open Sources: Words, Circuits, and the Notation/Realization Relation in Live Electronic Music." In *Ashgate Research Companion to Experimental Music*, edited by James Saunders, 99–112. Farnham, Surrey/Burlington, VT: Ashgate.

Lacey, Kate. 2013. *Listening Publics: The Politics and Experience of Listening in the Media Age*. Cambridge: Polity Press.

Lee, Brant T. 2004. "The Networking Economic Effects of Whiteness." *American University Law Review* 53 (6): 1259–1304.

Levine, Victoria Lindsay, and Dylan Robinson, eds. 2019. *Music and Modernity among First Peoples of North America*. Middletown, CT: Wesleyan University Press.

Lewis, George E. "Improvised Music after 1950: Afrological and Eurological Perspectives." *Black Music Research Journal* 22 (Supplement): Best of BMRJ: 215–46.

– 2011. "Interactivity and Improvisation." In *Oxford Handbook of Computer Music*, edited by Roger T. Dean, 457–66. Oxford University Press.

Leydon, Rebecca. 2004. "Forbidden Planet: Effects and Affects in the Electro Avant-Garde." In *Off the Planet: Music, Sound and Science Fiction Cinema*, edited by Philip Hayward, 61–76. Eastleigh, UK: John Libbey.

Linson, Adam, and Eric F. Clarke. 2017. "Distributed Cognition, Ecological Theory and Group Improvisation" In *Distributed Creativity: Collaboration and Improvisation in Contemporary Music*, edited by Eric F. Clarke and Mark Doffman, 52–69. Oxford: Oxford University Press.

Lipsitz, George. 2006. *The Possessive Instrument in Whiteness: How White People Profit from Identity Politics*. Philadelphia: Temple University Press.

Locher, Carl. 2014. *Dictionary of the Organ: Organ Registers, Their Timbres, Combinations, and Acoustic Phenomena*. Authorized translation from 4th (1912) edition by Claude P. Landi. New York: E.P. Dutton.

Lutter, Mark. 2015. "Do Women Suffer from Network Closure? The Moderating Effect of Social Capital on Gender Inequality in a Project-Based Labor Market, 1929 to 2010." *American Sociological Review* 80 (2): 329–58.

Manning, Peter. 2013. *Electronic and Computer Music*. 4th ed. New York: Oxford University Press.

Mauer, Barry. 2010. "Glenn Gould and the New Listener." *Performance Research* 15 (3): 101–7.

McCartney, Andra. 1994. "Creating Worlds for My Music to Exist: How Woman Composers of Electroacoustic Music Make Place for Their Voices." MA thesis, York University (Canada). ProQuest (AAT MM99600).

– 1995. "Inventing Images: Constructing and Contesting Gender in Thinking About Electroacoustic Music." *Leonardo Music Journal* 5: 57–66.

– 1996. "Creating Worlds for My Music to Exist: Women Composers of Electroacoustic Music in Canada." *International Alliance for Women in Music Journal* 2 (2): 16–19.

– 1999. "Sounding Places: Situated Conversations through the Soundscape Compositions of Hildegard Westerkamp." PhD diss., York University (Canada). ProQuest (AAT NQ46305).

– 2006. "Gender, Genre and Electroacoustic Soundmaking Practices." *Intersections: Canadian Journal of Music/Revue canadienne de musique* 26 (2): 20–48.

McKeon, Michael. 2005. *The Secret History of Domesticity: Public, Private, and the Division of Knowledge*. Baltimore, MD: Johns Hopkins University Press.

Mcmillan, Barclay, et al. "Arnold Walter." In *The Canadian Encyclopedia*. Historica Canada. Article published 12 June 2008; last edited 31 January 2019. https://www.encyclopediecanadienne.com/en/article/arnold-walter.

McNeilly, Kevin. 1996. "Listening, Nordicity, Community: Glenn Gould's 'The Idea of North.'" *Essays on Canadian Writing* 59: 87–104.

Mishra, Jyoti. 2009. "The SOS Guide to Choosing a Modular Synth." *SOS: Sound on Sound* (April 2009). https://www.soundonsound.com/techniques/sos-guide-choosing-modular-synth.

Montgomery, Jim. 2020. "The PtT Project (Pass the Track)." *The CEE (Canadian Electronic Ensemble)*. 15 August 2020. https://www.canadianelectronicensemble.com/http:/www.canadianelectronicensemble.com/2020/the-who-starts-first-project/.

Mumma, Gordon. 1975. "Live-Electronic Music." In *The Development and Practice of Electronic Music*, edited by Jon H. Appleton and Ronald C. Perara, 286–335. Englewood Cliffs, NJ: Prentice Hall.

Neill, Ben. 2002. "Pleasure Beats: Rhythm and the Aesthetics of Current Electronic Music." *Leonardo Music Journal* 12: 3–6.

Overton, Adam. 2006. "Invisible Performance and the Virtuosic Body." *Contemporary Music Review* 25 (1/2): 173–82.

Palombini, Carlos. 1993. "Machine Songs V: Pierre Schaeffer: From Research into Noises to Experimental Music." *Computer Music Journal* 17 (3): 14–19.

Peters, John Durham. 1997. "Realism in Social Representation and the Fate of the Public." *Javnost – The Public: Journal of the European Institute for Communication and Culture* 4 (2): 5–16. doi: 10.1080/13183222.1997.11008643111.

Pinch, Trevor, and Frank Trocco. 2002. *Analog Days: The Invention and Impact of the Moog Synthesizer*. Cambridge, MA: Harvard University Press.

Pitman, Walter. 2008. *Elmer Iseler: Choral Visionary*. Toronto: Dundurn Press.

Rea, John. 2011. "The Teacher." In *Weinzweig: Essays on His Life and Music*, edited by John Beckwith and Brian Cherney, 75–101. Waterloo, ON: Wilfrid Laurier University Press.

Robinson, Dylan. 2020. *Hungry Listener: Resonant Theory for Indigenous Sound Studies*. Minneapolis: University of Minnesota Press.

Rodgers, Tara. 2010. *Pink Noises: Women on Electronic Music and Sound*. Durham, NC: Duke University Press.

Ross, Sara Gwendolyn. 2016. "Preserving Canadian Music Culture: The Intangible Cultural Heritage Management of Urban Spaces of Culture and the Case of the Iconic Toronto Music Venue the Silver Dollar Room." *Architecture_MPS* 10 (2): 1–30.

– 2017. "Development versus Preservation Interests in the Making of a Music City: A Case Study of Select Iconic Toronto Music Venues and the Treatment of Their Intangible Cultural Heritage Value." *International Journal of Cultural Property* 24 (1): 31–56.

Sanden, Paul. 2013. *Liveness in Modern Music: Musicians, Technology, and the Perception of Performance*. New York: Routledge.

Schaeffer, Myron S. 1963. "The Electronic Music Studio of the University of Toronto." *Journal of Music Theory* 7 (Spring): 73–81.

Schaeffer, Pierre. 1966. *Traité des objets musicaux: essai interdiciplines*. Paris: Éditions du Seuil.

Schafer, R. Murray. 1977. *The Soundscape: Our Sonic Environment and the Tuning of the World*. New York: Knopf.

Schrader, Barry. 2001. "Barron, Louis." *Grove Music Online. Oxford Music Online*. https://doi.org/10.1093/gmo/9781561592630.article.42712.

Seabrooke, Thomas Jerome. 2008. *Bowie in Berlin: A New Career in a New Town*. London: Jawbone Press.

Sheikh, Iman. 2016. "The Politics of Music: Why the Canadian Music Scene Lacks Diversity." TVO. 25 July 2016. https://www.tvo.org/article/the-politics-of-music-why-the-canadian-music-scene-lacks-diversity.

Simoni, Mary, ed. 2006. *Analytical Methods of Electroacoustic Music*. New York: Routledge.

Small, Christopher. 1998. *Musicking: The Meanings of Performing and Listening*. Hanover: University Press of New England.

Smalley, Denis. 1986. "Spectro-morphology and Structuring Processes." In *The Language of Electroacoustic Music*, edited by Simon Emmerson, 61–93. London: Macmillan.

– 1996. "The Listening Imagination: Listening in the Electroacoustic Era." *Contemporary Music Review* 13 (2): 77–107.

– 1997. "Spectromorphology: Explaining Sound-Shapes." *Organised Sound* 2 (2): 107–26.
Snider, Roxanne. 1984. "The Composers' Frontier." *Maclean's*, 15 October 1984, 59.
Southam, Ann. 1981. *Natural Resources, or What to Do till the Power Comes On*.
Steenhuisen, Paul. 2009. *Sonic Mosaics: Conversations with Composers*. Edmonton: University of Alberta Press.
Stern, Jonathan. 2003. *The Audible Past: Cultural Origins of Sound Reproduction*. Durham, NC: Duke University Press.
Stone, Kurt. 1967. "Review: Music and Musicians of Canada. 17 LP discs. RCA Victor. CC/CCS 1007-23 (mono and stereo)." *Music Quarterly* 53 (3): 440–52.
Strachan, Jeremy. 2016. "Listening Out to Experimental Music in Canada: Places, Subjects, Places." *Intersections* 36 (2): 67–74.
– 2020. "Modernisms on the Air: CBC Radio in the 1960s." In *John P.L. Roberts, CBC/Radio Canada and Art Music*, edited by Friedemann Sallis and Regina Landwehr, 208–22. Newcastle upon Tyne: Cambridge Scholars Press.
Taylor, Timothy. 2001. *Strange Sounds: Music, Technology & Culture*. New York: Routledge.
Teruggi, Daniel. 2007. "Technology and Musique Concrète: The Technical Developments of the Groupe de Recherches Musicales and Their Implication in Musical Composition." *Organised Sound* 12 (3): 213–31.
Thistlewaite, Nicholas, and Geoffrey Weber, eds. 1998. *The Cambridge Companion to the Organ*. Cambridge: Cambridge University Press.
Tilbury, John. 2001. "Cardew, Cornelius." *Grove Music Online. Oxford Music Online*. https://doi.org/10.1093/gmo/9781561592630.article.04912.
Toynbee, Jason. 2000. *Making Popular Music: Musicians, Creativity and Institutions*. London: Arnold.
Tuck, Eve, and K. Wayne Yang. 2012. "Decolonization Is Not a Metaphor." *Decolonization: Indigeneity, Education & Society* 1 (1): 1–40.
Van Eyk, Jason. 2013. "Centrediscs: Showcases Canada's Composers." *Musicworks* 116 (Summer). https://www.musicworks.ca/reviews/recordings/centrediscs.
Vorachek, Laura. 2000. "'The Instrument of the Century': The Piano as an Icon of Female Sexuality in the Nineteenth Century." *George Eliot - George Henry Lewis Studies* no. 38/39 (September): 26–43.
Ware, Evan. 2013. "Ann Southam." In *The Canadian Encyclopedia*. Historica Canada. Article published 21 September 2011; last edited 16 December 2013. https://www.thecanadianencyclopedia.ca/en/article/ann-southam-emc.

Ware, Evan, and David Olds. 2013. "Larry Lake." In *The Canadian Encyclopedia*. Historica Canada. Article published 1 July 2009; last edited 16 December 2013. https://thecanadianencyclopedia.ca/en/article/larry-lake-emc.

Westerkamp, Hildegard. 2002. "Linking Soundscape Composition." *Organised Sound* 7 (1): 51–6.

– 2006. "Soundwalking as Ecological Practice." *The West Meets the East in Acoustic Ecology*. Proceedings for the International Conference on Acoustic Ecology, Hirosaki University, Hirosaki, Japan. 2–4 November. Reprinted online: https://www.hildegardwesterkamp.ca/writings/writingsby/?post_id=14&title=%E2%80%8Bsoundwalking-as-ecological-practice-.

– 2015. "The Disruptive Nature of Listening." Keynote Address, *International Symposium on Electronic Art*. https://www.hildegardwesterkamp.ca/writings/writingsby/?post_id=11&title=the-disruptive-nature-of-listening%27.

Williams, Peter, and Barbara Owen. 1988. *The Organ*. New York: W.W. Norton.

Woloshyn, Alexa. 2016. "Norma Beecroft. 2015. *Conversations with Post World War II Pioneers of Electronic Music*. Self-published with assistance from the Canadian Music Centre. E-book." *Intersections: Canadian Journal of Music* 36 (1):103–5.

– 2017. "Electroacoustic Voices: Sounds Queer, and Why It Matters." TEMPO 71 (280): 68–79.

Young, Gayle. 1989. *The Sackbut Blues: Hugh LeCaine, Pioneer in Electronic Music*. Ottawa: National Museum of Science and Technology.

– 1999. "Special Purpose Tape Recorder." *LeCaine: An Inventor's Notebook*. http://www.hughlecaine.com/en/sptape.html.

– 2004. "Hugh Le Caine: In Context, 2004." *eContact!* 6 (3): https://econtact.ca/6_3/young_lecaine.html.

Zareei, Mo H., Ajay Kapur, and Dale A. Carnegie. 2013. "Noise on the Grid: Rhythmic Pulse in Experimental and Electronic Noise Music." ICMC: 462–5.

Index

Italicized page numbers indicate figures or musical examples. Tables are indicated with *t* following the page number.

7 Below (CEE), 74, 133–4
7 Below (rehearsal space), xiv, 50, 74, 111, 133

accordion, 68, 133
acousmatic listening, 9–10, 128, 199–200, 240n2
acousmatic music, 9–11, 97–8, 240n2
acoustic ecology, 128–30
acoustic instruments: in the CEE's music, 67, 70, 90–1, 94–5, 98, 136; in contrast to live electronic music, 15–17, 22–5; in Southam's work, 171–3. See also *Consequences for 5* (Beecroft); *Fancye* (Jaeger), listening guide; *I Have Come Through* (Montgomery); *Increscents* (Grimes); piano; *Psalm* (Lake); *Quivi sospiri* (Jaeger); *Sparse Sunday* (Farah); violin
aesthetic listening: Demers's term, 127–8, 147, 200, 202; Robinson's term, 123, 198

aesthetic liveness, 86, 88
aesthetics of electronic music, 9–11, 52–5
Afrological perspective, 15–16, 109, 117–18. *See also* Eurological perspective; Lewis, George E.
agency, 16, 23–4, 99, 138, 141
Aitken, Robert, 155, 174, 238n3
All Wounds (Grimes), 45–6
Americanization, xv–xvii
AMM, 19, 20
analog technologies: ARP Odyssey, 44, 55–6, 219; the CEE's early use of, 3, 39–40, 55–7; EMS Synthi A, 39–40, 44, 55–6, 58, 81, 106; EMS Synthi AKS, 55, 59, 79, 81, 106; maintenance of, 56, 58–9, 81; monophonic synthesizers, 8, 55–7, 219; polyphonic synthesizers, 56–7; renewed interest in, xiv, 77, 78–9, 80–1; unpredictability of, 17, 21, 55, 80, 93–4; Yamaha CS-60, 57, 81, 220. *See also* Eurorack modular synthesis modules; modular synthesizers; Roland equipment
Anhalt, István, 13
Arnold (CEE), 44–5
Arts & Letters Club (Toronto): 2012 CEE performance at, 135–7;

2016 CEE performance at, 4, 8, 9, 23, 25; as space for chamber music, 9
Association pour la création et la recherche électroacoustiques du Québec (ACREQ), 14
Attention Elk! (Supertrio), 63–4, 241n11; listening guide, 200, 228–31, 229t, 230, 231
audience engagement: CEE members on, 95, 99; challenges of, xiv, 3–4, 103, 120–1; fascination with equipment, 3–4, 89–90; and perceived causality, 23–5, 84–5, 90–1, 95–6, 99; and virtuosity, 24–5, 84–5, 99–101, 103, 105; and visual cues, 3–4, 100–1, 103, 136. *See also* gesture–sound relationships; listening

Bach, J.S., 72, 165, 205
Bandcamp, 138–9
Banff Centre for the Arts, 62–4, 114, 130
Barron, Louis and Bebe, 14
beat-oriented electronic music, 53–4, 55, 82, 136
Beecroft, Norma, 13, 71, 155–6. See also *Consequences for 5* (Beecroft)
Bluffer's Lookout (2014 album), 73, 74–7, 109, 190. See also *This Is This* (Bolton)
Bolton, Rose: background and career of, 69, 70, 186; on the CEE's creative practice, 54–5, 111, 116, 119, 188; on the CEE's legacy, 191; on the CEE's members, 50, 66, 119, 178; contributions to the CEE sound, 74–6, 103, 119, 237n1; and EQ: Women in Electronic Music, xv, 70, 179, 181–2; on equipment, 94, 189; equipment used by, 59, 70, 91, 94; on gender in electronic music, 178; membership in the CEE, xviii, xviiit, 186; and the Music Gallery, 175, 186; in *This Is This*, 142, 143t, 144–6, 238n7. *See also This Is This* (Bolton)
brass, 68, 113, 136. See also *Consequences for 5* (Beecroft); *Improvisation #4* (CEE)
Bridgman, Billie, 42, 45–6
Buchla, Don, 7, 8

Cage, John: and the Eurological value system, 15–16, 118, 127; influence on the CEE, 15, 125–7; and instrumentalizing, 6, 17, 125–6
Canada, electronic music in, 12–14, 236n5. *See also* Canadian Electronic Ensemble (CEE); Toronto; University of Toronto Electronic Music Studio (UTEMS)
Canada, racializing hierarchies in, 176–7, 240n18
Canada Council for the Arts (CCA), 153, 177, 182
Canada–United States relationship, xv–xvii, 26
Canadian Centennial (1967), xvi, 26–7, 154
Canadian Conservatory of Music (CNCM), 66
Canadian Creative Music Collective (CCMC), 173–4
Canadian Electroacoustic Community (CEC), 14

Canadian Electronic Ensemble (1977 album), 43, 44–5, 174
Canadian Electronic Ensemble (1981 album), 43, 45–6
Canadian Electronic Ensemble (CEE): absence from scholarship, xii, 19; as chamber ensemble, 101–2; as a collaboration, 21–2, 94, 114–16, 119–20, 188; collaborations with other musicians, 60–3, 64, 67, 114–15; commissioning other composers, 48, 156, 159, 169, 170–1*t*, 171–3; as a community, 49, 50–1, 63, 83, 118–19; compared with other live electronic ensembles, 19–22; as creative outlet, 41; equipment, 3, 8–9, 55–9, 89–91, 110; exploring new technologies, 57–8, 125, 126; fluidity and flexibility, 64–5, 70–1, 79, 110; formation of, xiii–xiv, xv, 27, 38, 235n2; future and legacy of, xv, 190–3; group improvisation, 65, 71–2, 109–13, 114–16, 117–20, 126; humour of, 74; importance of, 48, 193; individuality within the group, 119–20; members as composers, 21, 43–4, 65, 133, 147; members as listeners, 122–3, 125, 131, 136, 149–51; membership (overview), xviii*t*, 49; and notions of liveness, 23–4, 89–91, 93–5; openness to different sound sources, 20, 125–6, 189–90; Pass the Track, 149–51; performance style of, 100–2, 127–8, 135–7, 141, 188; rehearsal process, 115–16, 120, 122–3, 132–3; self-referentiality, 119, 133; sound and aesthetics of, 52–5, 66, 81–3; spaces, 101, 110–11, 123–4, 126–8, 132–7, 174–5; as "weird," 54–5, 66, 69, 126; works (overview), xviii–xix, 45*t*, 60*t*, 61*t*. See also *individual members*; *specific works*

Canadian Electronic Ensemble (CEE), performances and events: (1971–72) before official founding, 38–40; (1972–85) original quartet era, 40, 41–4, 45*t*; 1979 European tour, 41–3; (1979) *The Music of Man*, 47, 100, 102; 1985 Holland Festival, 43, 47; (1986–96) trio era, 59–64, 60*t*, 61*t*; (2009–) sextet era, 71–2, 73–4, 79, 81; (2012) Arts & Letters Club, 135–7; (2015) Beecroft book launch, 156; (2016) Arts & Letters Club, 4, 8, 9, 23, 25; (2017) Canadian Music Centre, 103–4, 126, 237–8n1; (2020) Carnegie Mellon University, 73–4, 84, 115, 120, 122–3

Canadian Electronic Ensemble (CEE), recordings: *Bluffer's Lookout* (2014), 73, 74–7; *Canadian Electronic Ensemble* (1977), 43, 44–5, 174; *Canadian Electronic Ensemble* (1981), 43, 45–6; *Canadian Electronic Ensemble: Live* (1998), xiv, 64, 96–8; *Catbird Seat* (1990), 59, 62; *The Electronic Messiah* (1982), 43, 46–7, 165–9, *167*, *168*; *Live in Cabbagetown* (2013 [2008]), xiv, 64, 71, 72, 89, 112–14; *Supertrio* (1996), 59, 62, 63–4

Canadian Electronic Ensemble: Live (1998 album), 64, 96–8

Canadianization, xvi–xvii, 154
Canadian Music Centre (CMC), 70, 135, 162, 163–4, 179
Canadian new music scene, xiv–xv, 161–4, 173–7, 193. See also *Two New Hours* (CBC Radio 2)
Carlos, Wendy, 72, 165
Carnegie Mellon University, 2020 CEE residency: collaboration with Exploded Ensemble, 73, 115, 120, 122–3; lecture, 185–7, 188–92; overview, xiii, 71; performances, 73–4, 84, 115, 122–3
Caspin's Arrival (CEE), 97–8; listening guide, 231–3, 232*t*
Catbird Seat (1990 album), 59, 62. See also *Quivi sospiri* (Jaeger)
Catbird Seat (CEE), 59, 61
causality, 23–4, 95–6, 99. See also gesture–sound relationships
CBC Radio Canada: and Canadian identity, xvii, 139, 153, 157, 161–2; CEE members working for, 153–5, 157, 158–9, 160, 183; as influential institution, 152–3, 154, 160–2, 163–5, 183. See also *Two New Hours* (CBC Radio 2)
CBC Television, 30, 47
CEE. See Canadian Electronic Ensemble (CEE)
Centrediscs, 163–4
Chaconne à son goût (CEE), 45, 46, 61
chamber music, 9, 67, 101–2
Chapman Stick, 68–9, 75–7, 87
Ciamaga, Gustav, 30–2, 35, 38, 56, 185–6
classical music. See Euro-American classical music
collaboration: within the CEE, 21–2, 94, 114–16, 119–20, 188; between the CEE and other artists, 60–3, 64, 67, 114–15, 188; in electronic music, 16–17, 18–22
Columbia-Princeton Electronic Music Center, 11, 15
CompuServe, 67, 68, 139, 186
Consequences for 5 (Beecroft), 156, 157; listening guide, 209, 210–11*t*, 211–16, *212*, *213*
corporeality: liveness of, 88–91, 92, 95–6, 97, 112, 114; and virtuosity, 23, 24–5, 96, 105, 108. See also gesture–sound relationships; humanization of electronic music; physicality of instruments
counterpoint: in *I Have Come Through*, 216, 218*t*, 219; in Montgomery's music studies, 36; in *Psalm*, 225–6, *226*, 227*t*; in *Quivi sospiri*, 220, 224, *224*
COVID-19, 124, 134, 149–51
Croft, John, 85–6, 88, 91, 92
Cruz, Lina, 64, 70, 114
Cvejić, Žarko, 107

Davies (CEE), 133
Demers, Joanna, 123, 127–8, 147, 200, 202
digital technologies: and the analog/digital debate, 77, 80–1; and gesture–sound relationships, 3–4, 23, 86, 96, 103; as technological development, 8–9, 25, 56–7, 68. See also laptops
disability, 108, 237n8
Dobinson, Michael, xvii–xviii, xviii*t*, 65–6, 67, 71
drones: in *Attention Elk!*, 228–31, *229*; in *Psalm*, 225, 226*t*; in *Sparse Sunday*, 76

drum beats, 54, 136–7, 233–4. *See also* beat-oriented electronic music; pulse
Dyno-Soar, 44, 55, 56

Echoplex, 156, 189. See also *Consequences for 5* (Beecroft)
écoute réduite (Schaeffer). *See* reduced listening (Schaeffer)
editing, 114, 150. *See also* studio-based electronic music
Egermann, Hauke, 95–6
electronic dance music (EDM), 53–4, 202
Electronic Messiah, The (1982 album), 43, 46–7, 165–9, *167*, *168*
electronic music, historiography of, xii–xiii, 11, 19, 179
electronic musical instruments, early history of, 5–8
elektronische Musik, 10, 88, 93. *See also* Nordwestdeutscher Rundfunk (NWDR)
Elmer Iseler Singers, 46–7, 165–9
Emerson, Gina, 95–6
Emmerson, Simon, 23–4, 87, 97, 99
EQ, Women in Electronic Music, xv, xvii, 70, 179–82, 240nn19–21
Esprit Contemporain, 159–60
Euro-American classical music: composer-centred nature of, 16, 117; concert rituals of, 95, 101–2, 127–8; gesture–sound relationships in, 3–4, 22–3, 85; harmony in, 205, 206; influence on electronic instruments, 6–7; musical hierarchies in, 126, 127; role of the performer in, 17, 22–3, 24–5; structural listening in, 52, 198, 201; taught at the University of Toronto, 27–9,

117; virtuosity in, 100, 101, 103, 105, 107. *See also* Eurological perspective
Eurological perspective, 15–16, 117–18, 120, 127. *See also* Afrological perspective; Lewis, George E.
Eurorack modular synthesis modules, 4, 77, 80–1, 87, 90, 106–7. *See also* modular synthesizers
exclusion, 12, 153, 156, 176–7. *See also* gender inequality; racial inequality
Exploded Ensemble, 73, 115, 120, 122–3. *See also* Carnegie Mellon University, 2020 CEE residency

Fancye (Jaeger), listening guide, 205–9, *207t*, *208*, *209*, 241n8
Farah, John Kameel: background and career of, 72–3; on the CEE's members and creative practice, 50, 73, 116; contributions to the CEE sound, 72–3, 75, 103, 104–5, 119–20; equipment used by, 59, 72–3, 111, 118, 188; as improviser, 73, 103–5, 111, 234; membership in the CEE, xviii, xviii*t*, 72, 186; and the Music Gallery, 175, 186; on Pass the Track, 149; in performance, 84, 104–5, 113, 233–4; *Sparse Sunday*, 74–7
fidelity, liveness of, 88, 91–2, 114
financial investment in equipment, 57–8, 70, 81, 192
fixed listening (Robinson), 123–4, 127, 147, 148
form. *See* structure
funding, 70–1, 132, 163, 177

gatekeeping, 164, 177. *See also* exclusion

gender and listening. See *This Is This* (Bolton)

gender inequality: efforts to counter, 153, 164, 179–82, 183–4; in opportunities for composers, 154–6, 157–8, 160–1, 179–82; and stereotypes, 177–8, 180–1; as a systemic issue, 120, 152–3, 173, 175–6, 183–4

gender roles, 63, 173, 179–82

gentrification, 130, 134

gestural surrogacy, 97–9

gesture–sound relationships: in the CEE's performances, 3–4, 84–7, 89–91, 95–6, 99–103; and digital technologies, 3–4, 23, 86, 96, 103; in Euro-American classical music, 3–4, 22–3, 85; and human agency, 22–5, 98–9; and virtuosity, 95–6, 99–101, 103, 106–7. *See also* audience engagement; corporeality

Golani, Rivka, 62, 164, 173

Gould, Glenn: friendship with Jaeger, xi, 154; ideas about recording, performance, and listening, 109, 139, 141, 147, 148; influence on Farah, 72

Gray, John S., 65, 135. See also *No Dim Pearls* (Gray)

Green, Owen, 102, 110–11

Grimes, David: background and career of, 37–8; departure from the CEE, xiv, xviii*t*, 38; as founding member of the CEE, xv, xviii*t*, 27, 37, 40; on *Increscents*, 202–3; and *Two New Hours*, 38, 158–9. See also *Increscents* (Grimes)

Gruppo di Improvvisazione Nuova Consonanza, 19, 20

Honisch, Stefan, 108

humanization of electronic music, 24, 92–3, 107

hungry listening (Robinson), 123, 130, 148

I Have Come Through (Montgomery), 54; listening guide, 216–17, 217, 218*t*, 219

improvisation: Afrological vs. Eurological perspectives on, 15–17, 109, 117–18; in the CEE's performance practice, 65, 71–2, 109–13, 114–16, 117–20, 126; in *Consequences for 5* (Beecroft), 213–14; "goes first" improvisations, 72, 104, 120–1, 126, 150; as a group process, 16–17, 20–1, 114–16, 119–20; in *Pass the Track*, 149–51; and unpredictability of equipment, 21, 117. See also *Improvisation #4* (CEE)

Improvisation #4 (CEE), 54, 113; listening guide, 233–4, 234

Increscents (Grimes), 38, 160; listening guide, 202–5, 203*t*, 204

indeterminacy, 15–16, 37, 118

Indigenous perspectives, 123, 130. *See also* Robinson, Dylan

institutional connections, privilege of, 137, 152–3, 163–4, 175–7, 182–3. *See also* networks

instrumentalization, 17, 20, 85, 116, 125–6. See also *Natural Resources* (Southam)

interactivity, 23, 88, 90, 94–5, 120–1. *See also* agency; audience engagement

International Rostrum of
  Composers (IRC), 157–8, 161–2
intimacy, 124, 139–40, 146–7,
  150–1, 197
Iseler, Elmer, 165–6, 169. *See also*
  Elmer Iseler Singers
Iyer, Vijay, 90, 95, 109, 112, 113

Jaeger, David: on audiences, 91, 95,
  99; background and career of,
  xi, 32–4, 164, 205; on Canadian
  new music, 161–3; as CBC Radio
  Canada producer, xiv–xv, 33,
  153–5; on CEE members, 3, 64,
  66, 187; on CEE performances
  and events, 42–3, 62–4, 135;
  on the CEE's musicking, 54,
  112, 159, 188, 190; on *The
  Electronic Messiah*, 165, 166,
  168, 169; and equipment, 4,
  57–9, 89, 106, 118; as founding
  member of the CEE, xv, 27, 37,
  38–40, 185; and the International
  Rostrum of Composers,
  157–8, 161–2; membership
  in the CEE, xvii, xviii*t*; as
  Possibilities Portmanteaux (with
  Montgomery), 40, 109, 111; on
  Southam, 171, 172–3; in *This Is
  This*, 143*t*, 144, 145; and *Two New
  Hours*, 129, 157–9, 161, 162. See
  also *Fancye* (Jaeger), listening
  guide; *Quivi sospiri* (Jaeger); *Two
  New Hours* (CBC Radio 2)
Jaeger, Sally, 141, 143*t*, 144
jazz, 15–16, 111, 118

Karen Kieser Prize, 35, 160, 161
Keane, David, xii, 48, 52
keyboard interfaces, 4, 6–8, 23–4,
  87, 92

Kieser, Karen, 35, 45–6, 63, 70, 153.
  See also Karen Kieser Prize
Kramer, Lawrence, 100, 105, 107

Lacey, Kate, 137, 138–9, 198
Lake, Larry: at the CBC, 129, 153–5,
  158–9; on *Chaconne à son goût*,
  46; death of, 35, 71, 73–4; Farah
  on, 50; as founding member of
  the CEE, xv, xvii, xviii*t*, 27, 37,
  38–40; Jaeger on, 3, 50, 168; and
  Kieser, 35; in performance, 113,
  135–6, 233–4; and Stillwell, 68,
  69, 73, 139, 186; and technology,
  3, 81, 119; at the University of
  Toronto, 27, 34–5; works, 35.
  See also Psalm (Lake); *Two New
  Hours* (CBC Radio 2)
laptops: the CEE's use of, 3–4, 59,
  74–5, 90, 103; and gesture-
  sound relationships, 3–4, 23, 86,
  103; as a tool for live electronic
  music, 3–4, 8–9, 59, 68
Le Caine, Hugh, 8, 12–13, 30–1, 39,
  92
Lewis, George E., 15–16, 109, 114,
  117–18, 138
listening: author's perspective on,
  113, 142, 144–7, 197–8, 214–15,
  216; and gestural surrogacy,
  97–9; and improvisation, 113,
  115; and live CEE performances,
  102–3, 120–1, 125–8, 135–7;
  overview, xiv, 148, 197–8; and
  place, 122–4, 128–32, 135–7;
  and values, 123–4, 130–1; in
  virtual spaces, 137–41, 149–51.
  See also audience engagement
listening, modes of: acousmatic
  listening, 9–10, 128, 199–200,
  240n2; aesthetic listening

(Demers), 127–8, 147, 200, 202; aesthetic listening (Robinson), 123, 198; fixed listening (Robinson), 123–4, 127, 147, 148; hungry listening (Robinson), 123, 130, 148; reduced listening (Schaeffer), 118, 123, 128, 199–200; self-reflexive listening (Robinson), 148, 198, 201–2; structural listening, 52, 198, 201–2

live electronic music: in contrast to acoustic performance, 15–17, 22–5, 85, 105; emerging from studio practice, 8, 10–11, 15, 39; history of, 6–8, 19–22; technological knowledge needed for, 17–18, 105–6. *See also* Canadian Electronic Ensemble (CEE); gesture-sound relationships; improvisation; liveness

Live in Cabbagetown (2013 [2008] album), 64, 71, 72, 89, 112–14

liveness: and human agency, 22–5, 84–5, 91–2, 120–1; and live albums, 88–9, 114; overview, xiv, 85–7, 88; Sanden's categories of, 88–9, 91–2, 93–5, 101. *See also* audience engagement; improvisation; live electronic music

Marx, Leo, 89–90
McCartney, Andra, 178
mediation, 84–5, 87–8, 90–1. *See also* Sanden, Paul
MEGAJAM, 60, 71, 114
Menuhin, Yehudi, 47
Messiah (Handel). See *Electronic Messiah, The* (1982 album)
MetaMusic, 78, 111, 186–7, 236n7

metre, 54, 55, 82, 172, 222. *See also* pulse
mmmm, 66
modular synthesizers, 7, 69, 77, 78–81, 106, 189. *See also* Eurorack modular synthesis modules
Montgomery, James: background and career of, 13, 31, 36–7, 185–6; as CEE archivist, xiii, 79, 236n7; on the CEE's future and legacy, 191–2; on the CEE's musicking, 37, 96, 188, 189–90; on collaboration, 62, 63, 171; on *The Electronic Messiah*, 166, 168, 169; and equipment, 55–6, 57–8, 93, 105–6; as founding member of the CEE, xv, 27, 37, 38–40, 185–6; membership in the CEE, xvii, xviii*t*; as Music Gallery artistic director, xiv, 36, 174–5, 186; in performance, 4, 100–1, 136; as Possibilities Portmanteaux (with Jaeger), 40, 109, 111; in *This Is This*, 143*t*, 144–5; at the University of Toronto, 29–30, 31, 32–3. *See also I Have Come Through* (Montgomery)
Moog, Robert, 7, 8, 12, 34–5, 80
Mozetich, Marjan, 159
Musica Elettronica Viva (MEV), 19–20
Music Gallery (Toronto), 41, 96–7, 134, 173–7, 186
musicking, 49, 102, 110–11, 122–3, 124
musique concrète, 9–10, 31, 199–200

Natural Resources (Southam), 125, 169, 171–2, 239nn14–15

networks, 137, 152–3, 161–3, 175–7, 182–3. *See also* institutional connections, privilege of
New Music Concerts (NMC), 36, 155, 158
No Dim Pearls (Gray), 54, 100–1, 135–7, 233
Nordwestdeutscher Rundfunk (NWDR), 10–11
nostalgia, xiv, 49, 80

oboe. See *Psalm* (Lake)
obsolescence, 58–9, 81, 105–6, 110
Olnick, Harvey, 30, 33, 34
Ontario Council for the Arts (OAC), 153, 177, 182
organ. See *Fancye* (Jaeger), listening guide

Pass the Track, 124, 149–51
pedagogy, 29–30, 31–2, 66
performance practice, 22–5, 86, 88–91, 93–5, 127–8. *See also* improvisation; liveness
performance spaces, 4, 101, 111, 126–8, 132–7, 174–5
Petric, Joseph, 62, 133, 164, 238n3
Petrowska Quilico, Christina, xi, 58, 62, 160, 219
physicality of instruments, 80–1, 85, 87, 89–91. *See also* gesture–sound relationships
piano, 44–6, 74–7, 94, 104–5, 173. See also *Consequences for 5* (Beecroft); Farah, John Kameel; *I Have Come Through* (Montgomery); Kieser, Karen; Petrowska Quilico, Christina; *Quivi sospiri* (Jaeger)
pitch: in *Attention Elk!*, 228–31; in *Caspin's Arrival*, 232t, 233;
in the CEE's sound, 53, 126; in *Consequences for 5*, 210–11t, 211–14; in *Fancye*, 205, 206–7, 208–9; in *Increscents*, 203–5, 203; in *Psalm*, 225, 226, 227t; in *Quivi sospiri*, 220–2, 221t, 224
place, 128–31, 132–7, 148. *See also* performance spaces
playback, 8, 58, 126. See also *Consequences for 5* (Beecroft)
positionality, 130–1, 198, 201–2
Possibilities Portmanteaux, 40, 109, 111
procedural liveness, 86, 88
Psalm (Lake), 54, 73, 94–5, 164, 241n6; listening guide, 225–6, 226, 227t
pulse, 54, 55, 82–3, 136–7, 233–4. *See also* beat-oriented electronic music; metre

Quivi sospiri (Jaeger), 54, 58–9, 201; listening guide, 219–22, 221t, 222, 223–4, 224

racial inequality, 120, 152–3, 154–5, 157–8, 160–1, 176–7
radio, as virtual space, 137, 139
recorded music, as virtual space, 137–41
reduced listening (Schaeffer), 118, 123, 128, 199–200
rehearsal, 115–16, 120, 122–3, 132–3
rhythm. *See* metre; pulse
Roberts, John Peter Lee, 154, 163
Robinson, Dylan: on fixed listening, 123–4, 125, 128, 147; on self-reflexive listening, 148, 198, 201–2; on soundscape compositions, 130, 131

Rodgers, Tara, 178
Roland equipment: DC-10, 58, 220, 224; Jupiter 8, 165, 166–8; MC-4 MicroComposer, 165–6; SE-02, 70; SH-5, 44, 55, 56, 57, 219
Royal Conservatory of Music (Toronto), 12–13, 26, 27, 72

sampled sound, 75, 112, 113, 140, 234. *See also* laptops; soundscape music
Sanden, Paul, 87–9, 91–2, 93, 101, 112, 121. *See also* liveness
San Francisco Tape Music Center (SFTMC), 19, 21–2
Schaeffer, Myron, 12, 30
Schaeffer, Pierre, 9–10, 92, 199–200, 235n1, 240n1. *See also* reduced listening (Schaeffer)
Schafer, R. Murray, 13, 128–9, 130–1
self-reflexive listening (Robinson), 148, 198, 201–2
settler colonialism, 123–4
Shadow Box (1988 album), 164, 227. See also *Psalm* (Lake)
Shadow Box (Jaeger), 133, 164
skill. *See* virtuosity
Small, Christopher, 49, 122–4. *See also* musicking
Smalley, Denis, 97–8, 200
Sonic Arts Union, 19, 21, 22
soundscape music, 128–32, 140
Southam, Ann: career, 12–13, 169, 171, 173, 239n13; music performed by the CEE, 62, 125, 160, 171–2. See also *Natural Resources* (Southam)
spaces. *See* performance spaces; place; spatial ecologies
Sparse Sunday (Farah), 74–7
spatial ecologies, 123–4, 148

spatialization, 92, 142, 143t, 144–6, 144
spatial liveness, 88, 89, 94–5, 112, 120–1
spectromorphology, 98, 200
spontaneity, 88–9, 93–5, 101, 112, 114, 118
Stillwell, Paul: background and career of, 68, 111, 186; on the CEE's social aspects, 50, 51, 83; on connecting with equipment, 58, 68–9, 77, 80–1, 87; and the editing process, 114, 150; on the evolution of the CEE's equipment, 3, 189; joining the CEE through Lake, 67, 68, 73, 139, 186; in live performance, 4, 90, 106; membership in the CEE, xvii–xviii, xviiit; and modular synthesizers, 7, 69, 77, 80–1, 106; on musical communication, 64, 66, 82, 111; in recordings, 75, 143t, 144–6, 149–50; and Sutherland, 78–9, 187; on the Toronto Sound Festival, 187. *See also* 7 Below (rehearsal space); *Caspin's Arrival* (CEE)
Stockhausen, Karlheinz, 19, 208
structural listening, 52, 198, 201–2
structure: in *Consequences for 5*, 209, 210–11t, 211–14; in *I Have Come Through*, 217, 218, 219; in improvisation, 113, 126, 198; in *Quivi sospiri*, 220–2, 221t, 224; in *This Is This*, 142, 143t, 144–6
studio-based electronic music: concerts of, 9, 39; history of, 5, 8, 9–11, 14–15; and humanization, 92, 93; live electronic music emerging from, 8, 10–11, 15, 39. *See also* University of

Toronto Electronic Music Studio (UTEMS)
Sunter, Robert, 165, 169
Supertrio, 61*t*, 62–4, 114, 130. See also *Attention Elk!* (Supertrio)
Supertrio (1996 album), 59, 62, 63–4, 109
Sutherland, David: and analog technologies, 59, 78–9, 81, 94, 106; on the CEE, 51, 188, 190, 191; on improvisation, 111, 115; joining the CEE through Stillwell, 78–9, 186–7; membership in the CEE, xviii, xviii*t*; music studies, 77–8
"Synthescope" Digital Synthesizer Ensemble. See *Electronic Messiah, The* (1982 album)
synthesizers. *See* analog technologies; modular synthesizers
Synthi A. *See under* analog technologies

"taketwoness," 109, 114
Tangerine Dream, 77, 82–3, 187
tape, 8, 10–11, 30–1, 40, 94–5. See also *Consequences for 5* (Beecroft); *Fancye* (Jaeger), listening guide; musique concrète; *Psalm* (Lake)
Taylor, Timothy, 80
technological sublime, 89–90
tempo, 165–6, 239n12
temporal liveness, 88, 89, 94–5, 112, 120–1
temporality, 109, 113, 149–50
texture: in *Caspin's Arrival*, 232–3, 232*t*; in the CEE's sound, 53; in *The Electronic Messiah*, 166–8; in *Sparse Sunday*, 75–7; in *This Is This*, 142, 143*t*, 144–7

This Is This (Bolton): analysis, 141–2, 143*t*, 144–7, *144*, *145*; live and recorded versions, 74, 237n3, 238n7
timbre: in *Attention Elk!*, 228–31, *229*; in the CEE's sound, 53, 55, 126; in *Fancye*, 206–9, *207*; in *I Have Come Through*, 217, *218*, 219
Toronto, 12–14, 26–7, 41, 134–7, 173–7. *See also* Toronto Sound Festival; University of Toronto; University of Toronto Electronic Music Studio (UTEMS)
Toronto Conservatory of Music. *See* Royal Conservatory of Music (Toronto)
Toronto Sound Festival, 181, 187
TRANZAC, The, 135
Trio Collectif, 62–4
trumpet. *See* brass
Two New Hours (CBC Radio 2): audience, 139, 161, 162; commissions, 33, 129, 159, 161; and Grimes, 38, 158–9; and Jaeger, 33, 129, 157, 158–9, 161–3; and Lake, 35, 158–9; programming, 129, 155, 157–60, 161–3, 239n6

United States–Canada relationship, xv–xvii
University of Toronto: CEE founding members at, 27, 40, 132; Faculty of Music, 25–30, 32, 34, 205; Farah at, 72. *See also* University of Toronto Electronic Music Studio (UTEMS)
University of Toronto Electronic Music Studio (UTEMS), xiii–xiv, 12–13, 30–2, 38–9
unpredictability, 17, 21, 55, 80, 93–4

Vietnam War, xv, 36, 38, 235n3
viola, 97, 98, 232–3, 232t. *See also*
    Wilcox, Laura
violin: electronic processing of,
    70, 76, 91, 205; and gesture–
    sound relationships, 91, 103; in
    Increscents, 202–5, 203t, 204; in
    Sparse Sunday, 75, 76. *See also*
    Bolton, Rose; Wilcox, Laura
virtuality, liveness of, 88, 97, 99, 114
virtual spaces, 124, 137–41
virtuosity: and audience
    engagement, 24–5, 84–5,
    99–101, 103, 105; in the CEE's
    performances, 84–5, 96, 99–101,
    103–7, 108; and corporeality, 23,
    24–5, 96, 105, 108; critiques of,
    107–8, 141; in Euro-American
    classical music, 100, 101, 103,
    105, 107

visuals, 90, 115, 188, 205–6
voices, 75, 139, 146–7. *See also*
    Electronic Messiah, The (1982
    album); *This Is This* (Bolton)

Walter, Arnold, 28, 30, 34
Weinzweig, John, 28–30, 38, 239n6
"weird" aesthetic, 54–5, 56, 66, 77,
    126
Westerkamp, Hildegard, xi, 13, 33,
    128, 129–32
Whale Oil (CEE), 44
whiteness, 120, 176–7, 182–3, 198.
    See also racial inequality
Wilcox, Laura, xviii, xviiit, 67, 96–7,
    231–3
Winnipeg Symphony Orchestra, 160
World Soundscape Project (WSP),
    128, 129, 130